The Theapeut

Established stories and myths, often culturally-specific, can be employed to great therapeutic effect with a wide range of clients.

The fourteen contributors to this book come from a multi-disciplinary background, and together have extensive practical experience of using stories as therapy. They look at story telling in its historical and cultural context and present a sound theoretical basis for its continued use in therapy.

Covering emotional themes such as anger, anxiety, fear, shame, guilt, splitting, separation and bereavement, the authors present many fascinating stories which they have found to be particularly beneficial in the therapeutic context. They show how story therapy can be employed practically in different settings – for example, within education, or as part of family therapy – and with different age groups.

The Therapeutic Use of Stories provides both a theoretical and a methodological framework for story telling as therapy and will be a valuable resource for all those working in the field of education, social work or health.

Kedar Nath Dwivedi is a Consultant in Child, Adolescent and Family Psychiatry at the Child and Family Consultation Service, Northampton, and a Clinical Teacher in the Faculty of Medicine, University of Leicester.

Contributors: Amit Bhattacharyya; Barry Bowen; Sonia Compton; Kedar Dwivedi; Susan Edwards; Damian Gardner; Mary Gray; Peter Harper; Sarah Hogan; Suzanne Lawton; Terence Lear; Ruchira Leisten; Margaret Pennells; Channapatna Shamasundar.

The Therapeutic Use of Stories

Edited by Kedar Nath Dwivedi

London and New York

First published 1997
by Routledge
11 New Fetter Lane, London EC4P 4EE

Simultaneously published in the USA and Canada
by Routledge
29 West 35th Street, New York, NY 10001

Typeset in Times by Routledge
Printed and bound in Great Britain by TJ International,
Padstow, Cornwall

British Library Cataloguing in Publication Data

Library of Congress Cataloguing in Publication Data
The therapeutic use of stories / edited by Kedar Dwivedi.
Includes bibliographic references and index.
1. Storytelling–Therapeutic use. 2. Mythology–Therapeutic use.
I. Dwivedi, Kedar Nath.
RC489.S74T47 1997
616.89'165–dc21   97–8846
                                                                         CIP

ISBN 0–415–15070–1 (hbk)
ISBN 0–415–15071–X (pbk)

With warm affection and esteem, this book is dedicated by the editor to Dr Param Hans Rai, of Azamgarh, India, who is one of the most delightful of all story tellers.

Contents

Notes on contributors

Dr Amit Bhattacharyya was born and educated in West Bengal, India. He came to England to train as a surgeon but had to give up for health reasons. He entered psychiatry in 1967 and retired from full-time employment in the NHS in 1992. Since 1993, he has been working as a consultant in psychotherapy. He uses various dynamic therapies and considers himself eclectic in approach. His interest in stories was kindled at the age of 12, when his first story was published in a Calcutta children's magazine. This was followed by several other publications in Bengali, including six children's story books. His brief literary career ended at the age of 21 when pressures of medical studies took over.

Barry Bowen is Psychiatric Social Worker at the Child and Family Service, Jersey, Channel Islands. He is a registered family and marital therapist and has presented workshops on family therapy topics throughout Britain for a number of years.

Sonia Compton works as a play therapist in Northamptonshire. She has experience of working with children with emotional and behavioural difficulties in both educational and therapeutic settings. She has also worked in the Department of Social Services in different capacities.

Dr Kedar Nath Dwivedi is Consultant in Child, Adolescent and Family Psychiatry at the Child and Family Consultation Service and the Ken Stewart Family Centre, Northampton, and is also Clinical Teacher in the Faculty of Medicine, University of Leicester. He graduated in medicine from the Institute of Medical Sciences, Varanasi, India, and served as Assistant Professor in Preventive and Social Medicine in Simla before coming to the UK in 1974. Since then, he has worked in psychiatry, is a member of more than a dozen professional associations, and has contributed extensively to the literature, including editing the well-received *Groupwork with Children and Adolescents* (Jessica Kingsley, 1993) and *Enhancing Parenting Skills* (John Wiley, in press) and co-editing *Meeting the Needs of Ethnic Minority Children* (Jessica Kingsley, 1996) and *Management of Childhood Anxiety Disorders* (Arena, 1997). He is also interested in Eastern, particularly Buddhist, approaches to mental health.

Susan Edwards has worked as a residential social worker in children's homes in Northampton for young people in local authority care, and with young people with emotional and behavioural difficulties. She helped set up information 'shops' in upper schools in Northampton as a part of one of the Department of Education's innovative projects. She has also worked for the Partnership Project in the West Midlands, helping gypsies and travellers to access various services. During her social work training she spent a training placement at the Child and Family Consultation Service, Northampton. She is now a Group Worker in a school in Northampton in a project sponsored through the Single Regeneration Budget.

Damian Gardner is a clinical psychologist working with adults. His interests include bereavement, theoretical issues in psychological therapies and gender issues. He is married with a young son and enjoys, among other things, reading and listening to stories.

Mary Gray is currently working as Play Therapist for the Council on Addiction in Northampton. She has studied play therapy at Roehampton and Hull, and has long experience of working with children in education, social services and health sectors. In her work, she offers individualized programmes incorporating focused play, drama, art and music.

Peter Harper is a Consultant Clinical Psychologist working in the Child Health Directorate in Northampton. He has a wide range of experience as a clinician, therapist, trainer and supervisor, both in the United Kingdom and abroad. He is a member of several professional organizations and is on the editorial board of *Child and Youth Care*. He has written a number of articles on working therapeutically with children and young people.

Sarah Hogan is Senior Nurse Manager at the Ken Stewart Family Centre, Northampton, where she has worked for many years in individual and group therapy with children, adolescents and families. She has previously worked as a voluntary supervisor for the local youth counselling service and a bereavement counselling service (GAP). Sarah also contributes towards the training and education of students and professionals from various disciplines.

Suzanne Lawton was a social worker in the Northampton Child and Family Consultation Service from 1988 until her retirement in 1996. She has also worked as a generic social worker in Warwickshire and Coventry, and before that as an infant teacher in Berkshire and Warwickshire. She is interested in preventive and treatment work in the field of child abuse.

Dr Terence Lear practises at the Turvey Centre for Group Therapy, near Bedford, and has been a leader in group analytic training courses. He is a former President of the Group Analytic Society (London). Formerly a Consultant in the NHS, he was responsible for the Psychotherapy Department at the Cheyne Walk Clinic, Northampton, where he had a special interest in the creative influences between therapists when bridging their different therapies.

Dr Ruchira Leisten is a Research Fellow in the Social Policy Research Group at the Nene Centre for Research, Nene College. She is an experienced researcher in the fields of family health and community care. She is also the module co-ordinator for the research methods course on the MA in Policy Studies. She is married with two young children.

Sister Margaret Pennells had been a social worker with the Child and Family Consultation Service since 1988, during which time she developed structured group work programmes, first for bereaved children and latterly for parents. Margaret also worked for CRUSE–Bereavement Care as a trainer and volunteer bereavement counsellor. She had been extensively involved in training professionals both locally and nationally. She was a member of the Good Shepherd Congregation. Sadly, Sister Pennells passed away during the completion of this book and will be greatly missed.

Dr Channapatna Shamasundar served in the Indian Air Force and also worked as a general practitioner. After specializing in psychiatry he served as a faculty member for twenty years at the National Institute of Mental Health and Neuro Sciences (NIMHANS), Bangalore, India, where he was Additional Professor of Psychiatry before retirement. His areas of special interest have included the training of general practitioners in psychiatry, psychotherapy and the philosophy of psychiatry and psychotherapy.

Preface

An integral part of my growing up in India was listening to stories from different people in a variety of contexts within my family, village, school and community. Amongst all these story tellers my grandmother, Rajeshwari, was perhaps the most unfailing and the most untiring. Even in her old age she was very brave and was full of energy, stamina and command.

When I graduated in medicine at the Institute of Medical Sciences, Varanasi, I joined the Faculty of Preventive and Social Medicine and became involved in a variety of projects in a rural community. This is where I had the opportunity to work with Param Hans Rai. We used to (and still do) affectionately call him Rai Saheb. He is a delightful story teller. He used to drop hints at the right places and at the right times about possible village meetings that he was organizing, and at the allotted time and place a large crowd of people would gather together. Rai Saheb would then tell them the most enchanting of stories, always with a beaming smile and much laughter. These stories brought people together and mobilized their energy and commitment for the creation of new social structures and practices, with a view to promoting community health and welfare.

For example, we had taken on a project to promote and improve the role of traditional birth attendants (Dwivedi and Rai 1971). The State maternity services did not have the resources to deal with all the births in the community. They had also been operating on a rather Westernized model, which did not sit happily with the traditional local customs and rituals. Such rituals involve the entire community in many days of singings and celebrations, and untiring support from the traditional birth attendants who also provide repeated massage to both the baby and the mother. These rituals, fuss and celebrations also provide a great deal of protection against postnatal depression in such cultures.

Unfortunately, in a climate of modernized attitudes the traditional birth attendants didn't feel valued enough. On the other hand, there was enormous potential for them to improve their practices on hygienic lines so that the chances of infection could be minimized. Rai Saheb took great delight in alluding to the stories of the birth attendants of Lord Rama and Lord Krishna (the gods from Indian mythology) and generated unbelievable enthusiasm and commitment from all parties concerned to get the best from both worlds, the old and the new.

Rai Saheb was born in 1938. After completing his education he worked in the 'Action' component of the research project on Health Education and Environmental Sanitation sponsored by the World Health Organization at the Planning Research and Action Institute, Lucknow. He then moved to work as a social scientist at the Institute of Medical Sciences, Varanasi, where I met him. He completed his PhD in Sociology and now teaches at the Postgraduate Department of Sociology in Azamgarh.

I learnt a great deal from Rai Saheb and I also began to enjoy telling stories. When I moved from India to the UK and from preventive and social medicine to psychiatry, I found the value of stories in therapeutic contexts to be equally important. My interest in the field continued to grow as most of my Indian stories, being rather unfamiliar here, were often listened to with great fascination.

Many colleagues – Amit Bhattacharyya, Peter Harper, Sarah Hogan and Mary Gray, to mention just a few – also began to talk about the real need for a book that would be practical for therapeutic purposes and also rich in the wisdom of stories. Therefore we met on several occasions to develop the idea further.

Although in recent years there has been a growing recognition of the powerful therapeutic effects of stories in a variety of therapeutic settings (and in fact there are now a number of books describing stories of good therapeutic value), there is still an enormous need for literature with a more clinical and practical emphasis. This need can only be met by offering a number of examples of using stories for therapeutic purposes and also by paying more attention to the practical and clinical aspects, showing how, when and what type of stories can be used in which situations with what effect. Such a book cannot deal with all the possible situations and settings, but we have aimed to cover a wide variety of areas and clinical methods of story therapy, along with descriptions of many fascinating and therapeutically potent stories.

The chapters have been written by experts in their fields with vast practical experience of using stories in their therapeutic work. It has therefore been a great privilege to put together the work of such an outstanding team of contributors from a variety of disciplines, and I have been fortunate in the excellent contributions received from each.

The book begins by examining the historical (chapter 1), theoretical (chapter 2) and therapeutic (chapter 3) contexts and perspectives for the use of stories. In chapter 4, Professor Shamasundar illustrates some poignant paradigms of psychotherapeutic nature from Indian mythology. An attempt is then made to focus on the practical aspects of story therapy around a variety of clinically important specific themes, such as anger (chapter 5), anxiety (chapter 6), shame and guilt (chapter 7), splitting, envy, jealousy and rivalry (chapter 8), separation, loss and bereavement (chapter 9), child abuse (chapter 12), learning disability (chapter 13) and the problems associated with old age (chapter 14). The therapeutic use of stories in the context of educational settings (chapter 10) and family therapy (chapter 11) is also included.

It is the enthusiasm and painstaking efforts of Edwina Welham, Luciana O'Flaherty, Hannah Dyson and others at Routledge that have made this work possible, so that it now has a body and wings to fly far and wide, and reach out to you.

The child mental health services have for a long time been a true 'Cinderella' service (Parry-Jones 1992), despite a number of recent pronouncements from the depths of official hearts, such as those of the Health Advisory Service (1995), the Department of Health (1995) and so on. Those who have the task of holding the purse strings are too numbed by their financial constraints to act upon these words, however sensible or authoritative. At least 5 per cent of children have mental health problems severe enough to require very specialist help, but only 1 per cent are referred; the fact is that the available resources are not adequate for a prompt response to the needs of even those who are referred. Inadequate resources have also compounded the difficulty of recruiting specialists to the vacant posts in our service.

We are, therefore, extremely grateful to Drs Sheila Shribman (the Medical Director of the Trust), Ken Lloyd (former Chief Executive of the Trust), John Rogers and Silas Sebugwawo (Consultants in Public Health), Jill Meara (Director of Public Health for the

District Health Authority) and Pat Troop (Regional Director of Public Health) for highlighting these needs as much as possible. I am also grateful to our other paediatric colleagues, including Drs Nick Griffin (Clinical Director of Child Health), Peter Daish, Fran Ackland, Cliona Ni Bhrolchain, Fiona Thompson, John Hewertson and others, for expanding their help in the field of child mental health, and to Brenda Baldwin, Jane Coles, Bob Butcher, Dick Edmunds, Vee Hales, Kevin Stafferton, Alan Phillips and others from the Child Health Directorate for their valuable support to the child mental health services. I am very thankful to Drs Jess Gordon and Ian Robertson who have kindly continued to fill – at least to some extent – the gaps created by their own retirements.

In such a climate, the timely emergence of this book will help towards the further exploration of more and more potent therapeutic tools. Similarly, within our service the arrival of Peter Marsden-Allen has brought exciting new possibilities of working with families in their homes, aided by videotaping and its playback, in order to provide a meta perspective to all family members, so essential for their transformational insight and change; Peter Kenny has now moved on to take up the challenge of another exciting venture – the co-ordination of therapeutic group work efforts in Northamptonshire in relation to child abuse; Sister Margaret Pennells, despite terminally malignant metastases in her bones, had been so active and enthusiastic with her work with the bereaved children that she had been a real inspiration, not only for our service but also for many others. Sadly, she passed away during the completion of the book and will be greatly missed.

I am similarly grateful to all the other members of our multi-disciplinary teams: Dr Tony Brown, Linda Flower, Peter Harper, Sarah Hogan, Frances Jones, Kay McCreadie, Clare Marshall, Dr Guru Nayani, Jan Pawlikowski, Paul Sellwood, Dr Marcus Thomas, Vyvienne Tipler and Margaret Wysling; to the trainee psychiatrists, Drs Sally Beeken, Brian Fitzgerald, Hilary Parrott, Husni Ahmad, Timothy Sales and Tanya Phillips (to mention only the most recent); and to the trainee psychologists, Rebecca Mitchell-Farmer and Catherine Dendy (again, to mention only the most recent) for their valuable contribution to the service. The trainee psychiatrists rotate to this service from the adult mental health services, the management of which has also been in turmoil, leading to an exodus of specialists. In spite of such a backdrop the trainees have brought tremendous strength to our service.

It is actually the secretarial and support staff who keep the place together. I am very thankful to my secretary, Naina Sadrani, and, in her absence on maternity leave, to Sharon Smith. I am also thankful to all those in the general office at the Child and Family Consultation Service – Mary Battison, Karen Amos, Deviani Vyas, Lynda Tyrer and Katherine Rogers – and, at the Ken Stewart Family Centre, Jean Kurecki and Brenda Smart.

My special thanks to Carol Weller, Dorothy Stephen and Angela Concannon from the library, for being so helpful.

The warmth and support of my family, Radha, Amitabh, Amrita and Rajaneesh, has also been one of the most important factors for me in this project. It has coincided with all the excitements of becoming grandparents of Siddharth, the most delightful baby.

Finally I would like to thank you, the reader, for taking the trouble to read and make full use of this book.

Kedar Nath Dwivedi

REFERENCES

Department of Health (1995) *A Handbook on Child and Adolescent Mental Health*, London: HMSO.

Dwivedi, K.N., and Rai, P.H. (1971) 'Training of traditional birth attendants', *International Journal of Health Education* 14, 1: 29–33.

Health Advisory Service (1995) *Child and Adolescent Mental Health Services*, London: HMSO.

Parry-Jones, W. (1992) 'Management in the National Health Service in relation to children and their provision of child psychiatric services', *ACPP Newsletter* 14, 1: 3–10.

Chapter 1

Historical backdrop

Amit Bhattacharyya

ONCE UPON A TIME...

One may wonder what the connection is between myths and therapy. Why should anyone know about our past ancestry when so much of it is shrouded in mystery and most cannot be verified? Why should therapists using 'talking treatments' find the legends, fables, folk tales and fairy stories fascinating when those therapies claim to have a scientific basis? Does it not cloud our critical judgement even further and delay the process of enlightenment? But Popper (1963) suggests: 'Science must begin with myths, and with the criticism of myths; neither with the collection of observations, nor with the invention of experiments, but with the critical discussion of myths, and of magical techniques and practices.' The connection may lie in the common quest in the study of myths and the investigation of the self. After all, a reconstruction of what has gone on, and how that affects what is now and what will be, is the aim of both types of enquiry. With that purpose in mind, we will examine myths and their universality in the history of human existence to see how that knowledge has been utilized in education, therapy and self-understanding.

Myths are about stories. Stories depict experience of life. Yesterday's stories become tomorrow's myths. They represent the culture, traditions, attitudes and values of a race or a nation. They show their dreams and aspirations and are handed down through the generations as history. Myths contain unconscious material in a disguised form to be absorbed and internalized by the listener for use in his or her personal life, and then in due course to be passed on to others. Myths try to answer such questions as where one comes from and where one belongs, so that an individual, a group or a race can find a context for being and a point of identification with their ancestors. Thus one can have ideas about birth and creation, as well as death and an ending and what happens after death.

Campbell, a great researcher into myths in modern times, says that without myths man loses the meaning of his inner life, and he blames many of the ills of modern-day living on the way we exist in a demythologized society. He made extensive studies of myths; in his four volumes entitled *The Masks of God* ([1959–67]1982) he explores their origins, purpose and dynamics in different cultures, drawing attention to the similarities between them.

Myths also give a framework for social systems and their norms and what might be called tradition. They also legitimize power, dynasties and ways of life. Until recently, the Japanese emperor was believed to be a direct descendant of Amaterasu, the goddess of the sun, thereby holding divine status. The Ynglinga saga of Sweden suggests the dynasty to have descended from the ancient fertility god/king, Yngvi-Frei. The Ranas of Mewar in Rajasthan, India, were similarly thought to have descended directly from the sun, and in the Mahabharata, the ancient Indian epic, the heroes, the Pandavas, were all sons of different gods. The Caesars were seen as living gods or were deified soon after their death. Perhaps through the ages the power of the ruler has always been strengthened by rituals performed giving him divine sanction and authority over ordinary people.

Myths also denote patterns of migration, political change, invasion and conquest and other historical information of a tribe or race. The Celtic mythology even gives dates of historical significance particularly relevant to the people of Ireland. Some say that the ancient Iranians and Indians originate from the same Indo-European race, giving as evidence the similarities between the languages and myths of the two civilizations. Two groups of Aryans (possibly the word was derived from Eran or Iran) might have fought a series of wars and one group emigrated to the east.

The common cult of fire and the rites of the ambrosial Haoma in Zend-Avesta, the religious text of ancient Persia, and those of Soma in Vedic culture seem too close to ignore, as their names suggest. Not only that, but those mythological figures seen as good in one culture are seen as evil in the other, although there are common gods as well. The Daevas are seen as bad in the Avesta, and yet Devas are the gods in the Vedic pantheon and are always seen to be fighting the Asuras. Indra, the great warrior and ruler of the gods in Vedic culture, becomes an evil person who deceives men in Iranian culture. Ahura (Mazda), the supreme god in the Avesta, sounds too much like Asura, in Hindu mythology. Both streams possibly had links with the Assyrians, and strangely enough the name of a great Assyrian king, Assura Mahipal, does mean in Sanskrit 'Asura, king of the world'!

The development of languages gives a clue to the common origins of tribes and their patterns of migration. To give just one example, there is an interesting link between the Slavonic language and Sanskrit: the word *Svarog* in Slavonic myths denotes the supreme elemental deity of the sky, and *swar* or *swarga* in Sanskrit means the sky or heaven.

It would seem myths perform a similar role to the sections of a tree trunk telling the history of the tree or the layers of the earth giving vital information to the geologist regarding their past. Like an archaeologist reconstructing parts of human history, a student of myths can paint a biographical picture of a race.

After conquests, the myths of the conqueror are gradually assimilated into the culture of the vanquished and the characters of the mythical figures of the former become acceptable in the latter. The stories of the Indian epic, the Ramayana, have been modified and incorporated into the culture of many countries of south-east Asia because of early conquests by Indian invaders, and have survived in spite of the later conversion of those countries to Islam.

History, on the other hand, may be rewritten to suit the prevailing mood. This is not very different from what happens even now. An enemy of yesterday may become the friend of today, as Orwell portrays in his book *1984*. The recent upheavals behind the Iron Curtain have already shown this to be possible, as demythologization of previous heroes occurs and new heroes take their places. One can already see how, in one Far Eastern country, a cult of myth is being promoted to enhance the stature of its president who has succeeded his father.

Myths and symbols are often interlinked, in that a symbol may refer to an underlying myth. This is where it differs from a sign. The symbol of the cross is not just a sign, but projects all that is meant by it. It is interesting that recent discoveries in China suggest that the cross as a symbol preceded Christianity and did not become a Christian symbol until well after the crucifixion. Sometimes a symbol may change its meaning if it comes to represent a different history. The swastika, which in Sanskrit is a symbol of peace, comfort and harmony and is used in every Hindu auspicious ceremony even today, was hijacked in its reverse form by the Nazis, bringing misery and terror to millions and representing opposite ideas to the original ones. A common symbol in the form of a national flag has inspired individuals and groups to great acts of courage and sacrifice.

Whether myths tell the truth of some bygone days or are totally unreasonable fantasies will be debated for ever. The very word 'mythology' hints at a combination of fiction and truth. One important characteristic of myths is their universality. Claude Lévi-Strauss (1978), the French anthropologist, has been one of several in this century to suggest that this is an important indication of a common framework of all human life. Campbell and Moyes (1988) describe it as like 'a song of the universe' which brings man in contact with his place in creation, opening his eyes to the 'radiance of the mind of God'.

The description of a deluge seems to be present in many cultures: in the story of Noah's Ark, in Indian and Chinese myths and elsewhere. Satyabrata Manu builds a boat to save mankind in India, Uta-Naphistim does the same in Assyrian myths and all the ancient American myths abound in this story. Even the Aztecs believed that a man named Coxcoxtli and a woman named Xochiquetzal escaped in a boat to land on top of a mountain – not Mount Ararat in this case, but Mount Colhuacan!

The myths of creation also show a universality. Many describe a chaotic amalgam or a limitless ocean from which differentiation takes place, creating the earth. From the fusion of Apsu and Tiamat, sweet and salt water, arose all creatures, according to Babylonian myth. Egyptian mythology describes how a piece of land rose out of the water; the spirit of the creator resided in this primordial water, or Nun, and from it developed all beings, which had lain dormant within it. Greek mythology refers to Chaos, from which everything is created. This is repeated in some of the American myths, and from Guatemala across to the Polynesian Islands.

Another set of cosmogonic myths involve a creator, a cosmic egg or a union of two divine parents. The Indian and Egyptian stories of creation are similar: in the Egyptian myth, a lotus appears from Nun and opens to reveal the primeval deity, while in the Indian version Brahma, the creator, is revealed in the lotus coming out of the navel of Narayana, lying in the endless sea. One meaning of Narayana is 'one who rests on water'.

Another common theme seems to be a sacrifice bringing about

creation, as in the Saharan myths regarding a dismembered serpent called Minia. This is comparable to the story of the sacrifice of Tiamat in Babylonian myth or one of the Indian versions, where the bodies of the demons Madhu and Kaitabha, killed by Vishnu, form the earth. The sacrifice is often associated with death and renewal, as in the myth of Osiris: after Osiris has been killed by his brother Seth, his body is divided up and scattered throughout the land. In the Arthurian legends, a similar renewal theme is described in the story of Gawain and the Green Knight.

With the advent of analytical thought and psychology, one aspect of the universality of myths has been studied extensively. The myth of the hero shows several common characteristics all the world over. Special features surround the birth of heroes. They are abandoned because of a prophesy, or they are illegitimate, and they undergo extreme hardship initially to survive. They then make good, and after many exploits, trials and tribulations return in triumph to the tribe. Often the death of the hero is dramatic.

Tylor (1863) and von Hahn (1876) were among the first to notice this common pattern. Later, Otto Rank, one of the followers of Freud, wrote *The Myth of the Birth of the Hero* (1959) to explain his theories of this universality. Other scholars, such as Campbell (1956) and Raglan (1956) have defined this further; although each has his own ideas, a common thread runs through their thinking. The myths of Oedipus, Perseus and Paris from Greek mythology, the stories of Karna and Krishna in India, that of Sargon from Babylon, Gilgamesh from Persia and Sigfreid from the Teutonic myths, the exploits of Tristan and Galahad in the Arthurian legends, the folk tale of Lachausis from Latvia and many others have an uncanny similarity. The story of Moses and even the life of Jesus have been considered by many researchers to have similar themes.

Apart from the central theme of triumph of good over evil, the success of the *Star Wars* movies may be attributed to the utilization of the hero myth. A prince is abandoned by his father who turns evil, the princess in distress calls for help, the prince leaves his isolation and after many hazards rescues her, finds his rightful place in society and ultimately destroys evil.

Myths also have an educational function; fables, parables and folk tales have been used in every society to educate and impart values. Fables often take a story form about animals and end up in a moral, whereas parables describe real situations which can be practised in life. Christ's parables in the New Testament are recognised as a powerful way of teaching. The Bible has an abundance of stories which educate. Most of the stories in the Jataka are told by the Buddha to teach his disciples through his past lives on his path to enlightenment. Religious teachers have always used allegorical stories and metaphors in this way. The tales of Confucius and the Taoist tales from China belong to this category. All such stories were spread by troubadours, travelling minstrels and monks.

The earliest fables known were probably told by Aesop, a story teller in the sixth century BC in Greece. The *Panchatantra* – 'Five Treatises' – was reputedly written in south India by Vishnu Sharma, but is also ascribed to Bidpai, in the third century BC. Here the old Brahmin devises animal stories to teach the ways of life, divided into five categories, to three unruly princes who have been given up as ineducable. A similar motive to teach five princes was the inspiration behind the *Hitopadesha* – the 'Book of Good Counsel' – in northern India. Another group of writings, including 'The Twenty Tales of Vetala' and 'The Tales of the Thirty-Two Fairies of the Throne of Vikrama', originated in India and depict various human dilemmas and their successful solutions.

Much later, stories of a cunning fox, entitled 'Le Roman de Renard', became popular in medieval France. The animal theme was further utilized in France by La Fontaine in the seventeenth century; his rhyming fables are probably some of the best known. Chaucer's *Canterbury Tales* also make use of allegories and fables, as do the works of Dante; a more recent example is George Orwell's *Animal Farm*.

Fairy stories and folk tales have always been a popular medium for imparting moral education and describing life experiences. Among the foremost exponents are the Danish writer, Hans Christian Andersen, and the German brothers Grimm, who incidentally had a great interest in the myths of the German people. These nineteenth-century stories are extremely popular. They can be taken as simple stories by children, but at another level they contain fundamental experiences of life appreciated all over the world. Beatrix Potter's stories, among many others, fall in this category. And although *The Arabian Nights* is ordinarily perceived as full of bawdy tales, the stories themselves portray life and all its vicissitudes, and most of them contain religious, moral and educational lessons.

MYTHS AND THERAPY

Freud, the pioneer of psychoanalysis and all the other 'talking therapies' that followed from it, realized the importance of myths in understanding human psychology. In writing about one of his fundamental concepts regarding sexuality, he says:

> You will be no less surprised to hear that male children suffer from a fear of being robbed of their sexual organ by their father, so that this fear of being castrated has a most powerful influence on the development of their character and in deciding the direction to be followed by their sexuality. And here again mythology may give you the courage to believe psycho-analysis. The same Kronos who swallowed his children also emasculated his father Uranus, and was afterwards himself emasculated in revenge by his son Zeus, who had been rescued through his mother's cunning. If you have felt inclined to suppose that all that psycho-analysis reports about the early sexuality of children is derived from the disordered imagination of the analysts, you must at least admit that their imagination has created the same product as the imaginative activities of primitive man, of which myths and fairy tales are the precipitate.
>
> (Freud 1926: 211–12)

Freud goes on to say how these archaic factors continue to thrive in the mental life of the child, who uses the history of his race, inherent in him in embryonic form. As a classical scholar, Freud used the Oedipal myth to explain a central thesis in psychoanalysis. This revolves round the development of the child and his struggles to cope with the triangular relationship between him and his parents, as it changes from a dyadic relationship between him and his mother to a time when he recognizes the father as his rival. Freud essentially describes this so-called Oedipus complex for a boy, but he also explains how a girl deals with this early conflict.

Freud's ideas in this area have often been trivialized or misinterpreted. One of his followers, Bruno Bettelheim (1983), writes about these misconceptions in defence of Freud. In Bettelheim's view, Freud's choice of certain terms such as *psyche* and *eros* seem to have been prompted by his knowledge of the Greek myths and their relevance in understanding fundamental principles of Freudian thought.

Segal (1990) writes that, 'Only in passing does Freud himself analyse myth. Because he always compares myths with dreams.'

Freud analysed symbols in dreams to understand the unconscious, and considered dreams to be 'the royal road' to such understanding (Freud 1900). One is reminded of the custom in ancient Greece, where, to achieve a cure, the sufferer had to sleep at the temple of Aesclepius in the hope that the god would appear in a dream and offer a remedy.

In contrast, C.G. Jung, an initial follower of Freud and later the father of analytical psychology, believed in the connection between dreams, symbols and myths. His analyses of dreams are much more to do with the individual dreamer and his uniqueness, and he sees the symbols as more personal to the dreamer than as offering a meaning which is all-pervasive. Jung (1978) warns against interpreting dream symbols to patients, in case the projections of the therapist are used to fill in the gaps, and stresses the importance of sticking to the context of the particular dream, 'excluding all theoretical assumptions about dreams in general – except for the hypothesis that dreams in some way make sense' (ibid.: 50). He says that dreams 'originate in a spirit that is not quite human, but is rather a breath of nature . . . we shall certainly get closer to it in the sphere of ancient mythologies, or the fables of the primeval forest, than in the consciousness of modern man' (ibid.: 36).

This understanding of the universality of dreams and symbols through his clinical experience with patients and his own analysis, in combination with a unique knowledge of the myths and rituals of mankind, allowed Jung to develop his theories of archetypes and the collective unconscious. He went far beyond what Freud called 'archaic remnants', and thought of archetypes as primordial images, an inherited part of the psyche and a biological norm for its activity linking it to the body, instinct and image. There are innate ideas of pre-formats, such as father, mother, self, hero, leader, etc., readying us for real experiences of life that surround us and revealing themselves by way of certain representational inner figures.

Jung sees a collective unconscious as a storehouse of latent memories of the cultural past, racial memory, the history of mankind and even of prehuman times, and also as containing possibilities for the future. This is in sharp contrast to Freud's ideas of the unconscious as encompassing the personal history of the individual, his fantasies, memories and associations over life. Jung believed that this understanding was essential for man to reach a spiritual and psychological integration within himself and with his environment. In his view, a person must achieve a uniqueness of their own through the process of individuation, but at the same time must remain related to the collective.

THEN AND NOW

Stories in therapy provide a template on which the patient can project his life story and make some sense of it all. The most powerful mechanism at work here may be that of identification, in that the patient puts himself in the shoes of the characters in the story and tries to emulate what the fictional hero does or does not do. If the story is unfolding and remains sufficiently vague, the patient may project and identify with the projection to work out a solution for his particular conflicts.

Case example

A woman in her thirties was very distressed because she was not making any progress in treatment. She seemed to have some insight but could not use it and went on making the same mistakes. She said, 'I am fed up. I come every week and tell the same story. You and I examine it and I understand. Then I come back next week and repeat the same problem, albeit in a different context! Why can I not learn?' She expressed her disappointment with herself and acknowledged that she had suicidal thoughts.

The therapist (A.B.) said, 'One needs to practise many times before any change can take place, and it involves pain. Who wants pain?' He then continued, 'There was this young man, a very long time ago, who did badly at school, not because he was stupid but because he did not apply himself enough. He did not realize this then. One day, he was so fed up with life that he decided to make an end of it all. He went to the river near his village, wanting to drown himself. As he was sitting thinking on a large stone slab by the river, the village women came to collect water from the river, bringing large clay urns which they carried on their heads. There were quite a few of them, and each waited for her turn. When it came, each one first filled her urn and then put it down on a large stone slab and had a dip in the river.

'As they waited and chatted among themselves, the young man became more and more impatient for them to leave so that he could jump in the river. Finally the last woman left, and as she went he noticed a great hollow in the stone slab. He thought, and realized that the hollow had been made by many women over the years, all having gone through the same routine of putting down their full urns and having a dip before they returned home. He thought how strange it was that the relatively soft clay had made such a mark on stone, and it occurred to him that, if he tried hard and persevered with his studies, one day he would learn and not be ridiculed by everyone as a dunce. He did not kill himself but went back to study hard, and in time he became a great scholar. His name was Panini; he lived in the fourth century BC and the grammar he wrote so long ago is still the most valid treatise on the subject in Sanskrit.'

At this point, the patient smiled and said, 'That's a nice story! Like a story from *Jackanory*. Have you got any children?' It is as well to say here that the patient had been the apple of her father's eye until her brother was born. She had tried all her life to be good and be loved by her father, but her perception was that she was always second best. The story captured for her two things: the need to persevere and her own longing for her father's love and acceptance, hence the enquiry about the therapist's children.

It was then possible to introduce the topic of the relationship between the patient and the therapist in the context of her earlier experiences, in the way she had been wishing for the therapist to meet that unmet need. The patient left happier, and in subsequent interviews she referred to the story.

Everyone seems to attach special significance to special names, and often these are culturally bound. Names revive in us stories and myths about some past figures and the listener or reader immediately understands what is being communicated. If someone is described as like a Buddha, or Peter, or Shylock, one has no difficulty in knowing what is meant. Some names or parts of a familiar story may not have any significance unless they are part of the culture of the listener. Similar and new myths are being created all the time. A Scrooge or a Walter Mitty immediately conjures up a mental picture for someone who is familiar with those characters. We know immediately what is meant by 'an ugly duckling' or 'sour grapes'. A story about a hero like Superman can create a rich imagery for a child. Everyone can remember how this has been exploited in advertising road safety for children!

In a similar way, a family name and its history can create a family myth which can have a significant influence in family life and can be used as a defence against the exploration of real issues

(Byng-Hall 1973) until the therapist can or is allowed to enter that myth. Use of stories in therapy can provide the key if the therapist and the patient have a common frame of reference; if not, a story may have to be spelled out in detail, developing a common language to place it in context as applicable to the patient.

Perhaps the most significant part a story or a myth plays in therapy is that it universalizes the dilemmas facing the patient, so that he does not feel alone any more. This phenomenon has been well recognized in a different context in group work, where the sharing of problems and their universality have been seen as important healing factors (Yalom 1975). A story tells the patient that he is not the only one to feel like this: others have done so before. This realization often brings relief and hope that he may find a solution to his problem as others have done.

Case example

A patient in her thirties was very bothered about the close relationship between her husband and his mother. At one stage in the patient's therapy, the mother-in-law became very ill and the patient felt guilty and ashamed of her secret wish that the mother-in-law would die, thus resolving the problem for her. She was able to talk to the therapist about this, as well as how the thought had made her feel. She was full of remorse and thought of herself as an evil woman.

The therapist (A.B.) commented that her feelings were not original. The patient asked what the therapist meant. The therapist then told her that a tribe in Zaire had thought about this in their myths long before the patient had done, and went on to explain that, according to this tribe's creation myths, death was unknown, as God had so decreed. Then one day death touched an old woman, and the tribe buried her. The old woman survived and thumped on the ground, begging to be let out. But her daughter-in-law kicked on the grave and said, 'No, no! Stay there and do not come out. Once you are dead you must stay dead.' So the old woman stayed underground. When God came to know of this transgression, He angrily said that from then on man would know death.

The patient was interested in the story and smiled with relief and slight amusement. It so happened that the mother-in-law recovered, and the patient was able to reassess their relationship more positively once she had been able to acknowledge the darker side of herself.

Psychotherapy in its wider sense is a type of intervention where drugs or other physical methods of treatment are not used. The interaction between the therapist and the client, the exploration and understanding of his past experiences and fantasies in relation to his present life, offer a solution to the problems the patient faces. Techniques in psychotherapy vary from active to passive: on the one hand are the psychoanalytic, one-to-one sessions, where the therapist helps the patient unravel his unconscious conflicts, their origins, the defences that keep them going and his resistance to change. On the other hand are the many active therapies involving drama, play, art and so on. The term 'passive' may be a misnomer here, as no therapy is exactly passive, but it describes the concept of the interpretative mainly listening type of therapy, as against the more expressive creative therapies.

In the main, the patient has to make some meaning out of what he discovers about himself and his environment. That is what gives him insight and power to survive or modify his life so that he enjoys better mental health. Most of these therapies will try, actively or passively, to help the patient to understand his present life in terms of his past experiences. That invariably means the reconstruction of a life story which may or may not be immediately available to the patient.

Holmes stresses the importance of a life story for the patient in quest of his identity as an essential requisite for psychotherapy. He says, 'Every psychotherapeutic case-history is, in a sense, a "fiction" – a story wrought collaboratively by patient and therapist from the raw materials of memory, history, dreams, transferential relationship and theoretical perspective. The urge to weave meanings out of experience seems fundamental to human psychology' (Holmes 1993: 127).

Eric Berne (1961), in enunciating his theories of transactional analysis, talks about recurrent life scripts which are complex sets of transactions, 'Exactly like the theatrical scripts which are intuitive artistic derivatives of these primal dramas of childhood'. The analysis of these scripts as they are replayed in the transference is a necessary part of therapy (Berne 1961: 116).

The importance of life events in psychiatric morbidity has been researched by various authors including Paykel (1978). Other approaches to helping to build a life story have taken the form of a life chart, a life book (Ryan and Walker 1984) and journal and diary writing (Brunel 1987). A more recent development in brief psychotherapy, cognitive analytical therapy (Ryle 1979, 1990), advocates a survey of the patient's life to identify 'patterns of unrevisable, maladaptive "procedures" described as Traps, Dilemmas and Snags' (Ryle *et al.* 1992: 401). All these have the common theme of recognizing autobiographical connotations in the problems of individuals.

Holmes (1993) calls this narrative capacity on the part of the patient a prerequisite in therapy and terms it 'autobiographical competence'. Even in cognitive therapy, it is important to know how the maladaptive thoughts generate in the first place, how they become generalized, selectively abstracted and distorted, and how a new incident triggers familiar patterns of reactions; in other words, a plausible causation has to be worked out.

The word association test first developed by C.G. Jung intended to create in the mind of the subject a temporary association between two words which meant something special to him and to him alone, giving the observer a clue to his inner conflicts. An important way in which stories can be used is for the therapist to create a story and allow the patient to develop and embellish it according to his realities and fantasies. This may also include stories which the patient creates and expands for himself. It is as if he is distancing himself from his wishes, dreams and realities, so that he can look at them and learn from them.

Projective techniques such as Rorschach have been used over a very long period of time to enable the patient to create a story with a standard picture or a diagram. The patient writes, as if on a blank blackboard, what he thinks of a particular diagram. Hoffman and Kuperman (1990) describe the use of TAT (Thematic Apperception Test) cards to treat a boy of 13 suffering from trauma following the accidental killing of a younger relative. What is often too painful to talk about in the first person can be projected on to somebody else; this distancing then makes the psychic pain bearable.

It would seem that the human mind often has to make up a story or a picture in order to understand and associate that understanding with something personal and meaningful. Berger (1989) stresses the importance of the literary metaphor which 'regards the therapist as the editor (and at times even the co-author) of the patient's developing novel or drama'. He goes on to say that therapy involves a reconstruction of the past and a deconstruction of the present, which then presumably helps the patient to resolve his dilemmas and conflicts. What is most important is to create a common language between patient and therapist, as Berger seems to suggest, to build a story that is mutually understood.

Case example

An intelligent professional man in his forties had always shunned conventional methods to achieve what he considered to be of value and within his reach, and prided himself on his originality. When he had been bypassed for a promotion, he had become depressed and wished that he had followed the time-honoured path, sacrificing his own innovative but unorthodox approach.

The therapist had been drawing attention to the strengths of the patient. One day the conversation had turned to his skill as a host. Knowing of the patient's great knowledge and interest in wine, the therapist asked him whether he had come across St-Véran, a wine from France. The patient said he had. The therapist then casually said, 'Of course, there was this rivalry between the nearby well-known Puilly-Fuissé and St-Véran. Puilly-Fuissé would not accept St-Véran into their fold. The villagers of St-Vérand, smarting under this rejection, made a determined effort to improve the quality of their wine and succeeded to such a degree that the other group want them to join with them now, as best quality St-Véran is almost as good as theirs and is also considerably cheaper.'

The patient laughed and said, 'I am like that, aren't I?' Then he added, 'At least I am cheaper, and as good.'

The art and science of story-making have been beautifully described by Ailda Gersie in her book *Storymaking in Bereavement* (1991). She draws on her vast experience and gives many examples of how she uses this form of therapy. She describes the reaction of Deirdre, a very deprived young girl, to the story of Deirdre and the Sons of Usna. The little girl, who refused to let anyone touch her, snuggled up to Gersie as she heard the story.

Training methods such as Gersie's are particularly useful for those working with children and families. Fine (1992) relates his methods of training family therapists. He sees the importance of stories as a way to teach as well as an expression of how to think, and does not hesitate to use a little literary licence to make a point.

Bibliotherapy has been described as 'guided use of reading, always with a therapeutic outcome in mind. Literature related to illness or problems as well as fiction or poetry may be incorporated as a therapeutic adjunct to help patients gain knowledge and insight' (Katz and Watt 1992). Many writers recommend searching for suitable material to use as a direct aid to therapy or to educating and giving insight.

Allegorical stories have been used by Fosson and Husband (1984) to allay the fears of children facing illness, medical procedures and hospitalization, with encouraging results. Poetry therapy has been used: Heller (1993) describes poignantly the case of a patient tormented by the death of her twin in embryo, where the survivor's resultant feelings of destructiveness, loss and the quest for reparation were paralleled by Coleridge's mariner in *The Rime of the Ancient Mariner*.

Imagery symbolizes the different parts of the psyche which need to be integrated, so that meaning can be found and sense eventually made of what now appears inexplicable.

Metaphors have a similar function, and again they are used extensively in family therapy. Like stories, they can distance the pain initially, but as insight comes through identification the projected unacceptable parts can be owned and integrated, making whole that which was fragmented before. Once again, these methods are probably used more in family therapy; however, they can and are used in many other situations, as described in Gordon (1978) and *A Teaching Seminar with Milton H. Erickson* (Zeig 1980). Barker (1985) writes extensively on the subject of metaphors, their origins, varieties and uses. The central principle is the construction of a story that means something to the patient.

Active therapies possibly started with drama and play therapies. J.L. Moreno, the founder of psychodrama, saw drama as a means of bringing what was inside outside. His innovative techniques would sometimes involve building up a play relating to the case history, or allowing the patient to create his own play in which the therapist and others would take part. Moreno (1959) describes how a man who had a delusion that he was Hitler prompted Moreno and his colleagues to immediately take up suitable roles around the character. The slightly modified sociodrama techniques (Bhattacharyya *et al.* 1971) use a similar theoretical perspective, and similar techniques are sometimes used in Gestalt therapy (Perls *et al.* 1951).

Jennings (1994) writes: 'If the theatre can be understood on the one hand as a separate reality within which we engage and interact with our imaginations, and on the other hand as intimately connected with all our lives and personal stories, we can begin to reflect on its therapeutic efficacy.' Here again we have a situation where the patient projects conscious and unconscious material from his life to create a meaningful story for himself; the therapist, in collaboration with him, can turn it into a healing process.

Play therapy with children is equally important in promoting a therapeutic milieu where imagination and reality come together. Anthony (1957) beautifully describes the development of such a group with kindergarten children. As the group progresses, the individual territories, themes and fantasies gradually merge and become more collective and diffuse, leading to integration. He suggests taking colour photographs to record the visual changes as the toys mix and territories disappear.

The myths, legends and stories follow a similar pattern: what belongs to the individual slowly becomes part of the group and then of the race, until there is a collective awareness which transcends boundaries and becomes part of the human experience. Their uniqueness in bridging imagination and reality, their near spiritual depth, their mysterious universality, all point to their significance in the history and life of mankind. They are not 'science' as such but, as Popper (1968) says, 'Science is not a system of certain, or well-established, statements; nor is it a system which steadily advances towards a state of finality.'

However, the power of myths and stories to cross civilizations and their boundaries over time while maintaining an affinity with the whole experience of life can be utilized at a deep level of the world of the unconscious, through dreams and symbols, to provide a meaning of being and belonging. Or, at a more practical and fundamental level, they can be used to facilitate a model, outside to be taken in, to encourage insight and ultimate acceptance of those unacknowledged, unseen and possibly rejected parts of oneself. That completes the circle and, like the circle, offers a wholeness and completeness that was not there before. That is why stories remain with us and we use them and shall go on using them all the time, to make one our inner and outer worlds.

REFERENCES

Anthony, E.J. (1957) 'Group psychotherapy with children and adolescents', in S.H. Foulkes and E.J. Anthony (eds) *Group Psychotherapy*, London: Karnac, 8: 192.

Barker, P. (1985) *Using Metaphors in Psychotherapy*, New York: Brunner/Mazel.

Berger, D.M. (1989) 'Developing the story in psychotherapy', *American Journal of Psychotherapy* 43(2): 248.

Berne, E. (1961) *Transactional Analysis in Psychotherapy*, London: Souvenir Press (1993 reprint), 116.

Bettelheim, B. (1983) *Freud and Man's Soul*, London: Chatto and Windus.

Bhattacharyya, A., Hicks, S., and Sturgess, P. (1971) 'Some experiences in sociodrama', *International Journal of Social Psychiatry* 17(3): 230–8.

Brunel, M.L. (1987) 'Introspective writing: its impact on psychotherapy and education', *Quebec Psychological Review* 8(2): 2–17.

Byng-Hall, J. (1973) 'Family myths used as defence in conjoint family therapy', *British Journal of Medical Psychology* 46: 239–50.

Campbell, J. (1956) *The Hero With a Thousand Faces*, New York: Meridian.

——([1959–67] 1982) *The Masks of God*, Harmondsworth: Penguin.

Campbell, J., and Moyes, W. (1988) *The Power of Myth*, London: Doubleday, 25.

Fine, M. (1992) 'Family therapy training: hypothesizing and story telling', *Journal of Family Psychotherapy* 3(4): 61–79.

Fosson, A., and Husband, E. (1984) 'Bibliotherapy for hospitalized children', *Southern Medical Journal* 77(3): 342–6.

Freud, S. (1900) 'The interpretation of dreams', in J. Strachey (ed.) *Complete Psychological Works, Standard Edition* vol. 5, London: Hogarth Press and the Institute of Psycho-analysis (reprinted 1964), 608.

——(1926) 'The question of lay analysis', in J. Strachey (ed.) *Complete Psychological Works, Standard Edition* vol. 20, London: Hogarth Press and the Institute of Psycho-analysis (reprinted 1964), 211–12.

Gersie, A. (1991) *Storymaking in Bereavement: Dragons Fight in the Meadow*, London: Jessica Kingsley, 219–20.

Gordon, D. (1978) *Therapeutic Metaphors*, Cupertino, Cal.: Meta Publications.

Hahn, J.G. von (1876) *Sagwissenschaftliche Studien*, Jena: F. Mauke.

Heller, M.B. (1993) 'The rime of the papyraceous twin', *British Journal of Psychotherapy* 10(1): 18–25.

Hoffman, S., and Kuperman, N. (1990) 'Indirect treatment of traumatic psychological experiences: the use of TAT cards', *American Journal of Psychotherapy* 44(1): 107–15.

Holmes, J. (1993) *Between Art and Science*, London: Routledge, 127.

Jennings, S. (1994) *The Handbook of Dramatherapy*, London : Routledge, 3.

Jung, C.G. (1978) *Man and His Symbols*, London: Aldus Books (Picador edition).

Katz, G., and Watt, J.A. (1992) 'Bibliotherapy: the use of books in psychiatric treatment', *Canadian Journal of Psychiatry* 37: 173–8.

Lévi-Strauss, C. (1978) *Myth and Meaning*, Harmondsworth: Penguin.

Moreno, J.L. (1959) *Psychodrama* vol. 2, London: Beacon House, 193–200.

Paykel, E.S. (1978) 'Contribution of life events to causation of psychiatric illness', *Psychological Medicine* 8: 245–53.

Perls, F., Hefferline, R.F., and Goodman, P. (1951) *Gestalt Therapy: Excitement and Growth in Human Personality*, Harmondsworth: Penguin.

Popper, K.R. (1963) *Conjectures and Refutations*, London: Routledge and Kegan Paul (fourth edition), 50.

——(1968) *The Logic of Scientific Discovery*, London: Hutchinson (revised edition), 278.

Raglan, Lord (1934) 'The hero of tradition', *Folklore* 45: 212–31.

——(1956) *The Hero: A Study in Tradition, Myth and Drama*, New York: Vintage.

Rank, O. (1959) *The Myth of the Birth of the Hero*, New York: Vintage.

Ryan, T., and Walker, R. (1984) *Making Life Story Books*, London: British Agency for Adoption and Fostering.

Ryle, A. (1979) 'The focus in brief psychotherapy; dilemmas, traps and snags as target problems', *British Journal of Psychiatry* 134: 46–64.

——(1990) *Cognitive Analytic Theory: Active Participation in Change*, Chichester: Wiley.

Ryle, A., Spencer, J., and Yawetz, C. (1992) 'When less is more or at least enough', *British Journal of Psychotherapy* 8(4): 401–12.

Segal, R.A. (1990) *In Quest of the Hero*, New Jersey: Princeton University Press, viii.

Tylor, E.B. (1863) 'Wild men and beast children', *Anthropological Review* 1: 21–32.

Yalom, I.D. (1975) *The Theory and Practice of Group Psychotherapy*, New York: Basic Books.

Zeig, J.K. (ed.) (1980) *A Teaching Seminar with Milton H. Erickson*, New York: J.K. Brunner/Mazel.

FURTHER READING

Campbell, J., and Moyes, W. (1988) *The Power of Myth*, London: Doubleday.

Gersie, A. (1991) *Storymaking in Bereavement*, London: Jessica Kingsley.

Jung, C.G. (ed.) (1978) *Man and His Symbols*, London: Pan Books (Picador edition).

New Larousse Encyclopaedia of Mythology(1959), trans. R. Aldington and D. Ames, London: Hamlyn.

Segal, R.A. (1990) *In Quest of the Hero*, New Jersey: Princeton University Press.

The story of Deirdre and the Sons of Usna can be found in Delaney, F. (1994) *Legends of the Celts*, London: HarperCollins.

Chapter 2

Theoretical perspectives and clinical approaches

Kedar Nath Dwivedi and Damian Gardner

Life is a continuous process of organizing or structuring of experience. We have a strong longing for order and sense but we live in a world that may not have any. As we do not have a direct knowledge of the world, our knowing requires that we interpret or ascribe meaning to our experiences, which become intelligible or comprehensible when seen in a historical sequence of beginning, middle and end. Thus, the lived experiences and events get turned into 'stories'. According to Brooks (1984: 3), it is the plot that 'makes events into story. The plot therefore, places us at the crossing point of temporality and narrativity.'

In this way we organize not only our experiences of the world but also our actions and, in fact, our very 'selves' that experience and act. 'An action is a moment in a possible or actual history or in a number of such histories. The notion of a history is as fundamental as the notion of an action' (MacIntyre 1985: 214). We structure our lives around specific meanings, as meanings attributed to events influence our behaviours. Thus, in order to express ourselves and make sense of our lives, we 'story' our experiences, because it is through this process of 'storying' that meaning is derived.

It is notable that narrative perspectives exploring this storying process have been independently developed in several disparate areas. These include social linguistics (Linde 1993), models of humanity and science (MacIntyre 1980: 70; Danto 1985), theories of human action (MacIntyre 1985) and social science research (Sarbin and Kitsuse 1994). In the works of the authors cited it is possible to discern a paradigmatic shift away from a modernistic empirical model of experiencing and conceptualizing the world. The new emphasis is upon the human construction of meaning and a perspective that highlights the imperative of coherent meaningful historical accounts articulated within a given sociohistorical context.

NARRATIVE IDENTITY AND LIFE STORIES

On first acquaintance the implications seem clear enough; for example, Brooks writes:

> Our lives are ceaselessly intertwined with narrative, with the stories we tell and hear told, those we dream or imagine or would like to tell, all of which are reworked in the story of our own lives that we narrate to ourselves in an episodic, sometimes semi-conscious, but virtually uninterrupted monologue. We live immersed in narrative, recounting and reassessing the meaning of our past actions, anticipating the outcome of our future projects, situating ourselves at the intersection of several stories not yet completed.
>
> (Brooks 1984: 3)

Again, Hardy comments: 'We dream in narrative, day dream in narrative, remember, anticipate, hope, despair, believe, doubt, plan, revise, criticise, construct, gossip, learn, hate and love by narrative' (Hardy 1968, quoted in MacIntyre 1985: 211).

These apparently simple statements, however, obscure complex and controversial views on the nature and status of life and fiction. On the one hand it can be argued that narrative structures bear no reference to life itself, but on the other hand they can be seen as originating in the structure of 'lived life'. The former position has been most forcefully articulated by post-structuralist criticism while a most influential proponent of the latter view is MacIntyre (1985). It is of interest that, despite the disparity of views, White and Epston (1989) have drawn upon both stances (that is Foucault and MacIntyre) in their formulation of the text analogy in family therapy. Freeman (1993), in his extended exploration of 'Rewriting the Self', also finds it possible to draw on both the 'lived life' and 'narrative fiction' stances.

Nevertheless, the reality of lived life as an origin for narrative identity is important if psychotherapy is to be anything other than random make-believe in its retelling of human life. Thus the starting point for an exploration of narrative and metaphor in psychotherapy must be a consideration of the way in which human action is only comprehensible as intelligible action, and this presupposes its being embedded within a historical sequence. To quote MacIntyre:

> in successfully identifying and understanding what someone else is doing we always move towards placing a particular episode in the context of a set of narrative histories, histories both of the individuals concerned and of the settings in which they are and suffer. It is now becoming clear that we render the actions of others intelligible in this way because action itself has a basically historical character. It is because we live out narratives in our lives and because we understand our own lives in terms of the narratives that we live that the form of narrative is appropriate for understanding the action of others. Stories are lived before they are told – except in the case of fiction.
>
> (MacIntyre 1985: 211–12)

The principle that organizes our experiences into narratives is described by Carr (1986) as the 'narrative structure'. However, one is never fully the author of the narrative that one lives out. MacIntyre (1985) observes:

> We enter upon a stage which we did not design and we find ourselves part of an action that was not of our making. Each of us being a main character in his own drama plays subordinate parts in the drama of others, and each drama constrains the others.
>
> (MacIntyre 1985: 213)

He concludes that 'the unity of a human life is the unity of a narrative quest' (ibid.: 219).

From this basic proposition – that life is itself of a narrative form and it is this grounding which gives life stories meaning – it is possible to theorize in a variety of directions. There is, first and foremost, the self-storying that occurs as a natural process through life (Butler 1963) and is explored at length in Freeman's (1993) analysis of narrative, memory, identity and the autobiographical process. Then again, there is the social role of life stories in regulating our presented sense of self, and establishing intimacy and negotiating group membership (Linde 1993). And third, while accepting the reality of our narrative structures in human life, it is also possible to analyse individual 'life texts' as representing the loci of a wider interplay of sociocultural stories which impact, often in a conflicting manner, on specific people's lives. Finally, if narrative and story are to be taken seriously as carrying meaning, then it becomes necessary to move beyond explicit historical accounting and to embrace the meaning in tale, fable and metaphor. For implicitly and explicitly, it is from the available cultural stock of stories that an individual's own stories will be understood and enacted (MacIntyre 1985: 216).

Shank (1990: 12) highlights the role of story in human memory and emphasizes that 'Human memory is story based'. Through these stories we can access a huge variety of our complex experiences. When we receive any new information, we try to connect it somewhere in our memory. The process of thinking, therefore, involves linking new ideas to previous experiences, and stories offer a large range of indices at various levels with which to link these ideas in different ways. Stories have many indices, such as time, place, sensory aspects of the context, conflicts, dilemmas, solution of a problem, and so on, and are therefore immensely helpful in the process of indexing. Thus, most of our thinking is in stories and most of the information that we receive in our day-to-day life is stored, retrieved and focused on in the form of stories (Shank 1990).

PSYCHOTHERAPY

> It still strikes me myself as strange that the case histories I write should read like short stories and that, as one might say, they lack the serious stamp of science.
>
> (Freud 1893–1895: 231)

Many theoretical models available to the psychotherapist tend both to contradict each other and to focus on selected fields or domains of human experience. In recent years, across a range of academic disciplines, a narrative approach to understanding human life has been formulated that promises a broad, coherent and creative framework for psychotherapeutic theory and practice. A range of approaches has been articulated that share an emphasis on the human being as story teller – homo sapiens as *homo narrans* (Russell 1991) or *homo fabulans* (Sullivan 1992).

Against this background it is of little surprise that a number of psychotherapists have explicitly articulated and advocated narrative, metaphor and text-analogical approaches to clinical practice (e.g. Mair 1989; Cox and Theilgaard 1987; Viney 1993). Together these authors offer a meta perspective on psychotherapeutic formulation and intervention. The potential to celebrate and create through 'self-storying', story listening, using and enacting is also, more or less explicitly, proffered as a means of enhancing both the experience and effectiveness of therapy (e.g. Freeman 1993: 21, 231). The creative possibilities of using story and metaphor are further enriched by the utilization of tales from diverse cultural traditions:

> Stories are the womb of personhood. Stories make and break us. Stories sustain us in times of trouble and encourage us toward ends we would not otherwise envision. The more we shrink and harden our ways of telling, the more starved and constipated we become.
>
> (Mair 1989: 2)

The most fundamental clinical application of story and metaphor is naturally the enabling of a person (or family or group) to 'tell their story'. In articulating their story clients will often themselves discover meaningful sequences and gain insights and coherence. To put this another way, when we lose something (like an object) we retrace our steps to find it. The same goes for when we lose our sense of self or have become unsure how to move forward in time (as most clients have who present to psychotherapists). In order to know where we are we need to review how we got there.

The power of telling a story should not be minimized. In a research study, Pennebaker *et al.* (1988) found that, relative to controls, students who wrote an essay about a personal trauma subsequently exhibited marked positive changes in cellular immune function as well as visiting health centres less frequently. In their study they emphasize that telling 'for the first time' involves confrontation and expression of inhibited thoughts, feelings and images as the traumatic event becomes narrated.

When spoken, these stories may attain a significance from the context in which they are told. It is of primary importance that they are truly heard – especially when the story may be one that has been the subject of private or general taboo, such as child sexual abuse (Williams and Watson 1994) or the experience of dementia (Woods 1989). Beyond this, the nature of the listener – their gender, age, race, status – may give added significance to the telling.

As the experiences and their narrative accounts are inseparable, psychopathology and psychotherapy can thus be seen as narrative phenomena: that is, as narrative deviations and as narrative restructurings respectively. Cox and Theilgaard (1987) observe that 'Psychotherapy is concerned with a story which is so disturbing that, however painful the telling may be, it must be attempted. The "teller" seeks an opportunity to explore, appreciate, and appropriate his story, so that it loses its hold' (ibid.: xxvi), and 'the presence of a narrator is a sine qua non of the therapeutic process. A large part of psychotherapy consists of a narrator slowly giving as much of his "narration" as he can' (ibid.: 233).

Whether written or spoken, the breadth of clinical application for allowing a story to be told is vast. For disempowered individuals or groups the opportunity to find a voice and tell a story can be especially beneficial, for example in life review work with older people, in the forming of a life story book with multiply abused children in care or in work with groups of female users of mental health services (Williams and Watson 1994). The premium here is on allowing the telling of stories that have been suppressed through the interplay of personal and public taboo. When the prohibition on the telling of certain types of story breaks down then people may seek out psychotherapy as a safe context in which to tell a story for the first time. Where the public taboo remains, the onus is on the therapist to offer an opportunity to the client to give their account.

Thus, much of the process of psychotherapy involves telling, listening, retelling, relistening, performing, and so on, of stories. These stories can assist the therapeutic process immensely as they provide materials and resources for deriving meaning, understanding and insight and, in fact, also offer a framework for transformation. As Roberts highlights:

> Stories can provide a resource and connecting focus for therapy. They offer a way to name our experiences without imposing a clinical language (which most often emphasizes pathology) upon people's lives. Also, we all have stories to tell: clients, therapists, people not in therapy, young, old, Black, white, Asian, Native American, Latina, Jewish, Moslem, Buddhist. Stories are a bridge across clinical and nonclinical populations, because in them we recognize our shared dilemmas. Moreover, the use of stories is not embedded in a particular model; no matter what the theoretical stance of the therapist, stories can be used.
>
> A central part of therapy is helping people link and understand the relationship of their stories to their own life. As clients share stories with therapists, it is not just the content that is important, but the story style as well. Exploring the kind of story-making with which they are familiar may help them to

better see what resources they have or have not had available to them. Working with the story styles can open up new possibilities for making meaning out of their personal histories.

(Roberts 1994: 22)

The essence of psychotherapy is the process of tapping into the power of these stories in order to discover ways of restoring the flow of meaning between past, present and future. It also involves utilizing these stories to access memories and imagination and to find the right voices and the right vantage points from which to hear, comprehend, create and tell stories. There may be stories that need to be loosened up; some may be shrunk, shrivelled or withered and require nurturing and elaborating, and others may have been silenced, requiring the right context for their revival (Roberts 1994). Kelly (1969: 335) notes that 'people are usually ashamed of seeing what they are not supposed to see, so there are the stories that are never told'. Sometimes they choose not to speak or the text may break down midstream: 'you can see older people wallowing, floundering a little as they make their way among teetering piles of past moments' (Hadas 1990: 76). In other situations the narrator may become silent or the story may contain materials that may have been 'too hot to handle' in the past, or the narrator may in fact be unaware of the material that has been deeply repressed. It is also possible that the narrator may feel too vulnerable about the fragile facets of the inner life and may become rather protective and diffident about disclosing it. Thus, when a narrator is unable to narrate what needs to be narrated, there could be a number of possible reasons (Cox and Theilgaard 1987).

The 'telling' of the story, however, may not be a verbal (written or spoken) occurrence. Stories may occur without words and they can be 're-told' without words. Hence in play therapy, art therapy, psychodrama and related therapies the therapeutic narration may be in a symbolic form, including those of bodily expression and symbol.

In such cases one could consider psychotherapy to be a translation. Here the therapeutic process is understood to take one form of discourse or meaning and translate this into another mode of account (typically words). The original form may be the symbolic language of dreams, visual fantasy or emotional and behavioural expressions. Such a process of translation is often the essential feature of the therapy of pre-verbal experience as words are put to events and experiences dating back to the time when the child was without language. Casement (1991: ch. 12) describes, through the use of case vignettes, how by avoiding a dogmatic approach to interpretation both dream material and the 'language of the analytic session' (e.g. lateness, silences) can lead to fresh experiences of discovery for client and therapist alike.

PSYCHOTHERAPY AS RETELLING THE STORY IN AN INTERPLAY OF NARRATIVES

> Rewriting the self involves more than the mere reshuffling of words. Indeed, it is rather more like the resurrection of the dead, a process of breathing new life into language, of imaginatively transforming it into something different from anything before.
>
> (Freeman 1993: 21)

From the narrative perspective, the goal of therapy – whatever the orientation and/or techniques of the therapist – will be on the construction with the client of a coherent, meaningful and adaptive self-account. Mindful of MacIntyre's analysis, such an account should respect the socio-cultural context and legacies into which individuals are born (MacIntyre 1985: 130) and acknowledge the potential moral implications of adopting one version of the past over another. 'For the story of my life is always embedded in the stories of those communities from which I derive my identity' (MacIntyre 1985: 220).

The process of this unfolding of a story in the therapy situation is influenced by a variety of factors, such as the context created in therapy and the responses of the therapist. Winnicott points out that:

> Psychotherapy takes place in the overlap of two areas of playing, that of the patient and that of the therapist. Psychotherapy has to do with two people playing together. The corollary of this is that where playing is not possible then the work done by the therapist is directed towards bringing the patient from a state of not being able to play into a state of being able to play.
>
> (Winnicott 1971: 38)

The unfolding of the story is bound to have an impact on the therapist, and the therapist's response would determine the further unfolding (or folding up) and the direction of the story. As Roiphe (1992: 28) puts it: 'A story can turn strangers into friends', and Coles (1990: 334) observes: 'This is what we do as we hear a story-teller speak: let our own imagination, our past experiences, our various passions and problems, help form images that accompany the words we're hearing.'

It can be argued that every telling is a re-telling. Nevertheless, we can distinguish re-telling from telling by the degree of active reconstruction in a narrative account. In other words, the therapist now becomes more than audience. The literary analogy is that of critic, or possibly editor. The therapist's task may involve shifting an emphasis, questioning conclusions, resequencing events to find new meanings, and so on. Russell (1991) argues that, though not explicitly stated, this is the essential feature of cognitive therapy, and indeed most schools of psychotherapy effectively operate as systems of retelling human life stories. In personal construct therapy this has become explicitly stated (Mair 1989; Viney 1993).

In reality the impact the stories have on the therapist and the way the therapist responds determine what follows. Cox and Theilgaard (1987: 235) highlight that: 'There is one cardinal distinction between the reader's response to the written word and the therapist's response to the spoken word. It is an unassailable fact that the therapist's response influences what follows, whereas the reader's response does not!'

As stories can have multiple indices, connections, meanings and significances, a therapist (or the narrator for that matter) may become aware of only a few of these. Hardy (1975: x) warns that narrative 'will almost always yield other significances. Narrative is hardly ever, if at all, simply and solely narrative.' And, 'When the narrator is a patient, whose narrative is disclosed during psychotherapy, the "other significances" often assume major proportions' (Cox and Theilgaard 1987: 232).

The response of the therapist is determined by the contents stirred up in the therapist's consciousness on the one hand, and the skills and the model of therapy adhered to by the therapist on the other. It is possible for a therapist of whatever school of therapy to respond in terms of stories. Jerome Bruner (1986) points out that:

There are two modes of cognitive functioning, two modes of thought, each providing distinctive ways of ordering experience, of constructing reality. . . . A good story and a well-formed argument are different natural kinds. Both can be used as means for convincing another. Yet what they convince of is fundamentally different: arguments convince one of their truth, stories of their lifelikeness.

(J. Bruner 1986: 11)

STORY AS A THERAPEUTIC PROCESS

A beautiful way of seeing therapeutic situations is in terms of a 'gift exchange ritual' (Ritterman 1983). Thus the patient and the therapist exchange gifts in the form of complaints, advice, stories, understandings, and so on. In such a context the story offered by the person to the therapist is to be received as a gift, unwrapped and admired. Just as one does not look into the mouth of a gift horse, so the therapist can't be disappointed by the gift of the story (however, one is not expected to receive a bomb in the form of a gift). The therapist can thus participate in a play of the stories as gifts for exchange. Having examined and admired the gift, the therapist, in turn, may offer the gift of an equally beautiful story.

> Therapeutic stories serve a variety of purposes. They are entertaining and generally short enough to hold the interest of the listener. More importantly, they give messages which talk directly to the unconscious of the listener with directives about love, power and healing.
>
> (Davis 1990: 3)

By responding in terms of stories, the therapist can offer multiple perspectives and possibilities rather than settled certainties. This is highlighted in an Indian story of a father and son who bought a donkey and were walking it back home through several villages. When the villagers saw the two men walking a donkey, they started teasing: 'Look at some fools who can't ride a donkey!' Having over-heard the teasing comments, the father decided to ride the donkey and the son continued to walk alongside. However, in the next village the villagers appeared shocked to see this and said, 'Look at a selfish man riding a donkey with no regard for a child!' They decided to swap places, but in the third village the taunting comments continued. This time it was, 'Look at the selfish young man with no feeling for his old father!' Listening to this, they then decided that both would ride the donkey. So the conversations in the next village were about two strong but selfish men who had no regard for the welfare of a poor donkey.

Roberts (1994) emphasizes that:

Because each person carries a unique set of life experiences, stories provide multiple possibilities for each individual to make meaning of them. And hearing one story usually triggers another story. This is sometimes an unspoken process, where the individual scans the story in his or her mind but does not share it. Other times, it is shared immediately or later on.

(Roberts 1994: 5)

and that 'Stories are a unique tool to use in therapy because they appeal to people of all ages. We all think in stories and they can give voice to people of widely disparate developmental levels' (ibid.: 22).

In addition to stories from one's own life, one may offer or may be invited to tell any other kind of stories: imaginative, hypothetical, fairy stories and so on. There are immense therapeutic possibilities in stories that people already have, and these stories can be used in a variety of ways. They can be spoken, written, sculpted, revealed through the use of puppets and other props or acted out; 'story telling may be dramatic, imagistic, lyrical, and mythopoetic, but it always narrates, retails a sequence of events' (Hardy 1975: x).

Stories teach us new attitudes and belief systems. The main modus operandi of cognitive therapy is to change one's belief systems in order to change one's reality. Traditionally the cognitive therapists have employed logical approaches to achieve this. However, there is now a growing recognition of the value of narratives in reaching this goal, and a feeling that 'further investigation of narrative processes in cognitive therapy can broaden and deepen our understanding of the representational process underpinning adaptation and change' (Russell 1991: 241).

STORIES AS METAPHORS AND THEIR TRANSFORMATIONAL POWER

If psychotherapy is a re-telling, then the distinction between renarrating a life through psychotherapy and the use of metaphor and story within a given session becomes one of degree. Nevertheless, whether as the major intervention in a psychotherapy encounter or as a contributory intervention, we can distinguish loosely between psychotherapy as a renarration of identity and the utilization of small self-contained stories, tales, fables, proverbs and metaphors as specific operations within a given therapy session.

All therapeutic approaches and systems make explicit and implicit use of metaphors. An example is Freud's use of sexual symbolism as a means of decoding dreams, fantasies and 'unconscious' associations. Jung developed the 'animus' and the 'anima' metaphors, and Reich the 'orgone'. The humanists talk about 'peak experiences' , while the mechanists deal with 'little black boxes'. Berne has 'games', Perls has a 'top dog' and an 'under dog', Janov has 'primal' experiences, and EST graduates presumably get 'it'.

(Gordon 1978: 8)

It has been suggested that, from a neuropsychological point of view, the two hemispheres of the brain have different styles of information processing. The left hemisphere deals mainly with language and logic and the right with symbolism and the ikonic aspects of metaphors. It is believed that the information processed through the right hemisphere has a more rapid and effective impact on one's feelings and behaviours. Cox and Theilgaard (1987) point out that:

The linking of the two cerebral hemispheres takes place through the Corpus Callosum. And metaphor, seen from a neuropsychological perspective, integrates the ikonic mode of the right hemisphere and the linguistic mode of the left.

(Cox and Theilgaard 1987: xxvii)

Clinical experience leads us to the conclusion that conventional interpretative and supportive psychotherapy can be facilitated by the use of image and metaphor. We suggest that deep affective material in the patient's inner world can be contained, changed, or consolidated by the appropriate use of poiesis in which new resources are called into being. And these resources fulfil the criteria of poiesis because, as far as the patient is concerned, something has been called into existence, in the shape of new capacities and enhanced resilience, which was not there before.

(ibid.: 18)

Pines (1987) is also amazed by the power of such a simple language:

Psychotherapists are rediscovering that psychotherapy is not primarily a precise technology of accurately used words, as tools of effective interpretations. The depths of the mind are reached and touched by simpler words that speak in images and metaphors, speak in a universal, timeless language, predating contemporary ideas.

(Pines 1987: xxiv)

It is because a metaphorical language adopts a non-invasive approach that it reaches the depths and exerts a mutative effect. According to Cox and Theilgaard:

Metaphor exerts its mutative effect by energizing alternative perspectival aspects of experience. This means that material which the patient has endeavoured to relinquish, avoid, or deny so that it is 'safely' classified, categorized, and 'filed' away, appears again in the 'pending action' file.

(Cox and Theilgaard 1987: 99)

Thus, stories and metaphors contain both the ikonic and the linguistic modes and the therapeutic value of a metaphorical language is enormous.

There was a time, only a decade or two ago, when the local authority and not the parents decided which school a child would attend. One of us (K.N.D.) was once requested by a family doctor to see a child over her difficulties in attending the school insisted upon by the Education Department. Her parents wanted her to attend a different school. Each had a strong case, which they argued extremely well, but the result was that the child had missed a considerable amount of schooling. The parents painted a vivid picture of the murder of a child that had taken place on the street through which their anxious daughter would have to go to attend the school insisted upon by the Education Department. The Education Department had their own story of the effort that had gone into carving the catchment areas. They also had a very strong feeling that giving in to the parental request would not only mean reinforcing the child's irrational anxieties but would also mean opening the floodgates for other such requests for changes of school.

The more one tried to persuade the other, the more the other became entrenched in their position. As one talked to them, one felt an enormous pull to join their 'side', but this would have simply prolonged the polarization and the battle. Instead, a Burmese proverb that came to mind was shared with the parties concerned. Later, it was learned that both sides had begun to shift from their respective positions; in fact, the child started attending another nearby school that the Department agreed to approve. The mutative

Burmese proverb was: 'When two buffaloes fight, it is the poor tuft of grass that gets crushed!'

In situations of therapeutic impasse or massive resistance, indirect methods have been noted to be of particular potency and therefore of immense value (Haley 1973; Gans 1994).

ALTERNATIVE STORIES

The stories that we have about ourselves not only determine the meaning of our experiences, but also select out certain parts of the lived experience for the ascription of meaning and are constitutive or shaping of our lives. However, because there are certain parts of our lived experiences that have been neglected and not included in our dominant story, it is possible to utilize these neglected aspects (called 'unique outcomes' by White 1989) to resurrect alternative stories which will make sense. In fact, White offers a detailed therapeutic procedure which includes externalizing the problem, mapping the influence of the problem on the people and of the people on the problem, attending to the neglected aspects (unique outcomes), revising the relationships in the light of these discoveries (restorying) and performing the new story.

However, 'life experience is richer than discourse. Narrative structures organize and give meaning to experience, but there are always feelings and lived experience not fully encompassed by the dominant story' (E. Bruner 1986: 143). Thus,

> persons experience problems, for which they frequently seek therapy, when the narratives in which they are 'storying' their experience, and/or in which they are having their experience 'storied' by others, do not sufficiently represent their lived experience, and that, in these circumstances, there will be significant aspects of their lived experience that contradict these dominant narratives. . . . Those aspects of lived experience that fall outside the dominant story provide a rich and fertile source for the generation, or regeneration, of alternative stories.
>
> (White and Epston 1989: 22)

This restructuring is also possible because there is no absolute, correct or final reading of one's life, and

> Each account of the past is a reconstruction that is controlled by a narrative strategy. The narrative strategy dictates how one is to

select, from a plenitude of possible details, those that may be reorganized into another narrative which is both followable and expresses the desired point of view on the past. Accordingly, this reconstruction, like its narrative predecessor, is always subject to change.

(Schafer 1983: 193)

Psychotherapy, therefore, is a process of telling and retelling of stories.

People tend to organize their lives around particular problems. Using the text analogy, White and Epston (1989) help us to see this as an interaction of 'writers' and 'readers' around particular stories or narratives. There is thus a story of the problem which has acquired a career or a lifestyle.

'Externalizing' is an approach to therapy that encourages persons to objectify, and at times to personify, the problems that they experience as oppressive. In this process the problem becomes a separate entity and thus external to the person who was, or the relationship that was, ascribed the problem. Those problems that are considered to be inherent, and those relatively fixed qualities that are attributed to persons and to relationships, are rendered less fixed and less restricting.

(White and Epston 1989: 5)

The process of externalization opens up the possibilities for the various family members to separate themselves and their relationships from the problem, and frees them to describe themselves, each other and their relationships from a new and non-problem-saturated perspective.

WORKING WITH CHILDREN

It is through hearing stories about wicked stepmothers, lost children, good but misguided kings, wolves that suckle twin boys, youngest sons who receive no inheritance but must make their own way in the world and eldest sons who waste their inheritance on riotous living and go into exile to live with the swine, that children learn or mislearn both what a child and a parent is, what the cast of characters may be in the drama into which they have been born and what the ways of the world are. Deprive children of stories and you leave them unscripted, anxious stutterers in their actions as well as their words.

(MacIntyre 1985: 216)

Bettelheim (1976) illustrates the crucial importance of fairy tales in children's lives in, for instance, finding deeper meanings, restoring meanings to their lives, overcoming narcissistic disappointments, cultivating self-esteem, learning to cope with violent impulses, jealousy and cravings, and mastering many other emotional, cognitive and behavioural tasks of growing up. Fairy tales can state the existential issues, conflicts and dilemmas so briefly, succinctly and pointedly that a child can easily come to grips with these in their essential form:

> When all the child's wishful thinking gets embodied in a good fairy; all his destructive wishes in an evil witch; all his fears in a voracious wolf; all the demands of his conscience in a wise man encountered on an adventure; all his jealous anger in some animal that pecks out the eyes of his archrivals – then the child can finally begin to sort out his contradictory tendencies. Once this starts, the child will be less and less engulfed by unmanageable chaos.
>
> (Bettelheim 1976: 66)

Thus, for children, a favourite mode of communication is story telling. They really enjoy both telling and listening to stories. Dr Richard Gardner (1993) has developed the 'Mutual Storytelling Technique', utilizing the above principle in his therapeutic work with children and also incorporating some elements of humour and drama to augment its effectiveness. In this technique, the child is invited to make up a story, and the therapist helps in this process with prompts such as 'Once upon a time, there lived a . . . ', 'and that cat . . . ' and so on. When the full story is elicited the child is asked to talk about the moral or the lessons learned from that story. In addition, certain aspects of the story may be further clarified: for example, 'Why was the dog so angry with the cat?' The therapist then tells a similar story with complementary therapeutic lessons which are then looked into in discussion with the child.

FAMILY THERAPY

In family work, the people sitting talking in one room may span the whole possible age range. Stories can easily connect them all, offering:

> a way to understand concerns and issues on different levels at the same time. They can hold the complexity of people's lives in a

format all can understand. Great events and mundane details are interwoven in the tangled strings of our personal stories.

(Roberts 1994: 22)

Our meanings are almost always inseparable from stories, in all realms of life. And once again family stories, invisible as air, weightless as dreams, are there for us. To make our own meanings out of our myriad stories is to achieve balance – at once a way to be part of and apart from our families, a way of holding on and letting go.

(Stone 1988: 244)

Roberts (1994) illustrates different ways of working with stories in family therapy, suggesting that listening to family stories facilitates not only the therapist but also other family members in getting to know each other and their unique experiences in more depth. The therapist may even encourage stories on certain themes, such as discipline, health, intimacy, shopping and so on. Different family members working together may be able to pull together fragmented pieces of information on events, forming a coherent story, and to tap into the power of stories and restore the flow of meaning. They can also be helped to restore or 'reauthor' stories that have become dysfunctional and to draw upon their power of imagination to create and invent hypothetical stories, which can then provide valuable directions for the matters in hand.

General systems theory is the most common theoretical framework utilized by family therapists. The therapeutic value of meta perspective is a key feature of such an approach. In a family system, for example, someone can be seen as nagging and someone else as withdrawing. The more the one nags, the more the other withdraws. Similarly, the more the one withdraws, the more the other nags.

A wife may have the impression that her husband is not open enough for her to know where she stands with him, what is going on in his head, what he is doing when he is away from home etc. Quite naturally she will therefore attempt to get the needed information by asking him questions, watching his behaviour, and checking on him in a variety of other ways. If he considers her behaviour as too intrusive, he is likely to withhold from her information which in and by itself would be quite harmless and irrelevant to disclose – 'just to teach her that she need not know everything'. Far from making her back down, this attempted solution not only does not bring about the desired change in her behaviour but provides further fuel for her worries and her distrust – 'if he does not even talk to me about these little things, there must be something the matter'. The less information he gives her, the more persistently she will seek it, and the more she seeks it, the less he will give her.

(Watzlawick *et al.* 1974: 35–6)

Each can get stuck in seeing their actions as appropriate responses to the 'inappropriate' actions of the other. They are stuck in their own narrative identities and punctuations of the historical sequences. In order to see that they are both victims of the same systemic force, they require a meta perspective. Stories offer the best means of providing this distancing and meta perspective, which can be likened to moving from a state of sleep and dream to wakefulness. In a dream, for example, one may find oneself helpless, being attacked and about to be devoured by a tiger, but by waking up the tiger becomes a dream tiger, no longer as threatening as before.

STORY AND METAPHORICAL INTERVENTIONS WITHIN PROFESSIONAL SERVICE CULTURES

Stories and metaphors can also be used effectively within teams of professionals to transform an understanding of a client's situation or behaviour. Indeed, much of the communication about clients within service cultures is effectively the passing on of particular stories about people. Such stories have to be told, since within the service culture different agencies – family practitioners, social workers, voluntary agencies, and so on – may need to communicate about clients and to co-ordinate their work. At times the way these stories are communicated may perpetuate a fixed or unhelpful narrative form. An explicitly narrative perspective on human behaviour thus offers a range of options for how to restructure the way in which a given individual or group is understood, as well as underlying the importance and power of routine communications. Such an approach may be understood as offering alternatives to a caseness or diagnostic model. Susko (1994) advocates a narrative over a diagnostic model even in working with people with major psychiatric difficulties. One of us (D.G.) has found it useful simply to copy and/or co-author letters with clients when liaising with referring agents such as general practitioners. In doing this, there is the challenge of finding a common language to describe the client's 'story'. The process has clearly been beneficial for people, especially those with a life-long involvement with services which may never have really heard the client's own account of their life. Another simple intervention has been to narrate, with their permission and/or involvement, an older person's life story to care-givers in a residential home. The effect is powerful, as the actions of a so-called 'difficult resident' with 'incomprehensible problem behaviour' take on more understandable significance.

CAUTIONS IN USING STORY AND METAPHOR IN PSYCHOTHERAPY

As in all forms of psychotherapy, the use of story and metaphor is open to misuse and abuse. An approach which encourages creativity and intuition needs to be located safely in a context of experience, thorough assessment and appropriate supervision and training.

There are, in addition, specific issues raised by a narrative approach which have more general implications. In a context of power differentials it is easy to impose a language upon a client, to force a given 'reading' of their story, perhaps according to a particular account of human behaviour given by one or other therapeutic model (Hacking 1995). Particular sensitivity should be used in working with the stories of people from differing cultures, gender or age groups.

BEYOND THERAPY: STORIES AS MEANS OF EMOTIONAL CULTIVATION IN THE INDIAN THEORY OF *RASA*

Feldman and Kornfield (1991) highlight that:

> The priceless gift of any story lies in its power to spark a fire in our imagination. A great story has the capacity to transcend the boundaries of our personal worlds, with their sorrows and joys, and introduce the universality of human experience.
>
> (Feldman and Kornfield 1991: 7)

The Indian theory of emotions known as the *rasa* (extract, flavour, essence, juice) theory was established several millennia ago, as evident in Bharat's famous *Treatise on Dramatology (Natyashastra)*, an early treatise (200 B.C.) concerning the enjoyment and purpose of drama, story, dance, ritual, poetry, and so on (de Bary *et al.* 1958). The main purpose of these aesthetic forms was conceived to be catalytic (rather than didactic or cathartic) in order to activate and refine the emotions already present in the audience. The members of the audience, on the other hand, have to cultivate their own aesthetic sensibility so that they begin to respond

> in such a way that his or her emotion is transformed into a purely aesthetic, transcendental, and universal one, a *rasa*. The experience of the *rasa* is a glimpse of and, more important, an experience of the divine bliss inherent in all humans.
>
> (Lynch 1990: 18)

Although the naive Western concepts of emotions (including the many so-called scientific and the commonsensical) have been of rather passive (things that happen to us) irrational and mainly physiological phenomena, the social constructionists and cognitivists now emphasize that emotions are essentially culturally constructed appraisals. In the Indian concept, emotions are grounded not only in the self but also in play, music, food, scent, and so on. The mind and body are part of, and continuous with, one another and therefore are identical. *Manas* is considered to be the centre of both reason and emotions, unlike the irrational Western view of emotions. Lynch (1990), therefore, highlights that:

> Contrary to Western devaluation of emotion in the face of reason, India finds emotions, like food, necessary for a reasonable life, and, like taste, cultivable for the fullest understanding of life's meaning and purpose . . . in much of India there is no real distinction between mind and body, cognition and emotion, and asceticism and eroticism.
>
> (Lynch 1990: 23)

Uses of story and other art forms in the Indian philosophical system and in Indian cultural practices are not only for therapeutic purposes, but far beyond: for the higher purposes of life.

CONCLUSIONS

We have advocated here the adoption of an analysis of both human life and psychotherapy that is formulated around narrative, story and metaphor. Such an approach can be rooted in the reality of daily life while opening up creative possibilities for therapeutic change and movement. In doing so we view this approach both as a means of integrating differing psychotherapeutic theories and as providing a meta theoretical perspective on those theories. It is inherent to such an approach that theoretical perspectives lead to adaptations and innovations in clinical practice.

REFERENCES

In this chapter the terms 'narrative' and 'story' are used interchangeably. The term 'psychotherapy' is used in a generic sense, meaning all types of psychotherapy (such as family therapy, group therapy, cognitive therapy and so on) and not only psychodynamic psychotherapy.

Bettelheim, B. (1976) *The uses of enchantment: the meaning and importance of fairy tales*, Harmondsworth: Penguin.

Brooks, P. (1984) *Reading for the Plot: Design and Interaction in Narrative*, New York: Random House.

Bruner, E. (1986) 'Ethnography as narrative', in V. Turner and E. Bruner (eds) *The Anthropology of Experience*, Chicago: University of Illinois Press.

Bruner, J. (1986) *Actual Minds, Possible Worlds*, Massachusetts: Harvard University Press.

Burck, C., and Frosh, S. (1994) 'Research process and gendered reflexivity', *Journal of Systemic Consultation and Management* 5: 109–22.

Butler, R.N. (1963) 'The life review: an interpretation of reminiscence in the aged', *Psychiatry* 26: 65–76.

Carr, D. (1986) *Time Narrative and History*, Bloomington: University of Indiana Press.

Casement, P. (1991) *Learning from the Patient*, London: Guildford.

Coleman, P.G. (1986) *Ageing and Reminiscence Processes*, Guildford: Wiley.

Coles, R. (1990) *The Spiritual Life of Children*, Boston: Houghton Mifflin.

Cox, M., and Theilgaard, A. (1987) *Mutative Metaphors in Psychotherapy: The Aeolian Mode*, London: Tavistock Publications.

Danto, A.C. (1985) *Narration and Knowledge*, New York: Columbia University Press.

Davis, N. (1990) *Once Upon a Time . . . : Therapeutic Stories to Heal Abused Children*, Oxon Hill, Md: Psychological Associates of Oxon Hill.

de Bary, W.T., Hay, S., Weiler, R., and Yarrow, A. (1958) *Sources of Indian Tradition*, New York: Columbia University Press.

Feldman, C., and Kornfield, J. (1991) *Stories of the Spirit, Stories of the Heart: Parables of the Spiritual Path from Around the World*, San Francisco: HarperCollins.

Freeman, M. (1993) *Rewriting the Self: History, Memory, Narrative*, London: Routledge.

Freud, S. (1893–5) 'Studies on hysteria', in J. Strachan (ed.) *Complete Psychological Works, Standard Edition* vol. 2, London: Hogarth Press and the Institute of Psycho-analysis (reprinted 1964).

Gans, J.S. (1994) 'Indirect communication as a therapeutic technique: A novel use of countertransference', *American Journal of Psychotherapy* 48(1): 120–40.

Gardner, R.A. (1993) *Story-telling in Psychotherapy with Children*, London: Jason Aronson.

Gordon, D. (1978) *Therapeutic metaphors*, California: Meta Publications.

Hacking, I. (1995) *Rewriting the Soul: Multiple Personality and the Sciences of Memory*, New Jersey: Princeton University Press.

Hadas, R. (1990) *Living in Time*, New Brunswick, NJ: Rutgers University Press.

Haley, J. (1973) *Uncommon Therapy*, New York: W.W. Norton.

Hardy, B. (1975) *Tellers and Listeners: The Narrative Imagination*, London: The Athlone Press.

Kelly, G.A. (1969) 'Epilogue: Don Juan', in B. Maher (ed.) *Clinical Psychology and Personality: Selected papers of G.A. Kelly*, New York: Wiley.

Linde, C. (1993) *Life Stories: The Creation of Coherence*, New York: Oxford University Press.

Lynch, O.M. (1990) 'The social construction of emotion in India', in O.M. Lynch (ed.) *Divine Passions: The Social Construction of Emotion in India*, California: University of California Press.

MacIntyre, A. (1980). 'Epistemological crises, dramatic narrative, and the philosophy of science', in G. Gutting (ed.) *Paradigms and Revolutions*, Indiana: University of Notre Dame Press, 54–73.

——(1985) *After Virtue*, Notre Dame: University of Notre Dame Press (second edition).

Mair, M. (1989) 'Kelly, Bannister and a story-telling psychology', *International Journal of Personal Construct Therapy* 2: 1–14.

Ogden, T.H. (1985) 'On potential space', *International Journal of Psychoanalysis* 66: 129–71.

Pennebaker, J.W., Kieidt-Glaser, J.K., and Glaser, R. (1988) 'Disclosure of trauma and immune function: health implications for psychotherapy', *Journal of Consulting and Clinical Psychology* 56: 239–45.

Phillips, J.M. (1991) 'Narrative structures and psychotherapy'. Paper presented to the Philosophy and Mental Health conference held at St Catherine's College, Oxford, 28–30 June 1991.

Pines, M. (1987) Introduction to M. Cox and A. Theilgaard (1987) *Mutative Metaphors in Psychotherapy: The Aeolian Mode*, London: Tavistock Publications.

Pocock, D. (1995) 'Searching for a better story: harnessing modern and postmodern positions in family therapy', *Journal of Family Therapy* 17: 149–75.

Ritterman, M. (1983) *Using Hypnosis in Family Therapy*, London: Jossey-Bass.

Roberts, J. (1994) *Tales and Transformations*, London: W.W. Norton.

Roiphe, A. (1992) 'Children's books', *New York Times* 12 April 1992, book review section, 28.

Russell, R.L. (1991) 'Narrative in views of humanity, science, and action: lessons for cognitive therapy', *Journal of Cognitive Psychotherapy* 5(4): 241–56.

Sarbin, T.R., and Kitsuse, J.I. (eds) (1994) *Constructing the Social*, London: Sage.

Schafer, R. (1983) *The Analytic Attitude*, New York: Basic Books.

Shank, R.C. (1990) *Tell Me a Story: A New Look at Real and Artificial Memory*, New York: Charles Scribner's Sons.

Stone, E. (1988) *Black Sheep and Kissing Cousins*, New York: Times Books.

Sullivan, K. (1992) 'Homo fabulans: a reply to Smail', *Clinical Psychology Forum* 40: 3–6.

Susko, M.A. (1994) 'Caseness and narrative: contrasting approaches to people who are psychiatrically labelled', *Journal of Mind and Behaviour* 15: 87–112.

Viney, L.L. (1993) *Life Stories: Personal Construct Therapy with the Elderly*, Chichester: Wiley.

Watzlawick, P., Weakland, J., and Fisch, R. (1974) *Change: Principles of Problem Formation and Problem Resolution*, New York: W.W. Norton.

White, M. (1989) 'The externalization of the problem and the reauthoring of lives and relationships', in M. White (ed.) *Selected Papers*, Adelaide: Dulwich Centre Publications, 5–28.

White, M., and Epston, D. (1989) *Literate Means to Therapeutic Ends*, Adelaide: Dulwich Centre.

Williams, J., and Watson, G. (1994) 'Mental health services that empower women: the challenge to clinical psychology', *Clinical Psychology Forum* 64: 6–13.

Winnicott, D. (1971) *Playing and Reality*, London: Tavistock Publications.

Woods, R.T. (1989) *Aeolian Discourse*, London: Souvenir Press.

Chapter 3

Maps and meaning in life and healing

Peter Harper and Mary Gray

What today may be our most modern experiences, the fairy tale has known since ancient times. Only it speaks in a different, very simple and simultaneously very difficult and deep language and pictures.

(Dieckmann 1986: 39)

THE UNIVERSALITY OF STORIES

The creation and telling of stories has been used universally by cultures, communities and individuals to provide hope, meaning, purpose and understanding in life. Stories perpetuate knowledge and connect succeeding generations to the richness of their heritage. They are a vehicle through which people are able to develop understanding and coherence in their worlds. Stories provide a very fertile range of implicit communal resources for each individual facing the inevitable developmental conflicts posed by life. In assuming a meta position, stories provide access to universal symbols which, through the process of transformation, make it possible for the individual to address both the conflicts of daily living and the developmental dilemmas of life. Stories provide a map for the soul – a body of knowledge capable of providing shelter, healing, instruction and inspiration (Gersie and King 1990). Stories allow the individual access to realms in which reason does not journey.

Twentieth-century Western society, with its increasingly individualistic orientation, has seen a significant decline in the oral tradition – and with this decline successive generations appear to have developed an increasingly egocentric focus. Money and material acquisitions are frequently primary concerns, kinship and family ties are diminished, parents lack ways of imparting the implicit wisdom of stories to their children, and succeeding generations are deprived of the access to 'universal knowledge' which stories can provide. Unfortunately the constant change and the rapid pace at which we lead life in this century often preclude us from opportunities to experience 'the eternally unchanging' which stories have to offer. Television and film have become the predominant media through which 'stories' are conveyed. The imagination can be severely proscribed by such media, such that succeeding generations are in danger of being deprived of processes in which life tasks can be articulated, obstacles presented, universal wisdoms learned, wounds healed, problems solved and possible courses of action made clear. The sequential rhythms through 'darkness and light' which stories have traditionally woven have given way to the avoidance of 'hurt and pain' in the twentieth century. With the avoidance or denial of such 'shadow experiences', short-term expedience has replaced age-old processes which promote long-term resolution and personal growth. Immediate gratification and the constant striving to acquire that illusive position of 'having sufficient' have put considerable strain on the capacity of individuals to care for one another and to promote a true sense of community.

THE MULTIPLE PURPOSES OF STORIES AND STORY TELLING

In the 'old way', as people gathered together in groups (in close proximity to one another, often around the evening fire), no story was ever told in isolation. Stories often follow a sequence (rhythm) in which one story will evoke another. A question may be responded to by telling several stories, as the story teller draws on greater forces of communal wisdom, implicit in which are options and perspectives which can be healing, educative and nourishing (Estes 1994). Stories allow exploration and articulation of issues and conflicts which may otherwise be too dangerous or frightening to be voiced directly. Characters can be identified with; themes of the likely and the unlikely, the possible and the impossible, the desired and the practicable, and primal fears such as abandonment and annihilation, all can be woven into stories to facilitate exploration of individual and communal issues. Stories which convey meaning carry messages which are sufficiently general to allow the individual to identify with the aspects most pertinent to their personal circumstance or stage of life. In this way, the individual is able to draw on the 'collective' range of experiences and possible solutions which are beyond their own experience and resources. Stories can therefore provide a very powerful adjunct to psychotherapy and can aid the individual's mastery over internal process and external reality.

The process of sharing involved in the telling of and listening to stories creates opportunities for an intimacy which transcends the capacity of verbal description. In addition, it is contended that pro-social behaviour and its core ingredients of empathy, reciprocity and intimacy are promoted through the process level of story telling. This is a highly complex process and is often experienced simultaneously at various levels – at the level of personal consciousness, at the level of personal unconscious, at the level of the communal unconscious or transpersonal (Clarkson 1992a) and at the somatic level.

The multi-modal delivery of stories (auditory, visual and tactile) in many cultures provides a 'social blanket' within which important inter- and intrapersonal skills are able to nestle (Blakemore-Brown and Parr 1996). From a very early age, children who have been exposed to stories develop the capacity to define and articulate the feelings implicit in the characters and symbols of stories. A 2-year-old child, observed while at play with her mother selecting dressing-up clothes, lifted a witch's hat from the box and put it on her head. Her mother asked, 'Are you going to be a witch?' The child promptly took the hat from her head and handed it to her mother, saying, 'Mummy be witch, Mummy be witch.' The mother took the hat from the child, placed it on her own head and said, 'I be a witch.' At this the child took flight around the playroom. When cornered, she turned and, with a look of distress on her face, shouted at her mother, 'Don't be angry, don't be angry!' This brief observation demonstrates the way in which children exposed to the 'social blanket' provided by stories have the capacity from a very young age to interpret the character as the instrument of emotions.

Stories are not simply a means of entertainment and recreation. They have intellectual and educative functions and are potentially curative when they facilitate the safe rediscovery and reconsideration of the often denied shadow elements of our lives. In Hindu culture, individuals who are emotionally distressed are frequently managed by being read a pertinent story upon which to meditate. The choice of both the story and the words used to convey it are carefully selected to encapsulate the essence of the individual's dilemma and to inspire insight into possible avenues for its resolution.

Bettelheim (1976) cautions against the interpretation of the unconscious content of stories in work with children. He considers it to be both intrusive and potentially destructive, particularly

> if he [the parent or therapist] seems able to read the child's secret thoughts, know his most hidden feelings, even before the child has begun to become aware of them. . . . Adult interpretations, as correct as they may be, rob the child of the opportunity to feel that he, on his own, through repeated hearing and ruminating about the story, has coped successfully with a difficult situation.
>
> (Bettelheim 1976: 18, 19)

USING STORIES AND STORY TELLING IN THERAPY

Naming the previously unnamed

Stories have the capacity to 'name the previously unnamed', and to personify the content of internal psychic functioning, thereby making the content of unconscious material, memories of repressed experiences and previously denied emotions communicable in a way which is not necessarily personally threatening. Through stories, fairy tales, music and other art forms, material from the unconscious can gradually be allowed to seep through to consciousness, bypassing the restrictive potential of logic and rationality. Logic is frequently both protective (against experiences of pain) and restrictive. However, the liberation of such material has the potential to facilitate the cathartic release (and experience) of pain, and the possible redeployment of logic to develop problem-solving skills and solutions instead of maintaining the emotional impasse and avoidance of pain.

This process is epitomized by Ruth, the 6-year-old daughter of deaf parents. Father was a violent alcoholic who physically abused his wife. At the peak of the incidents of domestic violence, an older sibling would watch and wait for the moment when the fighting became dangerous for the mother, and would then phone the police. A younger sibling would punch and kick Father in a bid to protect Mother. However, Ruth, who was quiet and withdrawn and was described by her mother as a dreamy and sleepy child, was reported to be 'unaffected' because she continued to watch television during the outbreaks of violence. The clinical view was that she had coped with these incidents by becoming 'emotionally frozen', and therefore a therapeutic goal was for Ruth to begin to express her feelings more overtly. While reading a story (about going to a fancy dress party) during one of her sessions she asked why it was that the wolf ate Red Riding Hood. When asked which character she would be in the fairy story, Ruth immediately said that she would be Red Riding Hood. She identified her father and younger brothers as 'the wolves in her world', but was horrified when asked if she was ever a wolf! However, with a twinkle in her eye, she did acknowledge that her best friend might be a bit of wolf occasionally as she sometimes hit Ruth. On being asked what she did when her best friend hit her, Ruth replied, 'I hit her back.' She smiled in recognition to the comment, 'Ah, so you have got a bit of wolf in you after all.' In response to an inquiry about what Red Riding Hood might have been feeling when she encountered the wolf in the fairy story, she reported her feelings in terms of sound, replying that in her head and ears was a feeling of 'bang, bang, bang', in her heart a feeling of 'beat, beat, beat', and in her tummy a feeling of 'umm, umm, umm'. Using a sand tray and puppetry, the child relayed her version of the story of Red Riding Hood. Her story ended at the point at which the wolf ate Red Riding Hood. She smiled and laughed when told of the hunter and the original ending of the story, and said, 'Oh, I forgot about the hunter.' It was from this point in the therapeutic process that Ruth began to experience and express her feelings more overtly when her father was violent, thereby enabling her mother to notice how she was harmed by what she witnessed.

This vignette also demonstrates the way in which individuals frequently derive their own meaning from traditional stories by changing their endings (usually unconsciously) to coincide with personal life decisions and circumstances. Alternatively, the stories and fairy tales with which an individual identifies are capable of exerting an unanticipated influence on the course which an individual's life may follow. Stories and their associated symbols and images, which are heard and internalized in childhood, are often discarded at the conscious level only to be revisited as 'carriers of meaning and understanding' at particularly poignant moments in later life – at times of transition, uncertainty or emotional crisis.

Time and timing

Fairy stories are the gift of fantasy, capable of sustaining us through the pitfalls of everyday life. The therapeutic use of stories requires both the ability to listen to the story which the child tells, and the development or use of other stories to enhance understanding, to develop resources, to solve problems or to promote growth. The use of stories can be preparatory for other therapeutic work, though in many cases working through the metaphor requires an astute sense of therapeutic timing. When the moment at which stories are told is carefully chosen, both in terms of purpose and timing, and they are told by a trusted and respected person, they have the capacity to be life-changing.

Issues of time and timing in therapy are considered in Gersie (1996), and it is hoped that the importance of timing will be demonstrated by examples, in which both the 'moment' and the judicious use of timing have been crucial in precipitating a therapeutic shift.

Jane, a 12-year-old girl, and her family attended family therapy at various stages of her life. She had a speech impediment and was a slow learner who was having great difficulty making herself understood in her family. Jane was constantly being compared to her older, brighter sister and had become a scapegoat within the family. During the course of one of her sessions Jane related an incident in which she had become so angry and distressed that she had run away from home to the horse paddock she enjoyed visiting. 'And I told the horse. . . . ' Filled with mistrust, Jane suddenly stopped telling her story. She was encouraged to tell what she had said to the horse, but replied: 'No, you will think that I am stupid. Everyone thinks that I am stupid.' On further prompting she still refused, though she laughed and had a teasing look in her eye.

It was at this moment that telling Jane the story of the Goose Girl (from Grimm) precipitated a therapeutic shift. After hearing the story she was able to relate how she had told the horse all about what had happened at home that morning. She reported how she had run all the way home after telling the horse, because it had told her that today was the day that she had a play session and that she could tell her therapist all about it. The session was concluded in laughter.

Liz was a depressed 11-year-old girl. During the course of her therapy it became clear that she lacked a clear sense of 'self' and that she had no understanding of the cause of her depression. Liz's father had left the family four years previously, and Liz and her mother were very close. It was decided that Liz and her mother would be seen jointly, to do some life story work.

During the fourth session, Liz and her mother were both asked to draw the wound that had resulted from Father leaving. Liz drew a rather scientific diagram of her heart receiving an injury. Her mother drew a heart inside the ribs, with a piece floating away. Mother described her picture with great passion, using 'we' to include Liz as if they were one person. It emerged that Mother began to get depressed every autumn, through the winter, in antici-pation of the anniversary of her husband's departure. During the session Liz cried for her mother's pain. It was at this moment that they were invited to listen to the story of Persephone. As the end of the story approached, Mother began to cry uncontrollably. As she regained her composure, she said, 'I was horrible to do that to her.' The therapist responded by commenting that her tears would help to wash her wounded heart. From this time on, Liz was able to see that her mother's depression was not her own, and that she (Liz) had in fact felt glad and relieved when her father had left them.

Personal meaning and problem resolution in story telling

> Stories offer more than consolation, they provide encouragement to continue the formulation of questions rather than to abandon the search. Through identification with a hero or heroine, who shows the degree of patience, wit and courage needed to surmount setbacks, we learn to face our own fear and loneliness. Untethered by the constraints of reality, yet within a plausible structure, our story characters explore alternative actions until an answer and a way out is found. . . . Listening to the gripping tale we think about questions posed, problems created and approaches and resolutions which hold us captive to the process of solution.
>
> (Gersie and King 1990: 35)

Many internal experiences cannot be rationally articulated in a way that others understand them. Psychotherapy – the telling of one's own story – is one means through which this process becomes possible. Artistic expression (of whatever standard) and the creation of personal fairy tales during therapy constitute very important attempts to give form (Gersie and King 1990) to such invisible, internal mate-rial, thereby making internal processes more accessible to conscious examination and, where they are conflictual, to resolution.

In the act of 'telling' in psychotherapy the client gives the thera-pist access to their inner world, and in doing so is able to embark on a journey towards the resolution of trauma, the regaining of competencies and the development of new insights and meanings. A familiarity with archetypal motifs and symbolic meanings is of considerable psychotherapeutic value as it can enhance the therapist's access to and understanding of unconscious material and processes. Furthermore, the therapist's knowledge of their own internal map (Clarkson 1992b) is essential in providing a safeguard against the introduction of stories and meanings which reflect or answer the therapist's own needs and issues.

Case example

A woman training in therapeutic techniques reported her experience of the process of accessing 'internal material' through her identification with the traditional Heidi story. Her account provides moving and powerful evidence of the way in which individuals 'hold' and model characters from stories which have particular significance for them and their management of life issues. Although potentially inhibiting in some ways, such identification frequently facilitates coping in the short term. It is perhaps the task of therapy to facilitate an integration of the various parts of the self and to mobilize sufficient psychic energy to enable the individual to decide on different and wholesome outcomes to their 'life script'.

Heidi was the story which most captured my imagination during childhood, though it took me three months to recall this when asked to do so. On rereading the story I realized how closely my life story both resembled and was intertwined with the Heidi story. In the story, Heidi leaves her family following a catastrophe, and is taken to live with her grandfather who lives up a mountain. Heidi blossoms there, becoming the apple of her grandfather's eye and spreading happiness to all with whom she has contact. She becomes friends with Peter the goatherd and his blind grandmother, reading the Bible to her and singing hymns to God. Following concern that Heidi is not being educated, her aunt returns to find her a place in a family in which Heidi is to be companion to a sickly girl, Clara. Heidi is told that she can return to her grandfather whenever she wants, but she soon discovers that this is not true. She becomes homesick and unhappy, and begins to long for her grandfather. Heidi is unable to please the stern housekeeper, Fräulein Rottenmeier, and although she and Clara are friends, Heidi always wishes to be elsewhere. Clara's grandmother recognizes Heidi's unhappiness. She tells Heidi to always pray to God for her wish, but cautions her that if she does not get her heart's desire, this is God's will. However, if she is patient and prays and trusts in God, God will make her light-hearted and happy and fulfil all her wishes. In the story Heidi becomes increasingly homesick and ill. She begins to sleepwalk, and it is suspected that there is a ghost in the house. Concern about Heidi increases when it is discovered that she is the 'ghost'. Clara's father calls the doctor. The doctor recognizes that Heidi is pining for her grandfather, and that she will die unless she is reunited with him.

This is where my recollection of the story ended, and I long held the belief that the 'child within me' must die in order for me to survive. [In the original version, Heidi goes home to her grandfather and is joined by Clara, who once again learns to walk. The story has a very happy ending.] The intertwining of my life story with the Heidi story is easily recognized. My family has a history of alcoholism and my father was a cruel man who subjected me to multiple abuse. A catastrophe was precipitated by my mother's discovery of the abuse, and our family was torn apart. I was told that I would never see any of my immediate family again. I lived with my grandfather in Scotland (up a mountain) between the ages of 3 and 6. Thereafter I lived in a children's home where the matron bore a close resemblance to Fräulein Rottenmeier. I was very ill between the ages of 8 and 10, and, just like Clara, my legs would not work and had to be massaged regularly. My eyes had to be wiped open for me to see in the mornings, mirroring the blindness of Peter's grandmother. The children's home ghost was a repetitive terror to be faced each night as I walked to the toilet to avoid wetting my bed. I spent many unhappy years when I could not eat properly or even be tempted to eat by the promise of something special. Many of my memories were permeated with recollections of ridicule, derision and disbelief, as I was frequently called a liar when trying to tell of the abuse.

However, throughout my life (even during the years of abuse) I felt that God was in my life caring for me, and in line with the instruction from Clara's grandmother I prayed regularly and felt warm and cared for in God's presence. My whole life feels as though it has been about sharing my happy side, about being a companion, and about waiting for God to show me the road I must take on the map of my life's journey.

The Heidi story signifies much of my childhood experience, though it has only been with the increased safety that I have experienced as an adult that I have been able to undertake the long and difficult tasks of reclaiming my 'dead child'. This process continues, with each of the characters in the Heidi story representing different facets of my life's experience and resources. Just as Heidi derived great pleasure from being able to tell stories and read to Peter's grandmother, I too now get great pleasure from telling stories and helping children to discover and to make sense of their own maps and life stories. There have been many stories that I have heard as an adult that have helped me grow, though perhaps most pertinent in this process is the moment at which the story is told. A story told at the right time in someone's life can shine a light sufficiently bright to illuminate the way ahead on the map of life.

STORY TELLING AS A THERAPEUTIC PROCESS

Engaging in therapy may be precipitated by an individual's awareness that their journey through life is in some way blocked. Different descriptions of the manifestations of this 'block' are provided by the various schools of thought in psychotherapy. In psychoanalytic terms the individual's behaviour may be described as a 'repetition compulsion' as the individual deploys earlier developmental styles in a repetitive failure to 'circumvent a block'. In transactional analysis this process is evident in Berne's (1972) concept of 'life script'. This is a metaphor describing the early (pre-verbal) development of a 'life plan' which is compulsively lived out, with the individual engaging in 'passive behaviours' (ineffective problem-solving attempts) which are script reinforcing (Schiff *et al.* 1975). The child-based examples used previously in this chapter describe the various symptoms presented by the children (e.g. quiet and withdrawn) and provide clues to the manifestation of 'the block'.

Traditionally, myth-making structures have been applied to the creation and understanding of single 'stories' with Gersie and King (1990) and Lahad (1992) delineating very helpful frameworks for the analysis of stories and the resolution of 'blocks'. Therapeutic endeavours have been enhanced by the clarity of these parameters within which problems are exposed, courses of action formulated, solutions attempted, issues resolved and experiences reorganized and integrated into a whole. Equally it is possible to plan therapy at a macro level, taking account of the apparent 'developmental sequence' followed by individuals as they recount their own life stories which progress through the development of personal meaning, healing and the emergence of growth and change. This sequence is illustrated in the report of exercises and their associated stories told during the course of one person's therapeutic journey. Each step in the sequence is accompanied by a description of the exercise set, the process followed and finally some brief comment on therapeutic integration at the micro level.

Illustrative exercises and stories

A sequence of stories is recounted here with the kind permission of their creator, Grace, a 34-year-old woman who used stories to help her confront her childhood abuse, unravel many of the complications it had caused in her life and (albeit slowly and painfully) discover her creative potential. She was clear from the outset that she would be unable to tolerate a 'continuous' journey in the classical therapeutic sense, but that she would travel sporadically, engaging and disengaging as she felt able to deal with each new issue that emerged. The sequence of stories (and stories within stories) demonstrates the 'Russian matrioska doll effect' (Estes 1994) in which, when it is allowed to do so, the unconscious will focus on those internal psychic elements which require attention if resolution and integration are to be achieved. Although these stories are drawn from the therapeutic journey of one individual, the exercises may be useful in facilitating change when used singly.

Grace's first story emerges from an exercise which we have entitled 'Switching on the light'. The exercise, a gestalt therapy technique, is intended to identify (and name) the 'knot' (or block).

The exercise

Choose some symbols which encapsulate the feelings linked to significant family members or friends. Next, using dough, create an inanimate object, a monster or imaginary hero/ine, and give it a name. Then place it on paper, create an environment in which it lives and write a story (Oaklander 1988).

Grace wrote this story:

The symbol for my husband was a yellow band – a wedding ring, strong, circular and precious. A beautiful white flower which was delicate and perfumed symbolized my daughter, and for my son I chose circular arms which were warm and soft. From these symbols I chose to make a creature which looked like a white sacred cow, but it developed into a monster/dragon/serpent with yellow horns and a red split tongue. I wrote this story: 'Once upon a time there was a monster called Life, who travelled around the world spitting out lies wherever it went. Everyone feared it and ran away when it came near. It continued along life's road in the knowledge that it would only find peace in death.'

Mapping the meaning

This story demonstrates the way in which stories can be the vehicle through which issues and conflicts too frightening and dangerous to be voiced can be given expression in a metaphorical way. On reflection, Grace identified this as the moment in her therapeutic journey when she 'switched the light on' to reveal her core therapeutic issues or 'knots'. She describes the power and shock of this experience:

The process took my whole body by shock as it began with the happiest feeling of my adult life and then became my experiences which I'd kept hidden but which were linked to the violence and abuse perpetrated on me by my father. I was so disturbed by this discovery that I quickly destroyed the 'model' and gave it back to my therapist, hoping that I would forget that which I had seen. For my inner child life was intolerable, and death would be preferable.

The traditional Blackbeard story (Estes 1992) contains themes which may provide an opportunity to externalize at a 'once removed level' (Gordon 1995) similar fears to those described in the exercise above. The story may be useful in helping clients to value their intuition and to trust their experiences of fear when feeling vulnerable. In addition, the story provides some material to identify and begin to incorporate shadow aspects of rage and anger.

We have entitled the next phase 'Acknowledging the knot'.

The exercise

After using relaxation techniques to rid the body of physical tensions, imagine being in a bubble of your favourite colour. Breath in until your whole body is warm and peacefully bathed in it. Now tell your own creation story.

There are many creation stories which exist in different cultures. The story chosen by Grace in our example focused on the biblical story of Noah's Ark, the flood and the search for new land:

> Long ago and far away, the land was barren and dry. A tall and ancient tree stood on the horizon in the midday sun. The heat distorted the vision and the tree appeared to move from side to side. Stretched out in every direction around the tree on the parched land were tall yellow grasses. The air was still, breathless, as silent as death. In the distance a speck appeared in the blue cloudless sky. Slowly the speck grew larger and larger, bigger and bigger as it drew closer to the tree. The rhythmic beat of its long wings broke the silence as it neared the tree. The bird landed on a branch of the ancient tree, and although tired it needed to tell its story. As all around listened, the bird began in a whispered voice: 'Listen to me. I came to this place on the wing of disaster. My soft white feathers are tattered and stained from my long journey. This is my journey's end. I am but one year old and have been held a prisoner, locked in a cage in a pirate ship. A great storm blew up and the ship was tossed about on the sea, rolling around like a cork. My cage crashed to the deck, breaking open the lock . . . and I was free. Now I need rest, for I am tired and weary. I am hungry and thirsty and need to be replenished. I saw the tree and knew it would give me rest. Perhaps I can build a shelter here. But all around looks dry and barren. Maybe I'll die, for I see no water. I must find something or my life will ebb away. As I wait and rest the day is drawing to an end. I can hear sounds of insects wakening and coming out in the cool of the evening. Drops of dew form on the dry grasses. I think I will survive.'

Mapping the meaning

There is much that is symbolic in this story. For Grace, the tree was symbolic of her dead inner child. It was ancient and wise, and a vessel within which new life could find a dwelling place and survive. The bird represented the '6-year-old self'. The number 7 has particular significance in biblical terms, God having created the world in seven days. When Grace was 7 years old she had been 'tossed about' by a destructive storm in the sea of her life. Through this story she managed to 'acknowledge the knot' in her life and to discover the resources and hope located in her 6-year-old self. She described the somatic response she had to the story, with her body shaking at its impact. However, most poignantly, she commented that the story provided her with a containment which allowed her to explore her life through the relative sense of safety of the metaphor. Although the recognition was followed by a time filled with the (cathartic) release of pain and experience of considerable shame, the sense of safety which she experienced made it possible for Grace to continue her journey.

The ancient myth of Persephone is one in which some of Grace's issues are also contained. Beauty and innocence meet 'parental' trickery and manipulation, mother and daughter are separated and then re-united after a compromise which involves Persephone spending time in the Underworld as well as on Earth. These experiences mirrored many of those of our example, and the myth encapsulated for Grace the way in which she had survived by keeping (at least) two parts of her life separated. This provided her with markers of the opportunity to 'acknowledge the knot/s' and the therapeutic work which she needed to undertake in order to survive without being a prisoner of her past.

These moments of recognition were followed by periods filled with the cathartic release of pain and the experience of considerable shame. We have entitled this phase 'Feeling the associated pain', and describe some of the terrain in this part of the therapeutic journey.

The exercise

This third phase was discovered in an exercise of meditation and story telling linked to a family photograph. The exercise requires discussion of the setting and relationships of the family in the photograph, and may be linked to the use of a guided fantasy. In this case (by chance!) the guided fantasy is of a person walking, being followed by a bird. A gift is given to the person by the bird and a letter or story is written to someone in the photograph.

The story told by Grace illustrates the capacity of metaphor to facilitate the experience of deep and powerful personal material:

On a warm summer's day, a bird flies on the wing as I wander over the lush green hills and down the valley. The sun shone in my face, making me squint against the bright light. The grass under my bare feet felt like velvet and the gentle breeze smelt fresh and clean. As I neared the bottom of the valley, tiredness overcame me. Lying down on the lush green blanket, a dreamy feeling began to cloud my mind. As I closed my eyes and drifted into a relaxing sleep I felt like a baby in a mother's arms and all the pain drifted from my body.

The bird screeched and hovered above my head, high in the sky. It appeared to be communicating some kind of message to me. There in the palm of my hand was a flower, so small and beautiful – a delicate white colour, yet tinged with a pale yellow from the hot rays of the sun. It told me this story: 'I am glad you have found me, for I have waited for such a long time for you to come back and possess me once more. We were merely separated, and I could never have been taken from you. I will always be yours whether we are together or apart. I think that from now on you will understand. I am yours to show if you wish, or to keep from view. Now you need no longer fear separation. In that knowledge you will find peace and freedom and grow. This I know.'

Mapping the meaning

Through this story Grace demonstrates the way in which the 'Adult' within her is given a symbol of her Inner Child – a delicate, beautiful and perfumed flower which indicates that her Inner Child is not dead but alive. The symbol of the flower is woven into each of the stories in this matrix and holds hope for new life. It offers a clearer understanding of the deep yet distinct language of the unconscious and highlights the need for therapists to have knowledge of such symbols. 'Without this knowledge one often overlooks the symbol and does not even know it' (Dieckmann 1986: 59).

Nancy Davis's (1990) story, 'The Burned Child', contains many parallels to this description and when read to Grace by her therapist precipitated a profoundly cathartic experience for her in which she was able to release 'truly healing waves of tears' as she empathically reconnected with her 'lost/dead' Inner Child.

Gradually, given the right therapeutic ingredients, it becomes possible to begin the often arduous process of 'unravelling the knot'. The process continues to be immersed in symbols rich in unconscious meaning but perhaps involves greater cognitive integration than is recognizable at previous stages.

The exercise

The intention here is to allow the unconscious to take the lead and for the participant/client to draw a stroke of paint or crayon, the shape of which is familiar or has some significant connection to them. This is followed by an exercise entitled 'A new beginning'. The invitation to locate any beginning in life is given. The events preceding the new beginning are recalled, as is their impact on the future/outcome. Each is painted.

The stroke which Grace painted was an 'S' shape, though for some reason she felt strongly that she did not like the shape she had drawn. Her symbol of a new beginning was a wedding dress, and was founded in her experience of stability in her life with her partner – a stability which she had not experienced in childhood. She entitled her picture 'A celebration of life', but recalls that 'sick' was the word which best described her feeling state. As she progressed through the exercise, the dress in the original picture changed to become a volcano, spitting red-hot molten lava from its centre. Lava flowed down the mountain to form a land in a massive 'sea of despair'. This is her story which accompanied the exercise:

> Once upon a time there was a devil with a red and purple face, two horns and evil eyes which turned upwards and outwards towards the ears. It had a wide nose with white and yellow fluid running out over an open mouth which was screaming profanities so terrible they were not fit for the human ear. I was filled with rage and hatred and then noticed the shape of the letter 'S'. Somehow I was able to make links with my very first story and my experience of having been sexually abused. My life story was starting to make sense.

On rotating the picture Grace described a heartening metamorphosis:

> The devil's horns became the volcanic eruption. The eyes and nose became two graceful magnificent birds, facing each other and dancing.
> The screaming mouth flowing with yellow and white fluid produced a dramatic yet romantic moonlit sky. The picture

required a new title: 'Two lovers dancing on the face of the Devil'.

Mapping the meaning

Grace reported that during the course of her adult life she had actively avoided encounters with depression. Each time her experience was of the intensity of a volcanic eruption which so terrified her that she felt she could only survive by avoiding the experience and busying herself to preclude time for reflection.

This exercise provided the material for her to begin to integrate a new cognitive framework through which to understand her life. Her new imagery helped dissipate her shame, and encouraged her to look at the greatest struggle of her life as a poetic and graceful dance upon evil: a dance which had the capacity to bring forth the joyful realization that good can triumph over evil.

As with the process delineated at the micro level, the 'unravelling of the knot' results in a decrease in the emotional charge with which core issues were previously imbued, and for their resolution and reintegration into a now reorganizing self structure. This period of 'resolution and integration' is the penultimate stage in the therapeutic journey.

The exercise

Following progressive deep relaxation or hypnotic induction, the invitation is made to seek the supportive assistance of the unconscious in 'knowing that which needs to be known', and to then recall the earliest memory available to the client.

The image which Grace presented in response to this exercise was of a baby, breathless with fear, being held by the throat, but with its head bursting open. Following a meditation she related a story in which she embarked on a journey to climb a mountain.

The road to be followed was initially rough and narrow, but then disappeared altogether. The traveller had to scramble over loose rocks in a journey which was almost perpetually treacherous. As the traveller mounted the first ridge, he entered a woodland with a more gentle slope. The full moon was unable to penetrate the thicket to light the traveller's way. His heart pounded as he pushed his way past bracken and bushes in the undergrowth. The howl of a wolf sent cold shivers down his spine. The slope steepened once again, and the traveller's breath and heart quickened with the effort and the thought of what was to come. Quite suddenly the traveller climbed the ridge on to a plateau. . . . In front of me was fire, flickering brightly at the mouth of a cave. As the traveller neared the fire, the shape of an old man appeared from within the cave. The old man was bent over and walked slowly, beckoning to the traveller to sit by the fire on round smooth cushion-shaped stones. The warmth of the fire crept slowly through the traveller as the old man sat on the stone next to me. The traveller did not at first notice the bag he placed between us. Although the old man said nothing, the traveller could hear him in his mind's ear, telling him of a gift, a wonderful gift that the traveller had come to collect from him. He had waited many years for the joy which was now potentially his. However, the traveller became afraid and wanted to flee, being caught between not wanting to displease the wise old man and yet not wanting to reach into the bag and take the gift. The old man immediately recognized the traveller's thoughts and reached down into the bag, carefully lifting the gift from it. Without a sound he unfolded the paperlike tissue which covered the gift. Gently lying in the palm of his hand the gift was revealed: a beautiful, delicate, purified white flower, with yellow edges which shone brightly in the light of the full moon.

Grace reported responding at the somatic level: she felt an intense pounding of the blood in her head, her breathing was rapid and shallow and she experienced a tightening sensation around her throat. At this point she did not consciously recall the imagery of her earliest memory, but continued her story:

'I cannot take it . . . I cannot take it, please. . . . ' The old man smiled reassuringly, and I felt his warmth calm me as he told me I'd know where it was when I was ready. I smiled in great relief.

Mapping the meaning

Many memories which are more easily recalled are more recent ones, often related to adult dysfunction. Recollection of early material in this case gave direct access to powerful unconscious material which provided an unanticipated gift to Grace. The way in which she oscillates between relating this story from the subjective and objective positions suggests that, although the framework now exists, the process of resolution and integration is not yet fully complete. The links in the story speak for themselves, though it was pertinent that Grace felt a reluctance to give up the old familiar behaviour rather than accept the new gift, perhaps because its implications for her life were not entirely clear, or perhaps because it meant bidding farewell to a long-standing familiar element of her life.

The traditional tale of the Crescent Moon Bear (Estes 1992) contains many similarities to Grace's journey and her heroic and courageous search for solutions to her life's issues. She reported that after 'discovering' the story she was encouraged to embark on the final stages of her journey. This began when Grace encountered the five element story-telling process (Lahad 1996), and marked her entry to the phase we have entitled 'Therapeutic termination and regeneration'.

The exercise

This technique involves the therapist composing a story which has five essential elements chosen by the client. These elements are a character, a place, a season, a time and an object. The undertaking at this stage of the therapeutic process is most successfully facilitated when the therapist uses universal truths, e.g. 'it was a warm day on which the sun was shining . . . ', and encourages the listener to take charge of their own process and to feel and own the experience.

Grace was told the following story:

> There was once a fairy [the character] who was lost in the forest [the place]. The fairy had been there for a very long time, though she couldn't remember when she had first found herself there. The seasons of springtime, summertime, autumn and winter had come and gone many times. The fairy felt that she had possibly seen ten new moons. The fairy felt that the forest must be of a magnificent size, or alternatively she had just been walking around in circles.
>
> It was now wintertime again [the season], and although it was midnight [the time] and the moon was shining brightly, the fairy did not feel the cold. Her dress sparkled with a special magic which kept her warm. As the fairy looked around her to find her way she noticed something which she had never seen before. It was a small white flower [the object] with a yellow glow, gleaming as if the moon shone its magic moonbeams on to it.

Suddenly the fairy was taken up to an earlier memory, a place which seemed so far away, and yet so near. This land in which she now found herself was in fact a place which she knew very well. The grass was green and felt like velvet. As far as she could see the landscape was carpeted with primroses. Feelings of warmth and safety enfolded the fairy as she remembered being held in her mother's loving arms. The moon smiled a gentle smile on to the face of the fairy, and invited her to reclaim the beautiful small white flower which had always been hers.

Mapping the meaning

In the context of what was an intensely emotional time for Grace, she was encouraged to consider which elements of her life still needed her attention before she could graciously reclaim her flower.

Throughout her life, 'child' fears had overshadowed and stunted Grace's life experiences and growth. She had starved herself of love, food, gifts and even of relaxing holidays. Recognition of the presence of loving objects in her life, of her own capacity to love and the clarity that love, anger, pain and beauty could co-exist within herself, enabled her to gain closure on many of her core conflicts.

The astute reader will no doubt have noticed the repeated presence of important and sustaining symbols throughout the process of this therapeutic story-telling journey – the circular ring, the loving arms, the fairy who had been walking around in circles, the beautiful and delicate white flower, etc. In various combinations they had a presence in each of the stages of the journey we have described. Each of the phases and exercises allowed both resolution of some issues and preparation for the next conflict to be resolved. The monster called Life may still hold some archaic fears for Grace, but has largely been laid to rest. She continues to grow, sustained by her creativity, wisdom and capacity for empathy – all qualities which she rediscovered in the process of her story-telling therapeutic journey.

CONCLUSION

From an initial focus on the universality of stories and their capacity to promote growth and development at the individual,

group and community levels, we have also presented details of the
variety of ways in which stories can promote growth in
psychotherapy. Some have involved the telling of traditional tales,
others have involved the development and telling of personal
stories. The power of story telling as a curative method is perhaps
most poignantly captured by Bettelheim's assertion that:

> For a story to hold the child's attention, it must entertain him
> and arouse his curiosity. But to enrich his life, it must stimulate
> his imagination; help him to develop his intellect; be attuned to
> his anxieties and aspirations; give full recognition to his difficul-
> ties, while at the same time suggesting solutions to the problems
> which perturb him.
>
> (Bettelheim 1976: 5)

For children and adults alike, stories can provide a very useful
means for the development of ways in which meaning can be
'plotted' and a healing journey initiated.

REFERENCES

In the course of this chapter we have made reference to a number of stories
(the tales of the Goose Girl, the Burned Child, Persephone, Blackbeard
and the Crescent Moon Bear). We have deliberately not detailed the
content of these stories in the text. We hope that readers will seek them out
and discover, in the rich and fertile content provided by such stories,
meanings which are personal and unique. These and other stories can be
found variously in volumes of Grimm, the Greek myths, Estes (1992) and
similar texts.

Berne, E. (1972) *What Do You Say After You Say Hello?*, New York:
    Bantam.
Bettelheim, B. (1976) *The Uses of Enchantment*, Harmondsworth: Penguin.
Blakemore-Brown, L., and Parr, M. (1996) 'Positive parenting', *Young
    Minds Magazine* 24: 24–5.
Clarkson, P. (1992a) *Transactional Analysis Psychotherapy: An Integrated
    Approach*, London and New York: Tavistock/Routledge.
——(1992b) 'Systemic integrative psychotherapy training', in W. Dryden
    (ed.) *Integrative and Eclectic Therapy: A Handbook*, Buckingham: Open
    University Press.
Davis, N. (1990) 'The Burned Child', in N. Davis (ed.) *Once Upon a Time
    . . . Therapeutic Stories to Heal Abused Children*, Oxen Hill, Md:
    Psychological Associates of Oxen Hill.
Dieckmann, H. (1986) *Twice-Told Tales: The Psychological Use of Fairy
    Tales*, Wilmette, Ill.: Chiron Publications.
Estes, C.P. (1992) *Women Who Run With The Wolves*, London: Rider.

——(1994) *The Gift of Story*, London: Rider.

Gersie, A. (ed.) (1996) *Dramatic Approaches to Brief Therapy*, London: Jessica Kingsley.

Gersie, A., and King, N. (1990) *Storymaking in Education and Therapy*, London: Jessica Kingsley.

Gordon, S. (1995) *The Right to Feel Safe: A Protective Behaviours Manual*, Adelaide: Mission SA.

Lahad, M. (1992) 'Storymaking as an assessment method for coping with stress', in S. Jennings (ed.) *Dramatherapy, Theory and Practice*, London: Routledge, 2.

——(1996) Advanced Workshop of the BASICPh Group. Personal communication.

Oaklander, V. (1988) *Windows to Our Children*, Highland NY: Gestalt Journal Press.

Schiff, J.L., Schiff, A.W., Mellor, K., Schiff, E., Schiff, S., Richman, E., Fishman, J., Wolz, L., Fishman, C, and Momb, D. (1975) *Cathexis Reader: Transactional Analysis Treatment of Psychosis*, New York: Harper and Row.

Chapter 4

Psychotherapeutic paradigms from Indian mythology

Channapatna Shamasundar

INTRODUCTION

The contents of this chapter are based on the material gathered
during my sabbatical study, 'The Mental Health Concepts in Indian
Mythology', funded by the National Institute of Mental Health and
Neuro Sciences, Bangalore, in 1987–8. The ancient texts studied
were: the Vedas, the Upanisads, the Puranas, the Epics, the Jataka,
the Jaina stories and *The Ocean of Story*. The material thus gathered consisted of stories (anecdotes) and dialogues/statements. I will
use the word 'story' for both forms.

The stories have rich psychotherapeutic potential. One of the
mythological stories succinctly demonstrates this fact.

Story 1

A Brahmin father was not satisfied with the manner in which his
grown-up son was attending to his duties and responsibilities. He
told his son: 'I will narrate a story to you. Thoroughly consider it
and its meaning in your mind, and then do as you choose' (Mitra
1891: vol. 1, ch. 1).

It is as though mythological stories are meant only for such usage in
any culture. I believe that the therapeutic use of mythological
stories does not have any cultural boundaries, for the reasons
enumerated below.

• The story influences the therapy essentially by providing a paradigm
shift, there being a 'quantum jump' from one orbit of thinking to
another (Calder 1968) and the metaphor suggesting a new hypothesis (Domaingue 1992).

- The mythology is comparable to nature by virtue of its universality (Karenyi 1949), and the mythylograms represent primordially experienced archetypal images arising in the depths of the unconscious (Jung 1949, 1954).
- Mythology represents the repressed psychological problems (Boyer 1977), and most of the intrapsychic phenomena and the psychological problems are cross-culturally similar. For example, Scott *et al.*'s study (1991) of the effect of family environment on children, Lester *et al.*'s study (1991) of depression and the locus of control, and Poortinga *et al.*'s study (1993) of gestures.
- The mythological stories of a culture are likely to have their thematic counterparts in mythologies of other cultures, as explained by Penzer in his introduction to *The Ocean of Story*. He says:

India is the home of story telling. From India, Persians learnt the art and passed it on to the Arabians. From the middle east, the tales found their way to Constantinople, Venice and eventually to all Europe. Incidents in stories well known to every European child existed in India over 2000 years ago.

(Penzer 1968: viii)

In addition to their universality, the mythological stories also have multi-dimensionality of themes and meanings. As a consequence, it is difficult to categorize these stories rigidly or to academically discuss their contents. Further, the therapist and the client may each selectively recognize and assimilate uniquely personalized meanings from a given story. This has a bearing on how a story is chosen for therapeutic use. I prefer to depend upon spontaneity, using a story if and when it spontaneously appears in my awareness at any therapeutic moment. Even though I am not able to justify this method logically, it seems to work.

The Indian mythological stories span a wide range of themes. I have therefore selected four main thematic groupings for the presentation of a few representative samples:

1 few general themes;
2 conflicts, psycho and somatic symptom meanings and defences;
3 inevitability of miseries and ways of managing them;
4 mental health promoting behaviour.

It is hoped that the story-examples in this chapter will sensitize the reader not only to the therapeutic potential of the stories but also to their usefulness in terms of a wider range of choices in understanding a given situation. Depending on the clinical or therapeutic context, the story can be used to:

- stimulate free association or the historical narrative;
- facilitate insight;
- explain either the aetiological aspects or the principles of management;
- offer choices to re-orient one's values, attitudes, etc.

A FEW GENERAL THEMES

A few of the common problems encountered in therapeutic work, especially in work with families, are:

- obsessive isolation of the part from the whole, or an event from the process or the context;
- rigidly defended differences of opinion, partly related to the problem of part versus whole;
- the deficits in adequate communication.

Stories are particularly suited to the problem of part versus whole because the metaphor allows communication in a holistic manner, perceiving the global relationships (Fatic 1993). And the narrative stories have an integrative quality, integrating the diverse events and actions in one's life (Polkinghorne 1991). The following examples illustrate these points.

Story 2

Sage Vashista explains to his pupil, Prince Rama: 'Life and death, peace and trouble, joy and sorrow, etc., are all concomitants of this worldly life, and will be together in the same person. Similarly, delusions, anger, fear, faith and mistrust, intelligence and ignorance, etc., are all inseparable parts of living manifestation. Out of ignorance, some people understand these different qualities as existing independently, independent of the whole individual. But the wise know all these to be just different functional aspects of the whole, dependent on the whole, and simultaneous manifestations of the same' (Mitra 1891: vol. 6, chs 80–2).

Story 3

Lord Krishna instructs his disciple, Uddhava, concerning the Veda, the four most ancient scriptures representing all knowledge about the Divine: 'Different views of the same Veda are all acceptable because all points of view are implicit in every one of them, either as antecedents or as consequences. The reason for the apparent contradictions in understanding is that each philosopher is incapable of comprehending what is against his nature. He who understands this principle has no difficulty with any contradiction' (Tagare 1979: Skanda 11, ch. 22).

Story 4

Sage Vashista instructs Prince Rama: 'Whatever a man thinks or knows in himself, whether correct or incorrect, he supposes the same as true at all times, and expects to see or understand the same always. Therefore, it is the nature of man to be prejudiced in favour of his own ideas. This is, after all, the desire to see again and again according to their expectations. This leads them to the error of seeing before them whatever they desired to see. Therefore, this error of observation can be removed only by abstaining from desires, strong feelings like anger or hatred and expectations' (Mitra 1891: vol. 6, ch. 79).

Story 5

Once upon a time, the four sons of the king of Benares wished to see a judas tree. Due to many unforeseen circumstances, each one of them saw the tree on separate occasions at long intervals. Later, when they happened to share their knowledge of the judas tree, dispute arose. He who saw the tree in early spring described it as a burnt stump. He who had seen it in summer described it as a banyan tree. He who saw it in the rainy season described it as looking like a piece of meat. He who saw it in autumn described it as an acacia (Cowel 1895: vol. 2, story 248).

Story 6

Sage Yajnavalkya explains to his wife-cum-disciple, Maitreyi: 'One is not able to grasp the particular notes of a musical instrument by themselves without grasping the general note of that instrument. Thus, it is only by knowing or understanding the whole that the particular can be known or understood. He who thinks on each aspect of the totality does not come to know the whole because knowledge thus gained remains incomplete' (Jagadiswarananda 1951: ch. 1, vv. 7–10).

Story 7

The lady-sage Sulabha explains about ideal communication to King Janaka: For the correct meaning of speech to be conveyed, the following conditions are to be satisfied:

- there should be mutual harmony and goodwill between the speaker and the listener;
- the speaker must be free from motives of pride, anger, fear or deceit;
- the words must not be ambiguous, i.e. the meaning of different words must be distinct;
- the speech must be truthful and internally consistent (Ganguli 1970: Shanti Parva, ch. 321).

CONFLICTS, PSYCHO AND SOMATIC SYMPTOM MEANINGS AND DEFENCES

The richness of Indian mythology is summarized by Erna Hoch (1960: 87) in her statement: 'There is hardly any discovery of modern Western psychotherapy that cannot quite easily be confirmed by some precept, parable or proverb from the writings of the Indian religion.' A few examples given below demonstrate this observation in respect of conflicts, psycho and somatic symptoms and defences.

Story 8

While courting his third wife Kaikeyi, King Dasaratha had promised her he would fulfil any two wishes and she had reserved her right to present her wishes at a time of her choice. Much later, Dasaratha started the preparations to crown his eldest son, Prince Rama, born to his first wife, as the successor to the throne. At this point, Kaikeyi submitted her two wishes to the king for fulfilment, asking that Prince Rama should be exiled into the forest for twelve years and that her own son, Prince Bharatha, should succeed to the throne. King Dasaratha was shocked by this dilemma, and suffered intense agony and confusion. After regaining his senses, he directed an angry outburst at Kaikeyi, and later swooned and writhed restlessly on the floor, crying. In the meantime, in order to honour his father's promise, Prince Rama went away in exile into the forest. The king became severely ill and soon died (Raghunathan 1981: Ayodhya Kanda, chs 11, 12).

Story 9

The celestial sage Narada is a perpetual wanderer of the three worlds. Once, he saw an old lady sitting beside two old and ill-looking men and bitterly weeping. Narada asked her who she was and why she was weeping so. She replied: 'I am Bhakti [Lady Devotion], and these are my two sons, Spiritual-Knowledge and Renunciation. I am very sad because, though very young, we have become very old and ill. I do not know the reason. Perhaps you can tell me.' Narada replied: 'In this current age of Kaliyuga, nobody wants you and your sons, and no one cares for you three. Due to lack of love and care, the three of you have become dull, weak, diseased and prematurely old' (Tagare 1979: Skanda 1, ch. 2).

Story 10

There was once a cannibal demon in a forest who was emaciated and very weak in spite of adequately feeding himself. When he found a wandering Brahmin from a nearby village, he pounced to eat. The Brahmin pleaded to be let off. The demon offered a choice: 'You are a learned man. I will set you free if you explain to me why I am lean, pale and weak.' The Brahmin, who knew the demon's background history, said, 'The reasons are many. You are away from your relatives and friends who are not well disposed towards you, and you are grieving on that account. You also feel ridiculed and humiliated by them. You lack the courage and will to face the challenges back home' (Ganguli 1970: Anusasana Parva, ch. 124).

Story 11

King Nala lost his kingdom in a game of dice, and went wandering into the forest with his wife, Damayanthi. One night, while Damayanthi was sleeping, Nala thought: 'If she remains with me, she will have to suffer a lot of hardships; if I desert her now, she will somehow manage to reach her parents' kingdom and live in comfort till I redeem my kingdom.' Thus debating, he decided to desert his wife. Going away some distance, he came back again to assure himself that she was safe. Thus, as though his heart and mind were rent in two, like a swing he kept on going away and coming back many times. Finally, with a great effort, he left her. In the morning, when Damayanhi did not find her husband, she was consumed with grief, became restless, rushing hither and thither, sitting one moment and standing the next, and remained confused for a long time. After many a hardship she reached her parents' kingdom and palace. Eventually, she rejoined her husband after he had regained his kingdom (Ganguli 1970: Vana Parva, chs 62, 63).

Story 12

Sage Vashista explained to Prince Rama: 'The outer body receives the qualities of the inner mind. The thoughts and actions of the mind have their display in the several organs of the body, just as the pattern of leaves and branches of a tree is projected by the inner properties of the seed' (Mitra 1891: vol. 4, ch. 44).

Story 13

A cannibal she-demon lived in a forest. Over the years, the people of the surrounding villages learned ways and means of protecting themselves, either by making a detour around the forest or by chanting the protective sacred hymns. Gradually, the demon suffered from the scarcity of human flesh. She decided to worship god Brahma for a boon so that she might for ever reside inside human flesh. She worshipped Brahma. Brahma appeared and granted her the boon, saying, 'You shall reside in human entrails as a tiny, sharp needle called colic pain, causing acute pain to living beings, particularly those short-tempered, hard-working fools' (Mitra 1891: vol. 3, ch. 69).

Story 14

King Mahasena was attacked by a mightier king. In accordance with the counsel of his ministers, he made a truce with the aggressor and avoided a war. Yet within himself he burned with remorse, asking, 'Why did I submit to my enemy?' His hurt pride and his sorrow made him very ill, and he developed an abscess in his vital organs. His wise physician, who knew the nature of the illness, thought out a plan, taking the ministers and the king's relatives into his confidence. The king was falsely informed that his wife had died suddenly. Upon this, he fell down in a faint, and as a result of the sudden shock of grief the abscess burst. Eventually the king made a good recovery. In the course of time, he conquered his enemies (Penzer 1968: vol. 2, Story of the Clever Physician).

Story 15

Lord Krishna, the Divine Incarnation, was growing up as a child in the village. The entire community loved him, even though they did not know his incarnate state. They only knew him as a very endearing child in whose life miracles seemed to happen. The ladies and the maidens in the village loved him so much that they unknowingly began to enact his various mannerisms and behavioural peculiarities, as though they identified totally with him (Tagare 1979: Skanda 10, ch. 30).

Story 16

King Ravana had abducted Sita, the wife of Prince Rama. Rama besieged Ravana's fort with a huge army. Ravana's grandfather advised Ravana to return Sita to her husband and thus avoid a destructive war with Rama. Ravana became angry and accused his grandfather of malicious intent and of having been bribed by the enemy: 'You are saying these things because you cannot tolerate heroism in others. If I am at fault, it is one with which I was born, and it is impossible to change one's nature' (Raghunathan 1981: Yuddha Kanda, ch. 36).

INEVITABILITY OF MISERIES AND SUFFERINGS

In Indian mythology, the general theme of human miseries and sufferings concerns their inevitability and the individual's own responsibility for them, causally and remedially. This view is in contrast to the attitude of most clients, where an expectation is often implied that health is a condition free of symptoms and sufferings, which are to be eradicated by external agencies such as drugs and operations.

While describing existential counselling, Bascue and Krieger (1972) say that individuals are responsible for their own health situation, at least to the extent that they have the choice of determining their attitudes and behaviours towards any given situation. This, of course, is the essence of internal locus of control.

Story 17

Lord Brahma the creator told the celestial sage Narada: 'People will be immersed in innumerable miseries on account of their own actions and behaviour' (Shastri 1983: vol. 1, ch. 15).

Story 18

Consequent to a series of incidents, Narmadasundari was deserted by her husband, and she found herself marooned on an island. In dejection, she walked into the sea to drown herself. While thus wading through the waves, she thought, 'Mere escapism will not end my miseries. Even though I may die now, I will not be freed from the bondages of my past actions which will follow me to my next birth. I may as well face them and finish them off in this life.' She survived, suffered few hardships, and eventually became a Jaina-Nun and attained peace (Kumarji Pratham 1984: Story of Narmada Sundari).

The reference to the next birth is related to the Hindu/Buddhist/Jaina belief that the consequences of one's actions (called *samskaras* or *karmas*) are like debts which are repaid in the form of inevitable suffering. If such debts remain uncleared in a life, they will cause a next birth for 'repayment'.

The theme of this story reminds me of the common observation that clients and/or their families suffer more as a consequence of their efforts to avoid some unpleasantness, real or imagined.

The inevitability of miseries and sufferings ('Fate' or 'Destiny') need not and should not lead to despondency. They will have to be dealt with by determined efforts as the occasion demands and according to the resources and the prevailing circumstances. Moreover, these inevitable miseries seem to have a positive potential. Studying the literature on eminent people, Thervel (1993) found that a major requirement for sustained creativity is a challenged personality shaped by major misfortunes.

Story 19

Sage Vashista explained to Prince Rama: 'Fate [inevitability] and exertion [choice and effort] are like two rams fighting each other. Whichever is stronger wins. However, the human exertion will have to be righteous [lawful]. Apart from this, the word "fate" is an imaginary word for consolation' (Mitra 1891: vol. 2, chs 5, 6, 9).

Story 20

King Kalinga and King Astaka arrayed their armies against each other. Kalinga went to a famous sage, requesting him to forecast the outcome of the war. The sage consulted god Indra, and conveyed Indra's forecast that Kalinga would win the battle. On hearing this news, King Astaka instructed his warriors to concentrate all their energies on and around the enemy king. The battle began, and Astaka won. The sage was surprised that god Indra's prophecy had gone wrong. He asked Indra about this. Indra replied: 'Do not you know that we gods always favour those who make sincere efforts with courage and fixed resolve?' (Cowel 1895: vol. 3, story 301).

Story 21

King Dhritarastra was advised by his counsellor as to how to plan a course of action in a difficult political situation involving his son and nephew. 'You must first carefully consider the objective to be achieved and the prevailing circumstances, the means or the methods to be adopted within the limits of good behaviour, and your own ability as the executor of that action or that of an agent you may employ. You must also be ready not to be upset or unduly disappointed if your effort is unsuccessful' (Ganguli 1970: Udyoga Parva, ch. 34).

This attitude of not becoming unduly disappointed and discouraged into passivity or inaction is not unfamiliar to achievers, especially those in competitive enterprises like sport. As mentioned earlier, this is the attitude of internal locus of control or autonomy. Minsel *et al.* (1991) found autonomy and responsibility to be one of the components of mental health. Also, the internal locus buffers the effect of stressors (Kliewer and Sandler 1992), and is correlated with psychological maturity and hopefulness (Brackney and Westman 1992). Lubusko *et al.* (1994) found that the internal locus is correlated with return to pre-injury level of employment among severely traumatized brain-injury sufferers. Moreover, the internal locus enables the individual to bear the distress with dignity without resorting to pathological responses.

Story 22

Once, a cow and its calf were undergoing a lot of misery on account of ill treatment by their Brahmin owner. The cow intended to gore the owner to death. But the calf advised its mother against such a course of action: 'We are now suffering the consequences of our past actions. If you kill the owner, we will only be perpetrating the vicious cycle of actions and consequences. We can wipe out the consequences of our past actions completely only when we undergo them with dignity, courage and composure' (Shastri 1983: vol. 3, Koti Rudra Samhita, ch. 6).

MENTAL HEALTH PROMOTING BEHAVIOUR

Definition of mental health

The definition or description of the state of mental health is scanty in current professional literature, and also comparatively vague. For example, Wolman describes it as appropriateness of emotional responses, maintenance of social adjustment and balance between one's and others' needs (Wolman 1965: 1127–30); and as total functionality with optimal integration (ibid. 1123–4). Wolman (1973: 234) has also described it as a state of good adjustment and actualization of one's potentialities. Eysenck *et al.* (1972) describe it as performance of one's normal functions and the capacity to give others the same values one claims for oneself. The emphasis is on total functioning with adjustment in the social context.

In contrast to the above, the description in Indian mythology of an individual who is totally functioning with adjustment in his social context is remarkably comprehensive and practical. The descriptions are provided by Sage Vashista's instructions to Prince Rama (Mitra 1891: vol. 4, ch. 46; vol. 5, chs 15, 16, 77).

The individual attends to all the legitimate affairs of life in social, familial, personal and occupational areas in order to fulfil their own and family members' spiritual, affectional and material needs according to the role functions, abilities and circumstances and within the limits of righteousness (social-moral code) with an attitude of hope, confidence, sincere sense of responsibility and contentment.

The words 'righteousness' and 'contentment' are described in stories 23 and 24.

Story 23

Sage Vashista explained to Prince Rama: The righteous conduct can be acquired by practice and protects the individual in the long run from the effects of inevitable miseries and calamities of life. The righteous conduct is:

- earning one's livelihood by just means;
- being fearless and calm tempered;
- being polite, tolerant and avoiding quarrels;
- while interacting with others, responding only to their positive qualities and with one's own positive qualities;
- not allowing one's personal reasons to interfere with good conduct (Mitra 1891: book 6, ch. 170).

Story 24

Sage Vashista instructed Prince Rama: A man, though poor, is happy and healthy if he is contented. He is contented:

- who does not desire what is not righteous, what is beyond his needs and capabilities;
- who enjoys what he has rightfully possessed;
- who does not create numerous ideas of wish fulfilling, or ascribe false reasons for his failures or to untoward consequences of his desires (Mitra 1891: vol. 2, ch. 15).

Based on the above description, the attitudes and qualities of mental health are listed below. The mentally healthy man:

- is affectionate (fulfilling affectional needs of others);
- adjusts his behaviour according to his role, abilities and circumstances;
- is fearless and tolerant;
- responds to positive qualities in others with his own positive qualities;
- does not allow personal reasons/emotions to influence his own good conduct;
- is hopeful, confident and sincere in discharging his responsibilities and duties.

The Indian mythology describes different components of *socially desirable behaviour* in different texts in different contexts. For the sake of economy of expression, I prefer to call this *ideal behaviour*, even though it may sound somewhat judgemental. The sources of descriptions of ideal behaviour are: Ganguli 1970: Udyoga Parva, chs 33–7; Shanti Parva, chs 60, 75, 109, 160, 229, 230; Mitra 1891: vol. 3, ch. 6; vol. 6, ch. 198; Shastri 1983: vol. 3, ch. 5. The consolidated ideal behaviour is listed below:

1 Behaviour relating to the self:
- avoidance of idleness, purposeless speech and purposeless activity;
- courage and self-confidence;
- contentment, i.e. equanimity in the face of negative and positive results, events or circumstances.

2 Behaviour relating to interpersonal relationships:
- not allowing own behavioural response to be influenced by anger, hatred, vengefulness, fear or pride;
- sincerity and honesty in a manner comfortable with the prevailing moral code;
- compassion, affection, respect and goodwill for others;
- pleasant truthful speech, not speaking ill of others;
- congruity between thinking, feeling, speech and action;
- fairness and equability towards others;
- consistency in values and attitudes.

3 The overall behaviour must be righteous, as already described in stories 23 and 24. Its meaning is also described at different places

in the scriptures as behaving in such a way that the result will be long-term good to all creatures.

It is noteworthy that the above descriptions of mental health, righteousness, contentment and ideal behaviour share many common components and are all capable of cross-cultural and universal applicability. All of the above components have anecdotal representations, as is probably true in the folklore of all cultures. Many therapists may consider some of these components as moralistic. But the fact is that many of these components seem similar to the desirable therapist qualities familiar to mental health professionals.

In modern mental health literature, different authors describe the *desirable therapist qualities* differently, though conveying similar meanings. The qualities listed below are collected from: Rosenzweig (1936), Hoch (1960), Reisman (1971), Frank (1971), Kramer (1978), Garfield (1980), Luborsky *et al.* (1985), and Friesen *et al.* (1992).

1 General qualities:
   • genuineness, integrity, honesty;
   • empathy;
   • hopefulness;
   • self-confidence;
   • ability to monitor one's own behaviour.

2 Attitude and behaviour towards the patient/client:
   • unconditional positive regard;
   • acknowledgement of client's right and freedom;
   • trust in client's ability to get well.

Table 4.1 compares the components of mental health, ideal behaviour and therapist qualities whose meanings seem similar.

The similarities displayed in Table 4.1 are so striking that it seems as though the same individual is being described from slightly different points of view. This requires the more thorough attention of researchers in psychotherapy.

The implications of these similarities are:

• Being descriptions of an individual functioning fully in his social milieu, the components of mental health may be artefacts, as it is quite natural and perfectly logical for an ideal human to be totally functioning with adjustment in his social milieu. If this is so, it further strengthens the subsequent implications.

Table 4.1   Comparison of components of mental health, ideal
behaviour and therapist qualities

Mental health	Ideal behaviour	Therapist qualities
Hopefulness		Hopefulness
Confidence	Self-confidence	Self-confidence
Fearlessness	Courage	
	Honesty	Honesty
Sincere sense of responsibility and duty	Sincerity	Integrity
	Truthfulness	
Affectionate	Affectionate	Empathic
	Compassionate	
Responds with positive qualities	Respect and goodwill for others	Unconditional positive regard
Tolerance		Acknowledgement of client's rights
		Non-judgemental tolerance and acceptance
	Congruity between thinking, feeling, speech and action	Genuinity
Not allowing personal reasons to interfere with good conduct	Not allowing own behaviour to be influenced by anger, vengefulness, hatred, fear or pride	Ability to monitor own behaviour

- An individual who has cultivated ideal behaviour will be mentally healthy, and the converse is also true. A corollary to this is that one of the psychosocial etiological factors for mental illness is deviance from the ideal behaviour in one respect or another.

- The individual who is mentally healthy or has ideal behaviour will have a 'natural' psychotherapeutic potential. A logical consequence of this is the prospect of according heavy weighting to the development of ideal qualities as an essential part of training in psychotherapy.
- As indicated earlier, these qualities are probably universally and cross-culturally valid. This possibility is depicted as a fact in the next story.

Story 25

Once, King Naravahana Datta was counselled by his minister, Gomukha: 'To a virtuous [righteous] man, no country is foreign. A contented man is never miserable. Calamity does not exist for him who has endurance and perseverance. There is nothing impossible for the enterprising' (Penzer 1968: vol. 5, story 97).

The following are examples of some of the evidence available in the modern mental health literature concerning the correlations of components of ideal behaviour and mental health:

1 A controlled study by Paul *et al.* (1975) indirectly demonstrated the inevitability of suffering. Among 105 families that experienced sudden death, one group of 39 were offered preventive crisis intervention over 4–6 sessions, while the remainder were not. There was no difference between the two groups of families in terms of psychiatric and somatic consequences of stress.
2 Contentment is one of the components of mental health as shown earlier. Its opposite, namely sensation-seeking, is known to correlate with pathological behaviour like impulsiveness, alcohol and substance abuse, disinhibition, etc. (Earlywine and Finn 1991; Iso-Ahola and Crowley 1991). Kasser and Ryan (1993) found that the relative centrality of money-related values, aspirations and expectations was inversely proportional to psychological well-being and global adjustment and directly proportional to behaviour disorders and to lower social productivity.
3 In respect of congruity and genuinity, Mikulincer and Peer-Goldin (1991) found that subjective happiness is a function of the congruence between the ideal self and the working self.
4 In his exploratory study, Maslow (1954) listed the following qualities of self-actualizers which are analogous to the components of mental health listed in Table 4.1:

- they are not threatened by the unknown;
- they have spontaneity, simplicity and naturalness;
- they have the ability to accept themselves and others as they are;
- they are more autonomous;
- they have sympathy and affection in spite of contextual anger.

In this context, it is very tempting to speculate that the promotion of mental health in any culture (or country) can more economically be achieved through the promotion of ideal human behaviour by education and other mass-communications media.

CONCLUSIONS

Indian mythology is a rich source of stories for psychotherapeutic use. Other mythologies are very likely to contain stories with similar thematic content. Moreover, these mythological stories should be capable of cross-cultural use, by the very nature of their universality.

Stories from Indian mythology for psychotherapeutic use cover a wide thematic range. Two of the important themes are:

1 the inevitability of miseries in human life, and the guidelines as to how to face and deal with them;
2 a comprehensive and operational definition of mental health.

The components of mental health, ideal behaviour and desirable therapist qualities happen to be similar, if not the same. This similarity suggests that the ideal human behaviour (or desirable therapist qualities) will have both health-promoting and psychotherapeutic properties. Consequently, it is likely to be easier to promote mental health in a culture through the promotion of ideal human behaviour.

The health-promoting and psychotherapeutic properties of ideal behaviour are a fertile area for further research. In the meantime, it is worth considering the development of ideal qualities as a necessary part of the training of the mental health professional in general and the psychotherapist in particular.

REFERENCES

The help of Karen Amos in preparing the final manuscript of this chapter is gratefully acknowledged.

Bascue, L.O., and Krieger, G.W. (1972) 'Existential counselling for the dying', *Journal of Rehabilitation* 38 (2): 18–19.

Boyer, B. (1977) 'Mythology, folklore, and psychoanalysis', in B.B. Wohman (ed.) *International Encyclopedia of Psychology, Psychoanalysis and Neurology*, vol. 7, NY: Von Nostrand Reinhold.

Brackney, B.E., and Westman, A.S. (1992) 'Relationships among hope, psychological development and locus of control', *Psychological Reports* 70 (1): 864–6.

Calder, R. (1968) *Man and the Cosmos – The Nature of Science Today*, London: Pallmall Press, ch. 2.

Cowel, E.B. (ed.) (1895) *Jataka – Stories of Buddha's Former Births* (6 vols), Cambridge: Cambridge University Press.

Domaingue, R. (1992) 'Learning for discovery: establishing the foundations', *Journal of Scientific Exploration* 6 (1): 11–22.

Earlywine, M., and Finn, P.R. (1991) 'Sensation seeking explains behavioural dis-inhibition and alcohol consumption', *Addictive Behaviour* 16 (3–4), 123–8.

Eysenck, H.J., Wurtzburg, W.A., and Meili, R. (1972) (eds) *Encyclopedia of Psychology*, vol. 2. London: Search Press.

Fatic, A., (1993) 'The inter-dynamic theory of metaphor and applied psychology', *Communication and Cognition* 26 (3–4): 249–63.

Frank, J.D. (1971) 'Therapeutic factors in psychotherapy', *American Journal of Psychotherapy* 125: 350–61.

Friesen, B.J., Koren, P.E., and Koroloff, N.M. (1992) 'How parents view professional behaviours: across-professional analysis', *Journal of Child and Family Studies* 1 (2): 209–31.

Ganguli, Kesari Mohan (1970) *Mahabharata* (12 vols), Delhi: Munsiram Manoharlal Publishers.

Garfield, S.L. (1980) *Psychotherapy – An Eclectic Approach*, NY: John Wiley and Sons, 69–71, 244.

Hoch, E.M. (1960) 'A pattern of neurosis in India', *American Journal of Psychoanalysis* 20(1): 87.

Iso-Ahola, S.E., and Crowley, E.D. (1991) 'Adolescent substance abuse and leisure boredom', *Journal of Leisure Research* 23(3): 260–71.

Jagadiswarananda, Swami (1951) *Brihadaranyaka Upanisad*, Madras: Sri Ramakrishna Math.

Jung, C.G. (1949) 'Psychology of the child archetype' in C.G. Jung and C. Karenyi (eds) *Essays on a Science of Mythology*, Bollingen Series 22, NY: Pantheon Books, ch. 2.

——(1954) 'The practices of psychotherapy' in H. Reed, M. Fordham and G. Adler (eds) *Collected Works*, vol. 16, NY: Pantheon Books.

Karenyi, C. (1949) Prologomena in C.G. Jung and C. Karenyi (eds) *Essays on a Science of Mythology*, Bollingen Series 22, NY: Pantheon Books.

Kasser, T., and Ryan, R.M. (1993) 'A dark side of the American dream: correlates of financial success as a central life aspiration', *Journal of Personality and Social Psychology* 65(2): 410–22.

Kliewer, W., and Sandler, I.N. (1992) 'Locus of control and self-esteem as moderators of stressor-symptom relationship in children and adolescents', *Journal of Abnormal Child Psychology* 20(4): 393–413.

Kramer, E. (1978) *A Beginning Manual for Psychotherapists*, NY: Grune and Stratton.

Kumarji Pratham, Sri Muni Sri Mahendra (1984) *Jaina Stories*, Delhi: Motilal Banarsidas.

Lester, D., Castromayor, I.J., and Icli, T. (1991) 'Locus of control, depression and suicidal ideation among American, Philippine and Turkish students', *Journal of Social Psychology* 131(3): 447–9.

Luborsky, L., McLellan, A.T., Woody, G.E., O'Brien, C.P., and Auerbach, A. (1985) 'Therapists' success and its determinants', *Archives of General Psychiatry* 42(6): 602–11.

Lubusko, A.A., Moore, A.D., Stambrook, M., and Gill, D.D. (1994) 'Cognitive beliefs following severe traumatic brain injury: association with post-injury employment', *Brain Injury* 8(1): 65–70.

Maslow, A.H. (1954) 'Self-actualising people: a study of psychological health', in *Motivation and Personality*, NY: Harper Brothers.

Minsel, B., Becke, P. and Korchin, S.J. (1991) 'A cross-cultural view of positive mental health: two orthogonal main factors replicable in four countries', *Journal of Cross-Cultural Psychology* 22(2): 157–81.

Mitra, Vihari Lal (1891) *Yoga Vashistha – Maharamayana of Valmiki* (4 vols), Calcutta: Bannerji.

Mikulincer, M., and Peer-Goldin, L. (1991) 'Self congruence and the experience of happiness', *British Journal of Psychology* 30(1): 21–35.

Paul, R.P., Donald, E., Richard, V., and Vail, W. (1975) 'Prevention in mental health: a controlled study', *American Journal of Psychiatry* 132(2): 146–9.

Penzer, N.M. (1968) (ed.) *The Ocean of Story* (10 vols), trans. C.H. Tawny, Delhi: Motilal Banarsidas.

Polkinghorne, D.E. (1991) 'Narrative and self-concept', *Journal of Narrative and Life History* 1(2–3): 135–53.

Poortinga, Y.H., Schoots, N.H., and Van de Koppel, J.M. (1993) 'The understanding of Chinese and Kurdish emblematic gestures by Dutch subjects', *International Journal of Psychology* 28(1): 31–44.

Raghunathan, N. (1981) *Ramayana* (4 vols), Bangalore: Vigneswara.

Reisman, J.M. (1971) *Towards an integration of psychotherapy*, NY: John Wiley and Sons, ch. 4.

Rosenzweig, S. (1936) 'Some implicit common factors in diverse methods of psychotherapy', *American Journal of Ortho-Psychiatry* 6: 412–15.

Scott, W.A., Scott, R., McCabe, M. (1991) 'Family relationships and children's personality: a cross-cultural, cross-source comparison', *British Journal of Social Psychology* 30(1): 1–20.

Shastri, J.L. (1983)*Shivapurana* (4 vols), Delhi: Motilal Banarsidas.

Tagare, Ganesh Vasudeo (1979) *Bhagavata Purana* (4 vols, ed. J.L. Shastri), Delhi: Motilal Banarsidas.

Thervel, E. (1993) 'The challenged personality as a pre-condition for sustained creativity', *Creativity Research Journal* 6(4): 413–24.

Wolman, B.B. (1965) 'Mental health and mental disorders', in B.B. Wolman (ed.) *Handbook of Clinical Psychology*, NY: McGraw Hill.

——(1973) *Dictionary of Behavioral Sciences*, NY: Van Nostrand Reinhold.

Chapter 5

Management of anger and some Eastern stories

Kedar Nath Dwivedi

MIND MIXES THE REAL WITH THE UNREAL

If someone says something hurtful or insulting to us, we are very likely to become rather angry. Our heart rate, breathing, blood pressure, skin conductance, and so on, can change dramatically, as if someone has pushed a button. These changes can take place suddenly, usually without our knowledge and certainly without our permission. Once these changes have turned on, they tend to stay on for some time because the particular humiliating phrases, demeanours, gestures or looks that triggered the anger tend to reverberate within the mind and the mind becomes glued to these mental objects, so much so that it becomes difficult to notice the details of other things that may be happening around us. Even if someone tries to be nice to us we may not be able to notice or respond to this because the mind is already preoccupied with the negative mental object. When the feelings are strong, these can also spill over into action and we might end up responding in an equally hurtful manner, verbally, physically, or both.

Eventually we calm down and the concerned mental objects slip out of the consciousness as we become occupied with other matters. Thus the anger-generating mental objects then become dormant or latent, but may not remain so for ever because some time later, that day or maybe the next, even when there is a pleasant atmosphere, the memory of the humiliating incident may suddenly break into the consciousness, and once again the blood pressure, heart rate, breathing, skin conductance and so on can dramatically change. No one is being hurtful now; it is simply the memory of a past incident that is producing the changes. And this could go on happening many times in our lives, the mind and body reacting to images, ideas and memories, as if they were substantial and real. People who have had experiences of physical, sexual or emotional abuse, bereavement or disaster know how distressing these memories can be. Although memories, images and ideas may not be direct here-and-now real concrete or substantial experiences, their power is still enormous. Some stories or examples can underline this fact.

There is a story of a lady in intense pain with a terminal illness who went to see the famous American psychiatrist Milton Erickson. She told him that she had already tried various medicines for her pain and, if real medicines could not help, she had her doubts about talk-therapy being of any use, However, she added that she had nothing to lose by seeing him. Dr Erickson then began to verbally paint an imaginary picture. He asked her to suppose that the door of the room suddenly opened and a very hungry ferocious tiger entered, so that the lady and the tiger were now face to face looking at each other. And Milton Erickson continued like this for several minutes before he enquired about the intensity of her pain. She reported with great surprise that at that moment her pain had disappeared. This was because the mind was already preoccupied with another strong mental object, which was intensely charged although completely unreal.

The power of such mental objects is further illustrated in the fictitious story of a Tibetan Buddhist ritual involving the Hall of One Thousand Demons. The trainees of this tradition have to prepare for years, so that one day they become capable of entering this Hall and coming out not only unharmed but in fact further advanced on their path towards enlightenment. When a trainee is ready and is about to enter the Hall, the supervising Lama reminds the trainee that now he will be on his own; however, it will be extremely helpful for the trainee to keep the following three facts in mind:

1   All the mental objects that will appear in the trainee's consciousness (when the trainee is in the Hall) will be unreal. These are simply the trainee's own dormant fears that become magnified a thousand times; this is why the Hall is known as the Hall of One Thousand Demons.
2   All the reactions, such as shaking or fainting, that the trainee experiences within himself are real.
3   If the trainee can remember to keep on his feet whatever his experiences, eventually he will manage to come out of the Hall.

Not only the mental object derived from one's own past or imagined experiences but also objects unrelated to oneself can be equally powerful. For example, someone watching a horror film in the middle of the night might begin to feel very frightened. Even the windows and the curtains of the sitting-room might become frightening, as if infested with nasty creatures, although the same windows and curtains were so pleasant and warm during the day. Intellectually one knows that the television monitor consists of glass, electronics, light and shade and contains no creatures, no real blood or flesh; however, the viewer's mind and body react to the images as if they were real. Similarly an erotic film could make someone feel strongly aroused although no one in reality is doing anything to the viewer.

Here the reader can also do an experiment. You can try and imagine visiting your favourite greengrocer's shop and go to the corner where the lemons are kept. Then you could select a large juicy lemon and when you have bought it, take it home, into the kitchen, put it on to the chopping block and cut it into two halves. Take one of the pieces in your hand and slowly but firmly squeeze the entire half of the large juicy lemon on your tongue, feeling the intensity of the taste of its juice. Keep on going until you have tasted and swallowed all the juice squeezed out of that half of the lemon. Now the watering that you may notice in your mouth is real, although the lemon is not.

Thus, our minds are extremely skilled in mixing the real with the unreal, like water with milk. In Buddhism, working for enlightenment consists of cutting through these illusory processes. Ledi Sayada, a Burmese Buddhist monk, described these processes in terms of three levels (Dwivedi 1990). Accordingly, the first level consists of the dormant mental objects, like fire that is hidden in a box of matches. However, when the matchstick is struck on the box, the fire becomes manifest, just as the mental objects, striking at the consciousness, stir up the psycho-physiological changes within oneself. This is the second level. When this burning match comes into contact with other flammable objects they too get burned, just as the strong feelings coming into contact with external objects can spill over into verbal or physical action – the third level.

TAKING THINGS PERSONALLY

Anger is an inherent part of our living. Even from the Buddhist point of view, none of us can fully eliminate anger until we become enlightened. Considering the latent level, the ultimate reason for the generation of angry feelings is the sense of 'self' that we all habitually carry. This is why in the Eastern cultures so much emphasis is placed on learning to go beyond egocentric or narcissistic outlooks in life. The cultural practices associated with bringing up children and growing up in extended family systems are also aimed at the Eastern ideals of cutting through and mastering narcissism (Dwivedi 1992, 1993a, 1994a, 1994b, 1994c, 1996a, 1996b, 1996c).

Buddha pointed out that this sense of 'self' is a product of illusory processes of the mind. In fact, it is the extreme rapidity of mental phenomena that creates such a strong illusion of 'self', 'I', 'my', 'mine' and so on. If you look at a ceiling fan, you see three blades when it is stationary, but a rapidly moving fan creates the illusion of merging of the blades. Similarly a cartoon film is created by a number of still drawings which are then projected so rapidly that they create an illusion of movement, continuity, entity, solidity, being and intention. Our attachment to our self, our ideas, theories and relationships, which are all products of these illusory processes, is the basic reason which triggers us into anger. Buddhism is devoted to cutting through these illusory processes, but it is a gradual, a lifetime's – in fact many lifetimes' – task.

The anger management approaches of the modern mental health services, too, do not aim to eliminate the experience of anger altogether but to help one learn to better manage and regulate one's thinking, arousal and behaviour under provocation, if getting angry is not serving a useful function. A comprehensive programme for the management of anger should, therefore, consist of managing its various aspects at different levels. The analogy of a 'bundle' is very useful here. Anger can be seen as a bundle of different parts; cognitions (appraisals, beliefs and thoughts), affect (psycho-physiological changes and feelings) and behaviours (physical and verbal actions). Each part can be managed more easily if tackled separately. It is similar to tackling each stick from a bundle of sticks separately rather than as a whole bundle.

COGNITIVE RETRAINING

There are ways of quantifying one's tendency to anger with the help of self-report inventories such as the Anger Inventory (Novaco 1975; a 90-item inventory that presents hypothetical anger-evoking situations with a 5-point Likert scale to indicate the degree of anger) and the Anger Control Inventory (Hoshmand and Austin 1985; a 128-item inventory with 15 subscales and items in two sections: situations that engender anger reactions and individual responses to anger-eliciting situations).

The cognitive processes play a very important role in generating, maintaining and managing one's feelings, including that of anger. It is these cognitive processes that attach meaning to things in such a way that they trigger anger. Our automatic thoughts or private speech and belief systems play an important role in our construing things as we do. The incidents and situations that provoke anger might not do so if they were perceived or construed differently. Some of the common thoughts that might be conducive to producing anger may be: 'It is going to be dreadful', 'It is dreadful already', 'I can't let him get away with this', 'This is the story of my life', 'I am always rejected', 'They always end up humiliating me', and so on.

Thus, a typical cognitive therapy approach to anger management would be: (1) to identify various triggers that tend to stir up anger, (2) to map out various habitual thoughts, feelings, actions and consequences associated with these triggers and construct a plan to replace them with their useful counterparts, and (3) to keep an anger diary so that one makes a note of the situations that make one angry; the details of what happened, when and where, what exactly one felt, what thoughts went through one's mind, what irritated one most and what one actually did (for example, not showing anger, being verbally angry, being physically aggressive, leaving the situation, and so on). An attempt is therefore made to list all the mal-productive thoughts such as the ones mentioned above and then to explore the possibility of some helpful alternative thoughts: for example, 'I don't have to rise to the bait', 'I don't need to prove myself', 'There is no point in getting mad. They probably want me to but, I will surprise them', 'My muscles are getting tight. This is time for me to take a deep breath', 'My anger is a signal of what I have to do', 'The situation is getting difficult but I do have a plan of how to handle this', 'Let me remember to stick to the issues and not take things personally', and so on.

The following Buddhist story of Bharadwaj illustrates the power of such a cognitive shift. Some two thousand five hundred years ago, there lived in India an orthodox Brahmin, named Bharadwaj. He had three sons. In his cultural context the parental responsibilities included not only bringing up one's children and establishing them in the traditions and values but also getting them appropriately married. After the wedding of his youngest son, therefore, he felt very pleased that he had now fulfilled his parental responsibilities. However, when he discovered that his new daughter-in-law did not participate in the family rituals and religious worship, he was deeply shocked. He found out that she preferred to practise some kind of Buddhist meditation on her own instead. He therefore sent his youngest son to teach the Buddha a lesson. Mr Bharadwaj felt very strongly that the Buddha must be stopped from misleading the young generation. But his son returned from the Buddha having become converted to Buddhism. Mr Bharadwaj was deeply disappointed and therefore sent his middle son to the Buddha with a clear instruction to be duly abusive and aggressive to the Buddha, but the middle son too came back as a Buddhist. Similarly the eldest son was sent and met with the same consequence.

Finally, Mr Bharadwaj decided that he himself would have to teach a lesson to the Buddha. He suspected that the Buddha might have some hypnotic powers, and therefore, he felt that he needed to work up his anger so strongly that he could not be deterred from hitting the Buddha with his stick. He became determined to start abusing and swearing as soon as he approached the Buddha so that he could make himself angry enough. However, when the Buddha found Mr Bharadwaj swearing at him, he gently asked, 'Sir, do you sometimes receive guests or visitors?' Mr Bharadwaj said, 'Yes, I do. So what?', and then started swearing again at the Buddha. The Buddha then enquired further, 'Do any of these guests bring you gifts from time to time?' Mr Bharadwaj affirmed and continued with his swearing. The Buddha also continued with his questioning: 'So what happens if you don't accept any of those gifts?' Mr Bharadwaj said that they remained the property of the guests. The Buddha then smiled and declared, 'Similarly, I don't accept the gifts [abusive swearing] that you have been offering me; they remain your property!' Mr Bharadwaj was a very intelligent man. As he understood the meaning of what was being said, he too felt deeply disillusioned and joined the rest of the family.

TRANSFORMING NARRATIVE IDENTITIES

Problems often arise when we get stuck with ideas about ourselves that get in the way of changing ourselves. We need to transmute our dysfunctional narrative identity into a functional one. Letting go of one and getting into another requires a certain degree of distancing and a meta perspective. Fairy tales, fables, other stories and anecdotes can quickly manufacture a potentially therapeutic space for such a meta perspective to evolve so that alternative narratives and narrative identities can be explored. Letting go of the ones that one already has is not easy, though!

In South India, we hear of some greedy people who catch monkeys to sell to the West for the purposes of 'scientific' research. They have a unique way of catching these monkeys. They take a coconut shell, make a small hole in it, put in some rice grains and stake it to the ground. When a monkey sees the rice he puts his hand into the shell through the hole, takes the grains into his hand, so making a fist, and finds that the hole is too small to let him take his clenched hand out of the shell. As the monkey panics, he doesn't feel that it is safe to let go of the fist and gets stuck and caught.

The difficulties in letting go are also illustrated in a Buddhist story of two monks, a novice and his master. One of the practices of Buddhist monks involves refraining from physical contact with women. According to this story, these two monks were walking by a river. After a while, they saw someone drowning in the river. The master jumped into the river and rescued the drowning woman and then the two monks continued to walk to their monastery. When they arrived at the monastery, the novice took the master's permission and asked, 'Is it not true that we monks are not supposed to touch women? On the contrary, you were holding a beautiful young woman in your arms.' The master replied: 'I left the woman a long time ago at the bank of that river, but you seem to have been carrying her all the way in your mind.'

EXTERNALIZING

White (1989) describes an approach to therapy that involves 'externalizing' by encouraging persons to objectify, and at times to personify, the problems that they experience as oppressive. In this process the problem becomes a separate entity and thus external to the person – or the relationship – ascribed the problem. This allows the various influences on the problems and the problem's influences on the person and others to be easily mapped out. Such an exercise renders the problem or the narrative identity less fixed and less restricting.

There is a story of a monk who asks his master, 'I have a terrible temper and I can't cope with it. Please help.' The master says, 'Well, bring it to me and I'll see what I can do.' The monk hesitates: 'I am sorry, at the moment I haven't got it.' So the master suggests, 'Next time, when you have got it, bring it to me.' The monk confesses, 'I am not sure if I can do that.' The master then declares, 'In that case it is not yours,' and suggests that if it comes again the monk should get hold of it and then beat it away with a stick!

AFFECTIVE MANAGEMENT

The psycho-physiological changes during emotional experiences are supposed to provide us with energy for any actions that may be required. This energy can be so strong that the emotions may move us beyond our control. They have subtle but enormous power. Usually we are not aware of these psycho-physiological changes, at least in the beginning, and only become aware when they become intense. One of the reasons for not being aware of these changes is the fact that our minds get preoccupied with the mental objects that trigger them. It is therefore useful to train oneself to be able to shift one's attention away from the trigger to the physiological changes themselves at the earliest opportunity. The analogy of catching a snake is very helpful here. People who are in the business of catching snakes from the fields tend to say that it is much easier to catch a snake as soon as it puts its head out through a hole. However, when the snake has come out of the hole it is much more difficult to catch. Similarly, if one can be aware of the psycho-physiological changes at the beginning and use them as a signal to practise one or other form of relaxation, one can be more effective in managing one's anger. The attitude towards the psycho-physiological changes is very important. It is a matter of opening up to their energy and befriending them rather than fighting them. If we try to fight them we become controlled by them. This fact is brought home nicely by Milarepa in the following story.

DON'T THINK OF MONKEYS

Milarepa was a famous Tibetan monk. A gentleman who felt very agitated came to see Milarepa and said that there was always some kind of chattering in his mind and he could not feel peaceful or restful at all. He asked Milarepa for a way of stopping this chattering of the mind. Milarepa told him to go home and to stop thinking of monkeys. The gentleman said that thinking of monkeys was not a problem for him, because he never thought of monkeys and monkeys did not cross his mind. Milarepa was delighted to hear this and declared that in that case the practice of 'not thinking of monkeys' should then come very easily to him and that he should go home and continue to practise. The gentleman began to do what he was told, only to realize that the more he tried not to think of monkeys, the more he ended up thinking of monkeys.

Managing anger, therefore, involves awareness of the psycho-physiological changes on the one hand, and of accepting these changes *without fighting them*, easing into them and relaxing into them, on the other. By getting into them with this attitude, one realizes that these changes are transient and impermanent and have a life of their own. It is the indulgence in the triggering mental objects that keeps fuelling the psycho-physiological changes. With practice it is therefore possible to learn to transmute the emotion into a constructive process, like taming a tiger (Rimpoche 1987), transmuting a weed into nourishment, or turning coal into a diamond.

BEHAVIOURAL CHANGES

Anger and violence are intimately connected but are not the same things. Sometimes violence may be motivated by other factors such as greed or fear. However, aggression and violence are often the products of feelings of anger spilling over into action. The intensity of the arousal or the psycho-physiological changes often influences our cognitive processes to the extent that we don't think properly, tend to misperceive things, do not engage in effective problem-solving and end up executing certain familiar sub-routines which may be aggressive and violent, as if in a state of trance or mindlessness. Many of us can remember getting into our cars and reaching the usual destination without remembering the journey in between. The sight of a certain roundabout made us take a certain exit, or the sight of certain traffic lights automatically made us take the particular turning without having to consciously think and decide. Thus in anger management training dealing with one's behavioural aspects, it can be useful to practise alternative behaviours other than the habitual ones. Training in assertiveness, social skills and other forms of effective communication, negotiation or catharsis has also been found to be helpful (Harower 1993).

In child mental health services, the most common problems that the parents seek help with are conduct disorders. Parents may find it difficult to manage their children's defiance and antisocial behaviours. However, one often discovers that such behaviours have gradually evolved in children as their parents have unwittingly empowered them to the extent that they have gone beyond control. They often tend to forget that as they can empower their children to dare they can also empower them to control themselves.

There is a fascinating story of a yogi, sitting still in a state of meditation in a jungle. With the extraordinary psychic powers gained through his meditative practices, he discovers that a nearby mouse is being chased by a cat. The yogi, feeling pity for the mouse, turns him into a cat. Similarly, on some other day this cat is chased by a stronger beast and the yogi protects the cat by turning him into a stronger beast. The process continues until the mouse has finally turned into a tiger. The tiger then begins to lead a fearless life in the jungle. However, one day the tiger thinks to himself that he is essentially a mouse, although, except for the yogi, the whole jungle knows him as a tiger. 'If the yogi wasn't there I would *really* be a tiger.' Therefore he decides to kill the yogi and is about to attack when the yogi, realizing what is happening, turns the tiger back into a mouse by simply pronouncing, 'Become a mouse again.'

Many parents need some help in getting in touch with their own strengths and authority without resorting to punitive means. Sometimes giving up certain behaviours (such as punitive ones) may feel like losing whatever power or control one has over the situation and can be associated with feelings of complete helplessness.

There is an Indian story of a Swami who lived in a temple. He was worried about the fact that people had stopped visiting the temple because of a cobra living nearby. The Swami decided to try to persuade the snake not to bite people, as they were temple devotees and their intention of visiting the temple was such a pious one. The snake agreed, and gradually the temple began to be crowded with worshippers. One day the Swami decided to see the snake again and thank him for his support. When he went near the snake's residence he found the snake badly wounded in many places, looking very sad, hopeless and miserable. The snake explained that since he had stopped biting, people had lost all fear of him and even little children were unafraid of throwing pebbles at him or dragging him around. The Swami was shocked to hear this and pointed out that it was true that he had requested the snake not to bite people, but he had never stopped him from hissing!

PSYCHODYNAMIC INSIGHT

The psychodynamic approaches to exploring one's tendency to experience unbearable feelings in order to manage them better involve making sense of the stories behind these in their historical context. Some of these story lines are as follows (Dwivedi 1997).

When the parents are unable to protect a child from the extreme intensity of an emotion, the child experiences a psychic trauma threatening to disrupt all psychic functions. Subsequently such emotions are perceived as particularly dangerous. This leads to a dread of being flooded with such feelings (abandonment, hurt and so on). This dread then leads to the employment of defensive strategies (such as violent outbursts, induction of altered states of consciousness, substance abuse, soothing or distracting rituals and so on) at the slightest possibility of the dreaded feeling emerging into one's consciousness (Dwivedi 1993c; Krystal 1988).

Another way of making sense of aggressive behaviours is to think in terms of a toddler who becomes mobile, running, climbing and exploring the environment around. Various objects that are encountered can be very exciting on the one hand, but can also be frightening and dangerous on the other, with their potential to produce sharp loud sounds, electrocute, burn, bite, attack, cut, poison, slide and so on. The parents, therefore, have to keep a close enough eye to protect the adventurer from getting hurt in a jungle-like environment full of fierce and dangerous objects; if the parents are unable to provide this protection or become hurtful, abusive or damaging themselves, the children are left to rely upon their own primitive and aggressive instincts to defend themselves in such a dangerous world. Violence then becomes natural and habitual as the child grows. Such violent and risky behaviours are therefore desperate attempts to stimulate anxious concerns in the significant others, because of the conviction that they will not watch out unless they are forced to do so (Dwivedi 1993c; Willock 1983).

The experience of separation, loss and hurt can also arouse very distressing feelings and stress. From very early on children learn to cope with such feelings and develop a capacity to tolerate them as they mature. One of the ways of aiding this kind of learning is through developmental play such as peek-a-boo, tossing objects and finding them, waving bye-bye, hide and seek and so on (Kleeman 1967, 1973). When such a line of development is distorted but the need for such an interactive play continues, it can take on more and more hurtful and dangerous forms, even continuing later in life in such behaviour as running away or joy riding and being chased by police (Dwivedi 1993d; Willock 1990).

A child who is being abused, tormented, attacked or tortured and finds itself in a state of inescapable suffering may end up identifying with the torturer, as a natural psychological protective device. In this way it may be possible to emotionally detach and dissociate from the otherwise unavoidable pain. This process of 'identification with the aggressor' then leads (even when one is grown up) to behaviour outbursts originally belonging to the aggressor. ('Identification' is a psychological process through which one acquires the attitudes, views, feelings and behaviours belonging to someone else. This is a normal healthy process and takes place as a result of a close, usually loving or admiring, relationship. However, the same mechanisms may be involved in pathological situations.) These outbursts are usually triggered by the subtle reminders of painful past experiences. This process of identification can be so subtle and pervasive that the person is as if 'possessed' or 'bewitched' and looks, sounds, talks and attacks like the past perpetrator. Even the memory of the childhood abuse may be lost or, if remembered, the associated emotions are unavailable. However, there are many who have had such traumatic experiences in their childhood but do not inflict their pain upon others, particularly upon their children. They remember their own experiences and make sure that they never let their children experience what they themselves have been through. For these parents the pain and suffering was not totally repressed and they have found ways of coping with their emotions without pathological identification or dissociation (Dwivedi 1984; Fraiberg *et al.* 1980).

Sometimes the behaviours that are clearly aggressive, attacking, damaging, destructive and violent are in fact distorted proximity-seeking or deviated attachment behaviours. Anyone faced with disasters, loss or stress needs to seek proximity with certain attachment figures or familiar persons or environments, with the goal of obtaining some comfort, even though that very person may be the cause of the stress. If the attachment figures are unavailable or rejecting, or the intensity of the stress is extremely distressing, this proximity-seeking attachment behaviour can become disorganized and can manifest as being hostile and even violent. This intense desire to 'reach out and touch someone' therefore can become disguised, confused, violent and even fatal (Mawson 1987).

COPING WITH ANGRY OR VIOLENT PERSONS

In a situation where violence is likely to emerge, it may be possible to make use of the available body of knowledge for dealing with aggressive and violent situations, for example learning how to sense impending trouble, how to approach a potentially dangerous situation and what may be the right thing to do in different aggressive circumstances (Moran 1984). Even very simple things, such as one's body posture, demeanour and look, can either aggravate or calm a potentially dangerous situation. For example, it may be less threatening to stand with feet apart, looking relaxed and at a distance from a potentially aggressive person, avoiding eye contact (by watching the chest or the hands of the person), being and appearing relaxed (by checking for any tension in one's fist and face in order to avoid looking angry or frightened and by relaxing one's breathing – shallow breathing in a state of arousal may lead to impaired thinking, and shallow breathing can also produce a high-pitched voice, giving the impression of being frightened or angry). However, one has to remain ready for any action required, such as standing in such a way that the dominant foot remains behind, bearing the weight of the body, and the other foot is in front with the knee bent. Similarly, before talking to the person, it may be useful to think of some ways of introducing humour or empathy into the conversation and distracting the person's attention away from oneself. One may also need, if necessary, to acquire skills in restraining an individual in a way that is equally effective but less dangerous, such as restraining from behind or getting hold of clothing rather than limbs.

The way we respond to a violent situation can either calm the dangerous situation or make it worse. Our natural responses to aggression are usually quite different from the above. Within split seconds a whole range of ready-made psycho-physiological, cognitive and behavioural responses emerge, as if from nowhere. It is like being a puppet whose strings have been pulled. The responses are, at times, effective in handling the aggressive moment, while at other times they make things worse. It is also possible that a response may be useful in one situation but can make matters worse in another. For example, when we have healthy legs, jogging can be very useful as it helps to keep the legs healthy. On the other hand, applying a plaster cast can be an unhealthy thing to do to a healthy leg, but it can be very helpful when applied to a broken leg, for which jogging would be rather damaging. Similarly we need to cultivate different responses for different behavioural contexts.

Unfortunately, when we develop habitual responses we tend to use them in situations where such responses may not be productive and can in fact be self-defeating. If we fall in a quicksand our tendency would be to struggle. But the more we struggle, the more we would sink, and the more we sink the more we would struggle. Similarly, when faced with a violent situation our tendency is to respond in a frightened or angry manner. Either of these responses can fuel the violent situation further. It is difficult to fight fire with fire. The following stories of Angulimala and the anger demon illustrate this point rather nicely.

The story of Angulimala

There is a story of an Indian bandit called Angulimala. He had suffered so much in his life through the exploitative behaviours of others that he became a bandit and settled on an important trade route through a forest. With his feelings of revenge he took an oath to kill a thousand persons. In order to keep a count of his killings he kept a finger of each victim in the form of a necklace (hence his name, Angulimala, meaning 'the one with a necklace of fingers'). Whenever he saw a passer-by he would attack with his sword and the passer-by would either fight back or try to beg for his life. These responses or attempts to stop Angulimala only made him worse. The trade route became so dangerous that the king sent an army to capture Angulimala. However, the Buddha came to know of this and proceeded to save Angulimala from being executed. When Angulimala saw the Buddha coming, he felt delighted because he needed just one more finger to complete his necklace of one thousand. So he raised his sword to attack the Buddha. However, the Buddha continued approaching Angulimala with a smile so peaceful and serene that Angulimala, who had never experienced anything like it before, felt puzzled. This gave the Buddha just enough time to draw Angulimala's attention to his physiological and mental processes and his erroneous thinking in relation to happiness through vengeful killings, and to change his murderous intentions. Finally, the Buddha accepted him as a disciple in his order of monks.

The story of the anger-eating demon

This is a story from Samyutta Nikaya, a Buddhist book (I. 237–9, for translation see Burlingame 1991). It describes the nature of an anger-eating demon who thrived on people becoming angry. The demon, therefore, went around annoying people and making them angry. Once he went to the 'plane of thirty-three gods', gatecrashed up to the throne of the king of the gods and deposited himself on it; the king, Sakka, was away at the time. When the other gods found out, they became furious with the demon. The more they became angry, the more the demon grew bigger, shining and bright. When Sakka arrived, the gods informed him of what was going on. Sakka, therefore, approached the demon with great humility, without any sign of anger, and prostrated himself in front of the demon three times and appeared most welcoming. Thus the anger-eating demon was starved of feeding on any anger and could not survive. He kept on shrinking until he became almost negligible and went somewhere else in search of people whom he could make angry and whose anger he could relish.

CONCLUSION

Thus, the cognitive components play a significant role in the mechanisms involved in the emotional system. Perceptions, cognitive appraisals, values and beliefs greatly influence emotions such as anger and are, in turn, shaped by these emotional experiences. Such intricate relationships are further augmented by the fact that our minds often mix the real with the unreal and have a tendency to take things personally. In such a context, cognitive behaviour therapy (CBT) has a great deal to offer to the cause of affective management. In this chapter a number of Eastern stories have been included. For thousands of years such stories have conveyed the essence of several anger management strategies with which CBT also resonates. In addition, some possible psychodynamic stories which may contribute to the background of an angry, aggressive or violent individual have been described, along with a couple of Eastern stories that enrich the strategies for handling such difficult situations.

REFERENCES

Burlingame, E.W. (1991) *Buddhist Parables* (Indian edition), Delhi: Motilal Banarasidas Publishers.

Dwivedi, K.N. (1984) 'Mother–baby psychotherapy', *Health Visitor* 57: 306–7.

——(1990) 'Purification of mind by Vipassana meditation', in J. Crook and D. Fontana (eds) *Space in Mind*, Shaftesbury: Elements, 86–91.

——(1992) 'Eastern approaches to mental health', in T. Ahmed, B. Naidu and A. Webb-Johnson (eds) *Concepts of Mental Health in the Asian Community*, London: Confederation of Indian Organisations (UK), 24–30.

——(1993a) 'Coping with unhappy children who are from ethnic minorities', in V.P. Varma (ed.) *Coping With Unhappy Children*, London: Cassell, 134–51.

——(1993b) 'Conceptual frameworks', in K.N. Dwivedi (ed.) *Groupwork with Children and Adolescents: A Handbook*, London: Jessica Kingsley, 28–45.

——(1993c) 'Emotional development', in K.N. Dwivedi (ed.) *Groupwork with Children and Adolescents: A Handbook*, London: Jessica Kingsley, 72–7.

——(1993d) 'Use of interpretation', in K.N. Dwivedi (ed.) *Groupwork with Children and Adolescents: A Handbook*, London: Jessica Kingsley, 183–92.

——(1994a) 'Mental cultivation (meditation) in Buddhism', *Psychiatric Bulletin* 18: 503–4.

——(1994b) 'The Buddhist perspective in mental health', *Open Mind* 70: 20–1.

——(1994c) 'Social structures that support or undermine families from ethnic minority groups: Eastern value systems', *Context* 20: 11–12.

——(1996a) 'Children from ethnic minorities', in V. Varma (ed.) *Coping with Children in Stress*, Aldershot: Arena Publishers, 89–99.

——(1996b) 'Race and the child's perspective', in R. Davie, G. Upton and V. Varma (eds) *The Voice of the Child: A Handbook for Professionals*, London: Falmer Press, 153–69.

——(1996c) 'Culture and personality', in K.N. Dwivedi and V. Varma (eds) *Meeting the Needs of Ethnic Minority Children*, London: Jessica Kingsley, 17–36.

——(1997) 'Group work with violent children and adolescents', in V. Varma (ed.) *Violent Children and Adolescents*, London: Jessica Kingsley.

Fraiberg, S., Adelson, E., and Shapiri, V. (1980) 'Ghosts in the nursery', in S. Fraiberg (ed.) *Clinical Studies in Infant Mental Health*, London: Tavistock.

Harower, J. (1993) 'Group work with young offenders', in K.N. Dwivedi (ed.) *Groupwork with Children and Adolescents: A Handbook*, London: Jessica Kingsley, 233–44.

Hoshmand, L.T., and Austin, G.W. (1985) 'Validation studies of a multi-factor cognitive behavioural anger control inventory'. Unpublished manuscript, quoted in E.L. Feindler and R.B. Ecton (eds) (1986) *Adolescent Anger Control: Cognitive-Behavioural Techniques*, Oxford: Pergamon.

Kleeman, J.A. (1967) 'The peek-a-boo game. Part I: its origins, meanings and related phenomena in the first year', *Psycho-analytic Study of the Child* 22: 239–73.

——(1973) 'The peek-a-boo game: its evolution and associated behaviours especially bye-bye and shame expression during the second year', *Journal of American Academy of Child Psychiatrists* 12: 1–23.

Krystal, H. (1988) *Integration and Self Healing*, Hillsdale, NJ: The Analytic Press.

Mawson, A.R. (1987) *Transient Criminality: A model of stress-induced crime*, New York: Praeger.

Moran, J. (1984) 'Responses and responsibility', *Nursing Times* 4 April 1984: 28–31.

Novaco, R.W. (1975) *Anger Control: The Development and Evaluation of an Experimental Treatment*, Lexington, MA: D.C. Heath.

Rimpoche, D.A. (1987) *Taming the Tiger*, Eskdalemuir: Dzalendara Publishing.

White, M. (1989) 'The externalization of the problem and the reauthoring of lives and relationships', in M. White *Selected Papers*, Adelaide: Dulwich Centre Publications, 5–28.

Willock, B. (1983) 'Play therapy with the aggressive, acting out child', in C.E. Schaffer and K.J. O'Connor (eds) *Handbook of Play Therapy*, New York: Wiley.

——(1990) 'From acting out to interactive play', *International Journal of Psychoanalysis* 71: 321–4.

Chapter 6

Using metaphor and imagery
An illustrative case study of childhood anxiety

Damian Gardner and Peter Harper

Children's play, and their creation and enactment of stories, is richly permeated with metaphors. Such narratives provide important opportunities (for the therapist who is attuned to the child's aspirations and anxieties) to gain insight into the way in which the child arranges their life experiences, and to develop intervention strategies which will promote greater understanding and coherence for the child growing up in an often complex and bewildering world.

The symbols and metaphors so central to play and stories are essential tools which equip the child to separate internal experience, conflict and imagination from external reality. By transforming events in this safer 'one step removed' way (Gordon 1995), the initial experience of the child as a passive responder gives way to the development of the child's resources and understanding, thus facilitating increased mastery and influence over events and experiences shaping life (Bettelheim 1987).

The profundity of themes, conflicts and their resolution is perhaps the most explored area of 'childhood' imagery. The classic fairy tales have been analysed for the psychological themes – and their utility to children – by various schools of psychotherapy including, for example, object relations theory (Cashdan 1988) and transactional analysis (Karpman 1968). In all these analyses, however, the utility of the narrative as a mechanism for psychological growth is dependent on a deeply imaginative and intellectual engagement by the child. It is this facility of children to be entranced by images and metaphors – of their own or of others' making – that makes the narrative method such a powerful mechanism for change. The essence of the method is encapsulated by Bettelheim's statement that:

For a story truly to hold a child's attention . . . it must at one and the same time relate to all aspects of his personality – and this without ever belittling but, on the contrary, giving credence to the seriousness of the child's predicaments, while simultaneously promoting confidence in himself and in his future.

(Bettelheim 1976: 5)

The response of children to such material is an active one. Their creativity is stimulated within a context that allows them to express themselves and master an evolving understanding of the complex moral and social situations that impinge on their world. Furthermore, these processes can be developed not just by providing material (such as fairy tales) but can be elicited from children themselves. Sheila Wilkins, head of a small Yorkshire primary school famous for its children's success in winning poetry prizes, comments:

I try to give [children] a rich diet of language. Nursery rhymes and fairy stories for the young ones; quality fiction, mythology and poetry, including lyrics . . . and performance poetry, for the older children. When children are exposed to myth . . . chords are struck. Ideas are triggered. Strings are touched.

(*The Independent* 1995: section II, 4)

ANXIETY AND IMAGERY

The management of anxiety has always been of central concern in children's stories. First, the themes of tales that appeal to children reflect the core anxieties of childhood (loss, polarization of good and bad, resolution of oedipal conflicts, etc.). Second, the form of these tales (such as formulaic repetition in threes) allows predictability and structure to govern the underlying terror and violence of their themes. And third, the context of their telling can provide a secure base from which the child can imaginatively explore danger while being safely contained.

These features of fairy tales can be incorporated into therapeutic work that uses the child's own stories as the primary vehicle for change. The case study that follows describes an intervention with a 7-year-old girl whose presenting problem of arachnaphobia could be seen as indicative of more generalized anxieties within a systemic family context. The therapeutic process used allowed the child to confront and master fears at her own pace and under her own control to a degree not possible using traditional exposure therapy treatments. Furthermore, the use of the story-telling approach allowed this girl to explore issues and develop her own competence through the use of personally meaningful symbols. At the same time, by entering her world, therapy could proceed without imposing an alien adult structure. At the end of therapy her comment was that she had 'come to play'. One is reminded here in a very concrete form of Winnicott's ideas about play and containment as the basis of effective and creative therapeutic encounter (Winnicott 1971).

THE FRIGHTENING DAY: A CASE STUDY

Context of intervention

Mandy, aged 7 years, was referred by the family GP for anxiety management to the NHS Child Clinical Psychology Service. She had a history of generalized anxiety in a range of settings, including home and school. More recently, after encountering a large spider, she had a major experience of panic, followed by three days of intense distress.

At the time of the initial assessment Mandy was experiencing broken nights, barricading her bed with pillows and occasionally seeing spiders where none existed. Her parents had become extensively involved in the phobia, checking rooms, the bedroom and in particular the bed. They also offered considerable reassurance to Mandy.

There were problems in the family over boundaries and discipline. The parents were frequently interrupted by Mandy, but they never interrupted her. A variety of behaviours which the parents found irritating and difficult to control were reported. A good example was Mandy changing television programmes without consulting her parents. Father was frequently absent from the home because of his work, sometimes overnight, sometimes for as much as three or four days. Mother reported that she herself had a fear of spiders but that she could cope with them. There had been a recent change in the constellation of the family in that Mandy's half-brother, Simon (aged 17), had left the home some five months previously. Mandy was close to this brother and looked upon him as a companion and as a 'protector'. The boundary difficulties in the home involved more than just discipline. When Father was away from home, Mandy would share the parental bed with her mother, and resented having to leave to go into her own bed. Generally it appeared that over-protectiveness was a theme in the family. This was combined with a tendency to anticipate one another's needs.

As a baby Mandy was reported to have been very demanding, and was used to having her needs met immediately. During the course of the assessment she presented as an imaginative, sociable and clever child who had good social relationships and no problems in school.

A tendency to test out limits both in the initial joint session with her parents and in the first individual session was noted. Finally, Mandy seemed to be perplexed about the expression of strong emotions, particularly about 'getting cross'. While describing her response to seeing a spider she commented that her first feeling was to get cross, and that she would then scream. She was able to report her sensations as 'shivery feelings' and 'a fast heart beat'. In terms of any possible imagery, when asked what an enormous spider would do, she said very quickly, 'It would eat me up.' It also emerged that Mandy ceased to think during the encounter with the large spider, and that she now found it difficult to think rationally about spiders under any circumstance.

Intervention planning

Four possible interventions were considered in this case. Seeing Mandy alone, seeing Mandy with her mother, using a systemic family approach, and finally a combination of seeing Mandy alone and seeing the parents separately from Mandy. The last of these formats was chosen, with the decision being to intervene primarily with the subsystem considered most likely to change – Mandy – which was simultaneously the subsystem showing the most serious pathology (Clarkson and Fish 1988). A session by session outline of the intervention is given in Table 6.1.

Work with Mandy

Of the various possible intervention styles available, it was decided that the primary intervention would focus on the use of imagery and narrative. This style was particularly applicable to Mandy who was a creative and imaginative child. A major advantage of using such an approach was that it would make therapy more like play

Table 6.1 Session-by-session outline of intervention programme

Person/s seen	Goal of session	Key content of session
1 Parents and Mandy	Assessment/engage	Background details supplied
2 Mandy	Assessment/engage	Picture of family 'Imagined story' Rainbow's Frightening Day
3 Parents	Assessment/engage	Family issues. Parents' 'irritation' with Mandy
4 Mandy	Establish story as main technique	'Corrected' picture. Puppet of butterfly brought to session. New story — 'Swallowed by a Whale'
5 Mandy	Independent coping. Thinking in frightening situations	Policeman butterfly as teacher (new puppets made). Homework: Mandy asked to have a dream
6 Mandy	Problem-solving. Understanding and expressing emotions	Dream as a basis of sea monster story (swallowed). Hard for Mandy to express anger ('Being cross') see transcript

7	Parents	1 Checklist of problems at home 2 Spider issues and feedback 3 Other	1 Problems identified. Nagging demeanour. Answering back. Limit setting. Strategies. Goal of misbehaviour (attention). Time-out until Mandy is ready. Withdraw from negotiations 2 Mandy not asking for help with checks. Straight into bed. Laughed at close-up of spider on TV 3 Mandy missing brother
8	Amanda	Simon's absence	Policeman leaves Rainbow. Rainbow is cross. Rainbow changes name and becomes a policeman.
9	Amanda	Coping alone continued	Abandoned by 'Police Dog'
10	Parents	Review. Plan assessment. Plan termination	Parental changes. Spiders 'not an issue'. Problem-solving with: School, Home, Spiders
11	Amanda	Problem solving and assessment planning	Amanda asked to generate ways to show she is not scared of spiders: 1 Toys 2 Spider hunt 3 Hold spider. Also demonstration and information that she has coped with spider
12	Amanda	As above	Implementation
13	Parents and Amanda	Review and termination	

and hence less stigmatizing, awkward and unpleasant than standard *in vivo* desensitization may have been. Standard cognitive behaviour therapy seemed an unattractive model for working with this child, given her personality and age. However, the 'play/imagination' techniques envisaged were capable of incorporating a model of problem-solving in the promotion of thinking when anxious.

Simultaneously, work was planned with the parents. This was to comprise of advising them to withdraw from the ritual checks, and to work on boundary and discipline issues.

Account of intervention

The first session with Mandy 'set the stage' for the remainder of the sessions. It began with Mandy being asked to draw a picture of her family. The picture showed Mandy as the largest member of the family, with her brother the second largest, then the father and finally her mother. When asked who was the strongest, she said her brother was and then her dad. After that she said she was stronger than her mum 'with words', though her mother was stronger with her hands.

We then followed a new line and began what turned into the key content of the session. This was a story elicited from Mandy in the following manner. She was asked to close her eyes and make her body 'floppy' because she was going to 'another world'. When she got there she was invited to first describe the weather, and to then describe what the land looked like (she described a summer's day in a wood). She was then told that something was moving behind a tree and that she could see it; she was asked what it was. She said it was a butterfly. Through the use of non-directive prompts such as 'what happened next?', 'and then what?', etc., she generated the following story:

The frightening day

There was a butterfly and its name was Rainbow. A crow was after her, the crow had eaten up Mummy and Daddy and was going to eat her. She hid under a leaf because she couldn't get under the soil. Three butterflies were after her so she flew into the rainbow and was camouflaged, then she flew out of it again and the three butterflies were back after her. Soon the police butterfly came along and took the three butterflies to jail.

After Mandy had completed the story the therapist wrote it down with her and left spaces for her to illustrate it.

During this time Mandy alternated between playful bursts of creative energy and more thoughtful periods. She was completely absorbed in her story and drawing, and was surprised the hour had gone by. There were two or three occasions at the start of the session where it had been necessary to be slightly firm in making requests, but as the story emerged Mandy showed no inclination to stop what we were doing.

At the next session Mandy arrived holding a puppet of Rainbow the butterfly and was keen to talk about a butterfly dream she had had. She also brought a new family picture which showed a more orthodox representation of the different members' sizes. However, she had little to say about it.

In this and subsequent sessions, although they were character-ized by informality and spontaneity, the central task involved the use of manipulated story telling. This was done not only through 'talking' the story but also through drawing, play-acting and using puppets. The following excerpt from session 6 is fairly typical of the content of the therapy. It followed a discussion about Mandy's dream in which Rainbow encountered a frightening whale.

THERAPIST (T) Do you remember what Rainbow did in the story [last week] which was really clever? Which the policeman butterfly told her to do?

MANDY (M)   He tried to let her know that if . . . if . . . she has to try and handle it because she is growing older now.

T   That's right. And what did she have to *do*? She has to do something really special which she used to forget.

M   [interrupting] Think!

T   Yes, that's right, isn't it? And that's what Rainbow had to do when she saw the 'creature' last week. Then we had the sea over there [pointing] because at first she felt . . . do you remember what she felt first of all?

M   Shivery.

T   Yeah – and then she remembered to . . . [pause]

M   Think! When we actually did that, I, I tried to dream that dream . . . it was a bit scary at first.

T   Oh, did you? And is that what happened – and did Rainbow think in the dream?

M   Um hum.
T   So did Rainbow go 'Aaaghh'? [play imitating M's panic]
M   No, no. [laughing]
T   So even when Rainbow was inside this whale . . .
M   [interrupting] She just sat down . . . she felt her heartbeats were going a bit slow, she tried to relax . . . she thought, 'Right – nothing is happening . . . right, I am in the sea monster', and . . . then she heard the noise and came flying out the whale's mouth! [giggle]
T   I think Rainbow is ever so clever to make her heartbeat go slower and to relax, and to think. Were you pleased with the dream?
M   Yes.
T   Good.

The word 'relax' had never been used with Mandy, nor had it been suggested that she reduce her heartbeat.

TECHNIQUES TO PROMOTE CHANGE

Three techniques can be discerned that were used to promote change in Mandy through the use of this manipulated story-telling process. The first was symbolic manipulation of the story elements. For example, the policeman butterfly 'went away' just as her brother had done. That there was some form of symbolic significance to the elements in the story was suggested by the closeness of the parallels between some of the story material and events or people in real life. Also interesting were the parallels between her drawings: for example, the policeman butterfly bore a strong resemblance to her picture of her brother.

The most important symbol was clearly Rainbow the butterfly, which seemed to symbolize Mandy herself. Through the use of the stories Mandy could, in her imagination, explore and negotiate developmental growth vicariously as she was presented with a careful progression of more challenging problems to confront. The second technique was simple problem-solving: Mandy was frequently asked, 'How would Rainbow . . . ?' In responding to these questions Mandy concentrated hard and was always very thoughtful before replying. The third and final therapeutic process was that of *in imago* desensitization to fearful stimuli – though to stimuli that were pertinent and meaningful to her and more under her control than if she had been presented with descriptions of spiders. In practice, of course, these three processes were interwoven and inseparable.

One small feature worthy of note during the sessions was Mandy's statement that she could make herself dream things. Mandy was asked to do this at the end of session 5 and she returned with a dream. It is not clear whether this was a real dream or an imagined story made up before falling asleep.

Another feature of interest was that after Rainbow the butterfly became promoted to being a policeman (session 8), Mandy suggested that she should have a more grown-up name. This was striking, because a week earlier in supervision it had been commented that perhaps it would help the family if the diminutive 'Mandy' was altered to a more adult 'Amanda'. It seemed that in her stories Mandy anticipated this with her symbolic self!

Intervention with parents

Two areas of intervention with the parents were planned. One was directly applicable to the phobia, the other to do with more general issues of parenting. A third purpose – that of liaison/information exchange – was a further key role of the meetings with the parents.

As it turned out, the first of these interventions was never pursued. This was because by the time we met for session 7 (the first post-assessment session with the parents), Amanda had ceased to ask for any assistance in her checking for or coping with spiders. Instead with the parents we focused on managing behaviours they found 'irritating' or difficult to deal with, by using firm but appropriate limit-setting.

Outcomes

Many changes occurred during the course of treatment. Amanda saw spiders and did not become anxious. Indeed she took one spider outside on a book cover while her 10-year-old cousin was scared. This occurred after the fourth one-to-one session but only emerged later on. In the final pair of individual treatment sessions Amanda was asked to think of ways in which she could demonstrate that she was not afraid of spiders. Her suggestions included: 'making me hold one'; 'get some toy spiders and make them move across the room and me pick them up'; and 'spend days looking for spiders and put the biggest one we find in a box with some flies'. With some modification she did all these, with an emphasis on a 'spider hunt' and the creation of a 'spider house'. This involved searching the hospital for spiders which were collected in a transparent container and taken home.

There was no return of panic – rather Amanda seemed to be quite fond of and amused by spiders. For example, she giggled playfully when seeing a close-up of a spider on a person's face in a television programme.

Her frightening imagery had disappeared. When asked what would happen when she met an enormous spider she said that she would walk under its legs. This is very different from her earlier comment that it would swallow her up.

Amanda developed a wide range of cognitive coping strategies upon which to draw. There was also no sign of the 'anger-followed-by-confusion-and-panic' sequence that apparently characterized the traumatic encounter which precipitated her referral.

The parents were pleased – and somewhat surprised – both by the improvement Amanda had made with spiders and by positive changes in her behaviour and how they were able to manage it more generally. It is clear that some of the systemic issues remained unresolved in the family. However, the central problem of involvement in Amanda's phobia had been dealt with. It is hoped that the changes that occurred will continue to help the parents and Amanda through the remaining years of her childhood and into adolescence.

Interestingly, Amanda was well aware of the changes that she had made with spiders, but had her own explanation. She put the changes down to acquiring more information, particularly that they 'eat flies'! Although she liked coming to sessions she questioned whether she had needed to attend so often since she could simply have been told that spiders ate flies and were 'good' the first time she had been seen. Not surprisingly, this opportunity to explain the full intervention rationale was declined!

CONCLUDING COMMENT

We have written here a narrative describing how stories can be used to facilitate change. Our hope is that through engaging with this narrative readers may themselves be enabled to make changes – to think about, to be encouraged, to imagine themselves acting in new and productive ways.

REFERENCES

Bettelheim, B. (1976) *The Uses of Enchantment*, Harmondsworth: Penguin.
——(1987) *A Good Enough Parent*, London: Thames and Hudson.
Cashdan, S. (1988) *Object Relations Psychotherapy: Using the Relationship*, New York: Norton.
Clarkson, P., and Fish, S. (1988) 'Systemic assessment and TA psychotherapy with children' in P. Clarkson (ed.) (1992) *Transactional Analysis Psychotherapy: An Integrated Approach*, London: Routledge.
Gordon, S. (1995) *The Right to Feel Safe: A Protective Behaviours Manual*, Adelaide: Missions SA.
The Independent 8 December 1995, section 2: 4, 'Young Poets Society'.
Karpman, S.B. (1968) 'Fairy tales and script drama analysis', *Transactional Analysis Bulletin* 7(26): 39–43.
Winnicott, D.W. (1971) *Playing and Reality*, London: Tavistock.

Chapter 7

For better or worse
Stories associated with shame and guilt in therapy

Terence Lear

EXPERIENCING SHAME IN VARIOUS PROCESSES OF PERSONAL CHANGE

Listening to stories enthrals all ages, especially in childhood. Spontaneous story telling has the advantage that the tale told may be modified by the listener's responses. Often a story's hero or heroine goes from personal disadvantage to personal fulfilment, a time that requires the hero or heroine to overcome a powerful evil figure and to experience shame. Shame occurs with the process of growing up, in phases of education and training, in grief and some therapies.

Cinderella had experience of a loving mother who died. When her father married again, her stepmother made repeated harsh demands on her, such as extracting lentils mixed in ashes, and then denied her the promised reward of going to the ball. The story tells how two doves, from a tree which Cinderella planted on her mother's grave and watered with her tears, assisted her with that task. Bettelheim (1978) notes that this represents the influence of her mother in early years, which gave Cinderella a foundation of (basic) trust in regaining self-confidence and self-discipline to deal with her stepmother's demands. Both 'good' and 'bad' mothers, it seems, are necessary for the process, since her stepsisters do not fare so well, despite continuing favour from their mother. Cinderella endures shame and humiliation during the stages of her transformation from adolescent servant to royal bride.

A young man referred himself to me for treatment. He was well versed in psychoanalytic ideas and, telling his story, paraded his understandings of himself in a dispassionate way. I could discern nothing in what he was saying to suggest that these understandings had had some influence in promoting change in him or that the feelings they aroused challenged either of us. There seemed very little contact between us. I looked for my part in discouraging the revelation of feelings and decided to be more transparent with my own. Soon he became animated and disclosed his childhood longing to know his parents' feelings and experiences from their spontaneous telling, rather than to have them react to his own behaviour in terms of approval or disapproval. He soon learned how to avoid the latter by hiding his thoughts and feelings. Both he and they sidestepped any issues of mutual embarrassment which might loosen their attachment and bring about changes in their relationship, or in his growing up.

The sidestepping of shame, muddles and messy feelings is a defensive manoeuvre that many trained psychotherapists will recognize.

With some body cures, damaging agents and dead tissues are removed and replaced by new tissue, a time-consuming process. Should assessment result in the choice of analytic psychotherapy, what follows is an analogous process of personal transformation, comprising some changes of attitude and self-image (Lear 1991). Through telling a personal story, and relating with a therapist or with others in a group, a person may be enabled to endure episodes of shame and self-doubt, followed by gradual rebuilding of self-esteem and self-confidence, to be tested in that person's social context. This is akin to growing up and to educational processes. The gangly gauche youth seeks his fellows, with whom to live out this shameful phase. Generally he is no more regarded as requiring assistance from a therapist than are college students in further education (Lear 1995: 397) who are undergoing transformation towards gaining a professional persona, and are also to some extent withdrawn from usual society to share their oscillations of gloom and optimism, regressive enactments and self-doubts. Eventually they emerge as self-confident graduates. Confident, that is, until the next step of occupational learning is encountered. These processes and therapy processes may not be inherently different except that the therapy context carries a burden of shame, supposing a deficiency or weakness in the person, whereas developmental troubles are regarded as universal and unremarkable. Those wanting for themselves the changes associated with education and training have their absence of knowledge, understanding and preparation for further responsibility covered by their proud association with a prestigious educational institution, although their inner views of self may be uncertain and quite different from their outward presentation.

Whether or not there is shame associated with the context of human transformation, it is self-evident that it is central to the experience of personal change. Familiar ways of experiencing the self, and of how one is regarded by others, recede and are gradually replaced by a reformed self. Thus the patient's story in therapy may emerge in episodes or may be retold with additions or alterations over time. What was experienced in the recent and more distant past can be re-experienced by relating it to the therapist and to a group with other members, and the associated feelings can be named and owned. With these new understandings a person may then risk modifying his or her ways of relating in a social context. Often such insights follow rather than precede change. Thus a sense of self is derived from both the inner world and the outer world, including social relationships. A process of personal change means partial dismembering followed by the restructuring of self. An inner sense of fragility or fragmentation associated with relating to others, as though one were regarded as unacceptable by them as well as by oneself, may accompany this process. What follows such a shameful state is a desire to hide away or disappear altogether, or to become angry, critical and capable of launching envious attacks on others. Others close to the patient may also be suffering from the treatment process. It is important that this suffering be understood as a temporary and unavoidable phase. An uncritical therapist provides the opportunity for these disturbing feelings to be contained by the patient. In a group, other members may have similar stories, for instance of a parent who shames them. Often, it is an internalized parent or ideal self who would be regarded as disapproving, rejecting and pointing to failure. In group psychotherapy, while a person is being invited to consider the different realities of what would be expected of a child and of an adult, that person is also experiencing the acceptance of the group conductor and other group members and has a sense of the group as a whole, more or less. For those many patients with so-called narcissistic disorders, who are shame-prone, a group providing reasonably unconditional acceptance for long enough often prompts change towards more realistic, self-affirming attitudes – an important transformation indeed. It is as though any number of shameful experiences are followed through with new understanding and decisive statements, addressed to the self, to relate differently and to enact this despite some trepidation.

Jane Austen's account ([1816] 1985) of Emma's feelings of shame when facing up to her insensitivity about ridiculing Miss Bates, after having been carefully confronted with this by Mr Knightley, is a story of positive shaming (361–70). For his part, Mr Knightley wondered for a while whether he had put their friendship at risk. Emma set about making amends to Miss Bates which assuaged her guilt for the hurt which she had inflicted, although Emma's shame demanded a decision to change her attitude. Later Emma reviewed her relationship with Harriet in another turmoil of shame, extending to self-disgust (401–3). According to understandings which came to her, she resolved to halt her patronizing and controlling attitudes. This enabled Emma, with new self-confidence, to assert her right to consider the possibility of Mr Knightley as her future husband.

Feelings of embarrassment, blushing, confusion, self-doubt, unworthiness, humiliation, mortification, self-fragmentation, self-disgust, desolation, emptiness, anomie and the desire to hide or to disappear are various characteristics of being ashamed. How could it be otherwise, for the self is disturbed when a person undergoes changes in attitudes and ways of relating, as well as by changes in others' perception. The case can be put the other way: that in order to prevent personal change, being shamed and feeling ashamed must be resisted.

In the biblical story of Daniel (Daniel chapter 3), Daniel's protégés Shadrach, Meshach and Abed-nego were exiles from Judah living in Babylon. They were tried publicly for their refusal to obey King Nebuchadnezzar's command to worship a golden statue which he had set up. Others in that multi-ethnic society complied, but those on trial chose rather to be thrown into a furnace. Azariah ('only preserved' in Greek – the New Jerusalem Bible) prayed aloud in the midst of the flames, beseeching God in his mercy not to abandon them to shame, but rather to shame and disempower their tormentors. They emerged unscathed and unchanged, and found favour with the King. These men were unwilling to change their beliefs and religious practices, and by refusing to be shamed and holding fast to their ideals found the means of retaining their individual and corporate identity and culture as Jews in an alien culture. Although they were willing to be integrated with some functions of Babylonian society, they would limit any personal change. It was Nebuchadnezzar who changed his attitude and became respectful to the God of the Jews.

The same theme is found in Isaiah (Isaiah 50: 6,7 Authorized

Version): 'I gave my back to the smiters, and my cheeks to them that plucked off the hair. I hid not my face from shame and spitting. For the Lord God will help me; therefore shall I not be confounded: therefore have I set my face like a flint, and I know that I shall not be ashamed.'

Patients, too, resist shame and pain in treatment for short or longer periods and there is no appreciable change in some cases before the patient leaves treatment or the treatment becomes interminable. The therapist tries to distinguish between a slow process of change and no process, and may be surprised either way.

THE USE OF FAIRY TALES

Bettelheim (1976) unravels developmental threads and a variety of life lessons in many fairy tales, although he doesn't regard telling fairy tales as therapy. He asserts that the overt story can be linked by the child, in ways he or she may be silent about or unconscious of, to deepen the child's understanding of life. Both parents and children may gain insights in oft-repeated tales.

In conducting an analytic psychotherapy group, I have sometimes noticed change happening in a member. While the nature of the change may be clear, how it was initiated may not, although it is ascribed by the patient to the group experience. This incomplete analysis may trouble me until I conclude that the bother is mine alone and needless, since that person or other members will usually return to unfinished business when it matters.

Jacoby *et al.* (1992) use fairy tales directly in their method of analytic psychotherapy. Fairy tales are examined and some consensus sought to validate developmental themes discerned in them. Some aspects may be translated into Jungian analytic terms. One useful definition of 'evil' is that it obstructs development. When the 'evil' obstruction is dealt with, development follows, so the evil was part of the process.

The method includes listening to the person's own story. Should a fairy story occur to the therapist, the thought is relayed to the patient. A dialogue ensues which may continue after the patient reads the story. Otherwise, the way the tale unravels may inform the therapist as to how he or she and the patient are relating to each other (transference and countertransference). This may add greater choice to the therapist's responses and provide some inkling of the work to be accomplished.

Possibly this use of fairy tales would be resisted were a patient to feel cheated of an opportunity of creating with the therapist unique meanings of personal experience, rather as a child likes to sort out the ways in which he or she can be different from his or her siblings. On the other hand, if fairy tales represent part of a collective unconscious, then each individual's response to it would be particular to that person. Foulkes (1986) drew attention to how each person in a small psychotherapy group responds to a common group theme according to the level of experience most strategic for that member at that time, a phenomenon he called resonance.

DIFFERENTIATING GUILT FROM SHAME IN STORIES

Guilt refers to a wrong act or omission which may have been offensive, hurtful or sexually unacceptable. This can be accompanied by the fear of a victim's outrage, indignation and demands for reparation and punishment. Unlike shame, guilt does not involve the whole self. Unless accompanied by shame, a sense of guilt may be abstracted, from relating to a person to relating to a code of conduct or to winning or losing a legal battle. If shame exists, this may inform a person that he or she should feel guilty. Thus a person may be guilty yet not feel guilty, or may be guilty but may or may not feel ashamed. Shame affects the whole self, according to a person's own standards or those of the groups to which that person belongs and is identified with. Therefore shame seems idiosyncratic. Sometimes it is an inevitable falling short of an unrealistic and unmodified self ideal from the distant past.

Guilt associated with feelings or wishes to harm another or to engage in prohibited sexual experiences may be the content of a person's fantasy. Guilt to do with committed acts would be termed real guilt. Mittwoch (1987: 33) cautions against overlooking real guilt in therapy and emphasizes the possibility of a patient making reparation, even after many years, with great relief, since reparation, like punishment, discharges guilt when the person has paid the debt. It may be helpful, then, to assist a patient to distinguish between real and fantasized guilt. Fantasized guilt may emerge in a story from childhood or adolescence, or as that story gets portrayed in the feelings of patient and therapist during the session. Such re-enactment can be considered as a mirroring of the patient's inner world, a world peopled by those of past and present importance, and reflected with varying distinctness. Sometimes similar themes arise from the patient's dream associations. Once a guilt-laden memory from the past is put into words and identified for what it is, a fantasy belonging to a past context, it begs to become redundant. Similar clarification can occur with wishes in the relationship with the therapist that are relayed from the past, which, though they are respected and understood in the context of therapy, can have no social reality. These rather bald statements may be misleading, because I have not mentioned the struggles with resistance to getting in touch with such feelings and wishes.

Child abuse is different, because here the abusive parent is really guilty, and often ashamed as well. The child, on the other hand, isn't guilty but feels humiliated and is also ashamed by association with the parent – my parent is like this and I am his or her child.

Returning to cures, not all healing requires lengthy processes. In physical medicine, for instance, a dislocated joint may be reduced by a manipulation with little if any requirement for restitution of body tissues. By analogy there are relatively brief psychological or psycho-social manipulations which bring change enough or make possible subsequent healing processes. Cognitive therapy and structural and strategic family therapy would be examples of such methods. What I have described in dealing with fantasized guilt would be a manipulation, psychologically speaking, as would the use of interpretations. Care must be taken with interpretations in therapy since these are intrusions into private experience. Interpretations are liable to arouse shame, although such is the appeal of meaning and understanding that, when interpretations are accurate, any shame is easily forgiven.

CARE WITH SHAMING

Sometimes the one who makes a statement which shames another must beware of an angry reaction.

In another Bible story (2 Samuel chapters 11–12), King David commits adultery with Bathsheba while Uriah her husband is at war, and she conceives. David arranges for Uriah to be killed in battle so that Bathsheba can be his wife. Nathan the priest avoids David's shame–anger by telling a story of a powerful rich man with many sheep, who took a lamb that a poor man loved, to cook for his guest. David is outraged at this guilty act and says that the rich man deserves to die and should pay four times the value of the lamb. 'Who is he?' the king demands. Nathan replies, 'It is you, yourself,' and rebukes him for his adultery and murder. It is hard to bring a ruler to justice when he is also chief judge in the land, unless he condemns himself or, through a priest, is condemned by God. Nathan tells him that he is not to die but that the son born to him by Bathsheba will die and that calamity and slaughter will follow in his family.

Angry reaction when a person is shamed is a reaction to feeling weak, impotent or naked. Another reaction would be to hide, that is to withdraw and become depressed.

King David's predecessor, King Saul, was shame prone (1 Samuel 9:19). When Samuel marked him out for high office he was incredulous. Despite preparation, Saul was found hiding among the baggage when he was chosen to be king. He tried to hide socially, by going away from others, and then did so in a psychic sense, when he sank into depression. David entered his service, and by his respect and devoted attentions, such as playing to him on the harp and accompanying him as his armour bearer, assisted him to lift himself out of his gloom. After slaying the Philistine champion Goliath, David became a successful and popular army leader beloved by Saul's son and by one of his daughters. Saul became envious of him and sent him to attack the Philistines against great odds – just the tactic David himself would later use with Uriah – to have him killed. After one of David's victories, Saul hurled his spear to pin David to the wall while David was playing the harp for him. So much for David's therapeutic endeavours!

It is important for the therapist to be alert to any envy of the therapist by the patient. In the working alliance, some envious admiration and emulation can be an advantage when the patient is learning a method of analytic work, although there may be a destructive element as well. In transference relating, where an envious critical attack occurs it may be prudent to avoid a confrontational style or a clever interpretation, and ask if there is something in what the therapist is doing or saying which reminds the patient of someone. One of the advantages of the wounded healer is possession of unenviable qualities. For the therapist to be bumbling and fumbling at times may enable the patient's own resources to come into play, thus protecting the treatment opportunity from destructive envy. The treatment may be at risk from the therapist's envy as well. The patient may have enviable personal characteristics, or the attentions which the person gets from the therapist may be enviable in the therapist's thought of remaking a voyage of self-discovery. Once spotted, the therapist may remark inwardly, 'Well, who doesn't feel envious sometimes?' or, if subscribing still to a therapist ideal, may be swamped with incapacitating self-inflicted shame. These are key issues in supervision during therapist training. In brief, the trainee chooses to get involved with shameful processes which take time, so that an ordinary therapist may emerge, or to carry within him or herself a readily available ideal therapist. This ideal is perhaps a version of the trainee's therapist, thus sparing the trainee shame but also his or her necessary personal development. A therapist may be shaming and arouse anger with intrusive questions or by encouraging a patient to continue with a story which becomes over-revealing. This is particularly likely during assessment when insufficient trust has been built between patient and therapist. The role of the court jester was to tell shameful truths and risk wrathful consequences. The risk was diminished by artfully wrapping the truth in a conundrum or assisting those concerned to rise above shame with humour. The therapist's interpretations may also draw wrath from a patient. These are best kept to a minimum by encouraging the patient to find his or her own questions and understandings. In a group, other members can balance the patient's own severe self-criticism by bringing attention to overlooked positive aspects or qualities, should despondency be looming. On the other hand, should an important theme be broached and seem about to recede, then that would be the right time for a therapist's intervention. Assuming that an intervention makes clear from which sources in the patient's story it arises, it is generally better that, should the patient become angry with the therapist, the attack be borne nobly rather than justifications be proffered by the therapist for what was said. Later, a reminder that what was said evidently touched on something may be useful. Interventions too near the end of the session may be unwise since the opportunity for calming and more reflective dialogue would not be possible. It is well to be open to the possibility that an intervention was mistaken in some respect. Without some constraints over arousing shame, the therapist may share the fate of a bearer of bad tidings and be 'killed off' by the patient's departure from treatment.

A therapy group member may be critical and also criticized by another. The group conductor or other group members may have a different and uncritical view: one that seeks meaning in what happens without calling that person's acceptance into question. If other members do join in the criticizing, the conductor may question whether another theme in the group is avoided or whether this member is attacked rather than the conductor. When a member of a psychotherapy group becomes scapegoated, unless the conductor intervenes in good time to protect that person, he or she may leave the group shamed, angry and demoralized, while those remaining feel guilty and ashamed with a group issue remaining unresolved. Anger aroused by criticism and shaming may be directed in fact or fantasy towards the one who is critical. This anger may be experienced as shameful, too, and sometimes guilty feelings are associated with a wish to attack the other. A person may face up to shortcomings, resolve to reform and to make amends by acknowledging the rightness of the criticism and giving thanks for the others' courage and trouble. This amounts to that person containing discomforts and thinking through the foregoing. Otherwise excruciating discomforts can be pre-empted by repetitive penances such as strivings to overcome, through good actions, some unacceptable habitual way of relating. These are energy-consuming and hard to maintain, and are therefore unlikely to continue for long.

SEQUENCES OF SHAME, ANGER AND GUILT LEADING TO SYMPTOMS

It is possible to trace sequences of shame, anger and guilt leading to symptom formation through stories from recent relationships, the relationship with the therapist in a session and recourse to stories from the distant past. Helen Block Lewis (1985) refined this method and claims that in many cases this is enough and becomes a shorter analysis. In the analysand's stories, anger with the one who sees what is shameful is appreciated as inappropriate and evokes guilt about that anger. The guilt is followed with a wish to make amends, which if unsettled becomes an obsession. Shame may be momentary, like a jolt, and in this way goes unrecognized and overlooked. The person is simply aware of guilt and the urge to make reparations in the genesis of repeated obsessions fuelled by latent shame.

Lewis (1985: 108–20) describes a man who withheld from intercourse because he anticipated guilt should he deceive his fiancée, since he had no intention of early marriage. For her part, she was worried about his potency. In other words, what concerned him was prospective guilt, which she took to be his shame. Intercourse did take place when his work prospects improved and marriage was a reasonable probability. When she remarked to him what she had thought, he felt that this had lowered him in her estimation and hence in his own; then he did become impotent and the doubt about his potency became obsessive. His rage at being humiliated by her remark, felt as a (psychic) blow, was overlooked and the guilt associated with his anger was manifest in resultant obsessive doubt. This emerged in his analysis in much more detail, as did predispositions to obsessive doubt from his past family experiences, which were then clarified. Early in treatment, he developed obsessive doubt about the starting time of his session. Resentments in his relationship with his analyst, such as the inconvenience of getting to sessions and the payment for them, followed by embarrassing thoughts about what she was thinking about him during sessions, were seen as a sequence of embarrassment-evoking resentment, finally covered by the guilty thought that it was none of his business. The overlooked shame and resentment were then transformed into doubts about the time of the session. This shed light on the sequence leading to his loss of potency.

When someone is engaging regularly with the early family, individual psychotherapy with that person may be less successful because influences of the family can be more powerful than the dyad of patient and therapist. An individual presenting a cycle of control and release behaviours (Fossum and Mason 1986) may best be assessed and have therapy in the context of the family. Abuses may be subject to rigorous control accompanied by exemplary conduct and work which becomes demanding, energy-consuming and ultimately unsustainable. Release behaviour follows, with consequences so damaging that control measures are reinstated and so on. Sometimes one member of a family takes a controlling role and another a release role, or they alternate these roles without awareness of any connection between their behaviours. With younger children in the family it is possible to note sometimes whether or not the boundary between parents and the child is satisfactory. For instance, the child may have an alliance with one parent to exclude the other. This may not be clear if unwitting hiding tactics are used by family members. The child in a special relationship with one parent feels ashamed for this undue attention and for the exclusion of the other parent and perhaps siblings. A family session including grandparents may reveal how one parent relates with his or her own parents and how a deficient intergenerational boundary can occur from generation to generation. Family sessions may provide information about shameful episodes in the family necessary for all members' understanding of their relationships, an understanding which was not possible from their earlier spontaneous shared family stories.

SHAME BY ASSOCIATION

Nathaniel Hawthorne's great American novel *The Scarlet Letter* emerged in 1850, from New England. Hawthorne's forefathers settled in Salem, an unforgiving Puritan community with sinners in their midst. Adultery was punished with severe beatings and thereafter a sinner would be stigmatized by wearing, perforce, the scarlet capital letter 'A' on everyday clothing. This was not time-limited nor was reform expected.

The book's heroine, Hester Prynne, was such a sinner, a married woman who gave birth to a daughter by the Reverend Dimmesdale, conceived while her husband was away. In her trial she did not disclose the father's identity. Dimmesdale was ashamed, and frequently unwittingly held his hand to his breast where a letter 'A' might have been and punished himself with flagellations. His even greater shame was his cowardice, until he owned up to his own adultery when he was literally dying of shame. After many years of absence with her daughter, Hester Prynne returned alone to this community, still wearing the 'A' on her breast. Living on the edge of the community, she became an unobtrusive therapist in the long tradition of the wounded healer.

Hawthorne's distant ancestors were harsh Puritans and he associated himself with, and was sensitive to, their cruelties. He stated that he wished to take their shame upon himself and to expiate it in his writing and thereafter be freed to move to a more wholesome environment (1986: 11–14). Shame by association had occurred, too, because of the disrespect the Hawthornes showed his widowed mother. Later Hawthorne was ashamed probably because of having lost his post in Salem before his writing had flourished. This is what God said to Moses (Exodus 34:7): 'visiting the iniquity of the fathers upon the children and upon the children's children, unto the third and to the fourth generation'.

A man told me the story of how he came to England in early manhood just before the Second World War. In childhood he received scant attention from his father, who was a distinguished man, busy with the troubles of other people. During the war his father was killed in a concentration camp. He said that he didn't want to get to know me as a person, which, I suggested, showed that his retaliatory feelings towards his father were transferred to me. He went on to understand more about his early relationship with his father. Apart from sadness, he had thought little about his father's terrible death, not wanting to be associated with that humiliation. He related how he had underachieved and had unsatisfactory sexual relationships of which he was ashamed. He had wanted to be his own person and not to succeed because of his father's influence. Before treatment, he did innovative work, but despite prestigious settings and programmes it was little known. During treatment, he discovered that his father had been a hero because he chose to die by refusing a dishonourable task in the camp. He assisted in making this widely known. In parallel with that came personal success, with his projects gaining great acclaim and more satisfying personal relationships.

THE IMPORTANCE OF DISCRETION AND TIME BOUNDARIES

To finish at the beginning, the structuring of the therapeutic boundaries has an important role in the management of shame aroused by story telling in therapy. Making contact with a therapist involves admitting to oneself, to the one referring and to those it is disclosed to, that one's personal trouble requires outside help and understanding – an intrinsically shameful admission. It is important that the therapy is understood to be confidential, that trust means that a person can tell personal stories without the risk of social embarrassment.

In captivity, Brian Keenan (1993) didn't know where he was, who his captors were, nor, at times, who his fellow captives were. His fear of losing his mind subsided when he realized that his act of self-observation was enough to preserve his sanity. He knew that communication with another was immensely important and that mutual story telling was healing the injuries he was enduring. He tried to deduce how time and routine in the prison were structured. He and his friend created games to introduce more structuring of time. A false idea of keeping one's sanity in those circumstances was to maintain individuality and self-respect by being aloof from others. One of the prisoners did not communicate for a long time and when seemingly near psychosis was enabled to talk by Keenan's playful disclosure of his own bits of madness, which that tortured man could respond to. Time to reflect on the stories and rest are part of the healing process and require time alone. In Keenan's story, when privacy was almost absent, distancing himself from another was made possible by mutual banter and by rising above the shame of overexposure by humour. Too much isolation from others, or too prolonged close contact, can risk psychic disintegration from the effects of damaging shame.

Story telling in therapy brings a sense of closeness, and drawing apart occurs when there is fullness, fear or fatigue. Hence the length of the sessions and the time between sessions are necessary considerations. Individual or group psychotherapy sessions are often once or twice weekly. Some training courses hold many sessions over several days in spaced so-called 'block' weekends. Block weekend group psychotherapy was pioneered by Reik (1989, 1993). Two different frequencies were compared by Reik and Power (1995): one consisted of ten group psychotherapy sessions starting on Friday evening and continuing on Saturday and Sunday with intervals of ten weeks, and the other of four Sunday sessions at monthly intervals. The longer weekend allowed two nights for thinking through experiences and sometimes to dream about them. To anticipate one or two days to work on problems arising from their stories, thus reducing anxiety, culminated in better analysis and integration. Dreams have a special relevance for the whole group and that sense of the whole group seems to affect the sense of time, so that long intervals between weekends are tolerated well. Reik and Power write:

> Being together virtually for three days, often uninterrupted by influences of work, family and social life, intensifies the multi-transferential situation and increases the possibility of its resolution. The extended, continuous contact of group members with each other allows intimacy and trust; in the atmosphere of this shared participation, personal matters become group matters through resonance, instead of confessions of individuals. This approach alleviates the so often expressed fear of having to talk about one's problems in front of strangers. It is this fantasy of experiencing shame and guilt which keeps people out of groups.
>
> (Reik and Power 1995: 21)

Within a session, respite from shame may be sought in silence or humour. When a story has been disturbing, the story teller may return to it later, either him or herself or when another member's story introduces a similar theme. A break in treatment may be particularly disturbing and experienced as a loss of rhythm, of the opportunity to be listened to and be responded to and to respond and to feel support.

In a group session before a break, three members told stories of feeling rejected. I suggested that this was how the three – and others too, probably – were feeling about the break.

During a break there may be resentment and shame and sometimes withdrawal into depression. The patient may make contact with the general practitioner, presenting an apparently worsened condition, and risks being advised to change the treatment. Such advice may come from a spouse. Attention from the GP or others may be all that is required to reassure and tide the person over, something which is immensely important. Drop-outs during breaks may be prevented by preparation from the outset, but for those concerned holiday breaks can still be upsetting.

The requirement for the development of a satisfactory individual boundary, to maintain integrity on the one hand and to be able to emerge and be intimate on the other, lies in experiencing unconditional acceptance, in addition to that won by effort and the use of charm, for a lengthy period in early childhood. This is particularly important while the child's sense of self and separateness is developing. This self-confidence born of trust in relating with those outside the self, who can be internalized, provides an inner control of risk-taking in getting close to another or in refusing another's inappropriate advances. Without lengthy early unconditional acceptance, a person remains liable to low self-esteem and shame. Such people tell stories of literal or psychological parental absence due to illness, childbirth, work, loss of spouse or home, addiction, imprisonment, etc. Other patients recount occasions of boundary violation by sexual abuse, by intrusive, more or less subtle, questioning or by intrusive statements based on intuitive guesswork about a child's wishes or intentions. Their stories evoke from the therapist, or group conductor and group members, responses providing different and satisfactory attentions and respect for personal boundaries, in each of whom the human propensity for regression allows for reformation processes in therapy.

REFERENCES

Austen, J. ([1816] 1985) *Emma*, London: Penguin Classics.
Bettelheim, B. (1978) *The Uses of Enchantment*, Harmondsworth: Penguin.

Fossum, M.A., and Mason, M.J. (1986) *Facing Shame: Families in Recovery*, New York and London: W.W. Norton.

Foulkes, S.H. (1986) *Group-Analytic Psychotherapy: Method and Principles*, London: Karnac.

Hawthorne, N. ([1850] 1986) *The Scarlet Letter*, London: Penguin Classics.

Jacoby, M., Kast, V., and Riedel, I. (1992) *Witches, Ogres and the Devil's Daughter: Encounters with Evil in Fairy Tales*, Boston and London: Shambhala.

Keenan, B. (1993) *An Evil Cradling*, London: Random House.

Lear, T. (1991) 'Personal transformations in the group', *Group Analysis* 24(4): 441–54.

——(1995) 'Personal transformations during group analytic training: the role of the large group', *Group Analysis* 28(4): 395–406.

Lewis, H.B. (1985) 'Analysing sequences from unresolved shame and guilt into symptom formation', in Joseph Reppen (ed.) *Analysts at Work: Practice, Principles, and Technique*, New Jersey: Jason Aronson.

Mittwoch, A. (1987) 'Aspects of guilt and shame in psychotherapy', *Group Analysis* (Special Section: Studies of Shame, guest ed. T.E. Lear) 20(1): 33–42.

The New Jerusalem Bible (Reader's Edition) (1990), London: Darton, Longman and Todd.

Reik, H. (1989) 'A changed time structure: the effect on the analytic group', *Group Analysis* 22(3): 325–32.

——(1993) 'The creative capacity of boundaries within the block training experience', *Group Analysis* 26(2): 157–61.

Reik, H., and Power, K. (1995) 'Weekend patient groups update', *Group Analytic Contexts: International Newsletter of The Group Analytic Society* 6: 18–21.

Chapter 8

Splitting, envy, jealousy and rivalry

Amit Bhattacharyya

SCIENCE OR FICTION?

Analytic theories, to say the least, are contentious. Their critics say they are untestable as they are based mainly on clinical observations which are made to fit retrospectively to the beliefs of the particular researcher. They say these observations are subjective and interpretations made by the observer are likely to be seen as a corroboration of the theories they may espouse. Popper (1963: 38) considers analytic theories in this light and says that 'they were simply nontestable, irrefutable'. He admits that it does not mean that these observations are necessarily incorrect or that they are not of importance. But he insists 'that the criterion of the scientific status of a theory is its falsifiability, or refutability, or testability'.

The proponents of those theories, however, advance many arguments in support of their case. Holmes and Lindley (1991) sum up some of these views and explain why analytic theories remain valid in spite of the difficulty in proving that they are so. They state that many so-called scientific theories start from axioms, and analytic theories are no exception in starting with some assumptions; they should not be discarded because they cannot be tested using the measures commonly employed for other scientific studies. Observation of behaviour can lead to certain inferences, which do provide evidence. In the course of their development, they add, certain theories have indeed been refuted as clinical observations did not corroborate them. They also point out that a 'common-sense belief-desire psychology' is important for us to understand our behaviour in a rational way. One may point out that some prospective rather than retrospective research, especially in relation to attachment theories, strengthens the arguments in favour of the analytic concepts. This research on attachment gives valuable insight into personality development and the quality of maternal care.

IS IT I OR IS IT THE OTHER?

The contents of this chapter have to be considered in the light of such controversies. The topics refer to early relatedness in human life and some of their later consequences. That naturally means the infant–mother relationship and how the world of the infant forms between the subject that is the infant-self and the mother-object.

The object-relations theories start with the work of Klein, followed by others such as Winnicott and Fairbairn. They describe the dilemma of the infant in coping with the breast that feeds and the breast that withholds. Later this apparent division extends to its perception of the mother as a whole and is not confined to a part of her, the breast alone. It is not possible at this early stage of its development for the infant to integrate these two opposite concepts. The way the infant deals with the problem is by splitting the two into 'good' and 'bad' and it survives this split by projecting them to the mother and introjecting them from her in order to form a concept of the self. Initially, the two cannot mix or be cross-referenced. Stern (1985: 249) calls it 'double book-keeping with regard to experience and memory' and adds a third dimension of cognition.

Later in the course of development, the infant can integrate the two opposites and comes to realize that 'the good' and 'the bad' are aspects of the same person. That realization is a gigantic step forward for the infant in accepting the splits within the self and without in the object; thereby it accepts ambivalence resulting in a coming together of reality and fantasy and a union of its inner and outer worlds. The theory, therefore, deals with 'the transformation of interpersonal relationships into internalized representations of relationships' (Gabbard 1994: 38).

One of the problems of the theory is to define how and when the concept of self is formed in the first place. Kernberg (1976), Kohut (1971) and Mahler *et al.* (1975) describe their respective views, but all see the importance of the early mother–child relationship.

Splitting of the self and the object into good and bad has been extended further to understand fragmentation, as in psychosis. The term can also mean a defence mechanism by which the world can be seen similarly as good or bad.

Many children's stories pick up this early separation of the good from the bad. The uncaring stepmother and the wicked witch represent this separation. Bettelheim (1976: 78) refers to many fairy tales and draws attention to the opposites: 'The main message is that these must be integrated for human happiness.'

The well-known story of Dr Jekyll and Mr Hyde by Robert Louis Stevenson exemplifies this split which gets out of control; the novel has become almost like a shorthand for describing the two sides of human nature. It is said that Stevenson got the idea from a factual story of a man in Edinburgh, who by day was a respectable citizen but at night turned to burglary. The films about the Wolf Man describe a similar schism. Many present-day media characters such as Superman or the Incredible Hulk seem to display this split in certain episodes, and struggle to integrate and control the power of the dark side of themselves.

What Jung called the shadow needs to be acknowledged and put together for the individual to feel complete. Denial leads to splitting, and the split-off parts are projected on to others. Some of the Eastern philosophies see the integration of these two sides of the ego as essential in the path of self-awareness. Thich Nhat Hanh (1987: 63) puts this beautifully in a poem entitled 'Please Call Me by My True Names'.

I am the Mayfly metamorphosing on the
surface of the river,
and I am the bird which, when spring comes,
arrives in time to eat the mayfly.

For some, this integration does not take place satisfactorily and the initial split continues into adult life. Winnicott (1960) says that the result of such splits in the adult is to create 'a false self' to deal with an unsympathetic, overwhelming or negative world. Balint (1968: 110) writes, 'This false ego may be highly efficient, and even successful . . . but it bars access to the real self which thus remains immature. . . . The result is a lifelong feeling of futility, emptiness and unhappiness.'

Case example

A married woman in her forties has presented with recurrent depression. She says she does not know where she is going and what she wants. She thinks she has wasted her life, she does not even know who she is. She was sexually abused by two members of her family when she was a child and has always suspected that her mother knew about it but did nothing to stop it. The mother was now dead. The family was large and the mother was always preoccupied with a new baby. The patient has coped all her life by creating a front and by detaching herself from her feelings. She has always done what she sees as her duty but without being truly involved. Her question to the therapist (A.B.) was, 'Who am I?'

A.B. says, relating a story from the Middle East: 'A wise man is confused while on a visit to a strange town. He goes to a shop and asks the shopkeeper, "Did you see me come in?" The shopkeeper says, "Yes." The wise man asks, "Do you know who I am? Have you seen me before?" The shopkeeper answers, "No." The wise man asks, "How do you know then that it is I?" ' (Shah 1968: 206).

The patient laughs and says, 'I understand how he felt. When you do not know who you are yourself, how can you expect anyone else to know you?'

A few sessions later, the patient describes a recent sad incident when she had to visit a dying relative. She reports how the other visitors had admired her cool head, and yet she was extremely upset inside and could not express herself.

One of her abusers had also visited, and she had had to keep her mask on and behave as if nothing had happened. She was sad about her many masks.

A.B. comments, 'You are a bit like a chameleon.'

The patient asks, 'What do you mean?'

A.B. tells another story. A man sees a strange lizard and tells his friends that he has seen a red lizard. One of his friends goes to see this creature, but sees a green animal. A third one goes to verify and comes back after seeing a black lizard. All three start arguing and go together to the tree but fail to see the animal. They continue to argue as to which one was telling the truth. Another man comes along and says that they are all telling the truth because the creature they have seen was a chameleon.

The patient exclaims, 'You mean those parts of me are all me?' Then she pauses.

A.B. says, 'I wonder why the chameleon changes colour.'

The patient replies, 'It is frightened. It is protecting itself.' Her face changes and she says, 'I have been protecting myself all my life. No one protected me when I needed protection!'

Bollas (1987: 54), in giving a case history, remarks how 'the lack of a stable mothering process simply facilitated the widening of the ordinary splitting'. In the case example above, the patient has defended herself by creating a multitude of 'selves' and has nurtured them to fight recurrent depression and disappointments following what she saw as rejection from her mother in the first place.

The sense of self is vitally dependent on the early mother–child relationship. The mother acts as a mirror for the child and what the child sees in the eye of the mother helps him form an idea of what he is. Mahler *et al.* (1975) call it 'the mirroring frame of reference'. The ugly duckling had to see itself in the reflection of the water to be convinced that it was indeed a swan.

Pines (1984: 121) narrates a Russian story to illustrate how a fragile self is influenced by 'the mirror'. The story goes like this: a poor Russian goes to an inn for a night's rest. The inn is full and the innkeeper says that he can share the only bed available with a famous general. The man accepts and with trepidation gets into bed in the dark after undressing quietly so that the general does not wake up. Next morning, he wakes up early, dresses hurriedly and slips out of the room. In the mirror on the landing, he sees himself in a general's uniform and exclaims that they have woken the wrong man!

THE GREEN-EYED MONSTER

Another early emotion to be described is envy. Initially, it was not clearly distinguished from jealousy and rivalry. Freud and others, while acknowledging the boy's envy of femininity, concentrated on the female child's envy of the penis. Many of these theories have been examined, supported or refuted.

Klein (1957) refers to the earlier blurring of these concepts and firmly asserts that envy is primitive and relates to what happens between the infant and the mother. She sees jealousy as a later development. Essentially, envy is the result of a dyadic relationship, whereas jealousy is a triadic one. One feels envious of what another possesses and which one would like to have, but one is jealous of losing or being deprived of what one has.

With the envy of the mother for what she possesses comes a desire to destroy the object of envy, with resultant guilt and a wish to repair the damage. In the therapeutic situation, one common envy is what a patient feels occasionally for the therapist: for his ability, skills, knowledge and status. This is often manifested during treatment in confusion, inability to understand interpretations, a negation of earlier achievements, lack of concentration, etc. The therapeutic process takes this into consideration. At times, a declaration of lack of power on the part of the therapist may help the client to acknowledge his envy and gain insight. Cade (1982) writes about a similar technique in family therapy.

Case example

A man of 40 who has been in therapy for a little while comes one day, sits down and says he cannot remember a thing. He complains he has been coming for some time and yet he is not getting anywhere. The therapist, realizing that something is not right, waits and encourages the patient to talk about his feelings of despair.

The patient gradually reveals what has upset him. He has put in a lot of effort to support his local football club and they have gained a trophy. As a result, everyone had been given an award, including the previous secretary of the club, but the patient has been ignored.

He then talks about his disappointments in life and how deserving he thinks he is. Particularly, he is concerned in not having any real influence, status or a university education. He then asks the therapist directly whether he (A.B.) has been to university. A.B. remains silent.

The patient continues about the therapist, 'You must be clever. Now you have this office and you are important.'

A.B. replies: 'Status comes with office, but there is something besides what one sees.'

The patient asks, 'What do you mean?'

A.B. tells a story:

There was this great court official called Gopal who had been invited to a feast. The king was there and the whole court with him. As Gopal had gone without his ceremonial robes, no one took any notice of him, while other less important persons of rank were ushered in with appropriate pomp.

Thus rebuffed, Gopal returned home and put on his uniform and came back to the feast. This time, the host rushed out to welcome him and gave him pride of place, in front of the king. When the sweets arrived, Gopal started putting them in the pockets of his robe. Everyone laughed at his stupidity, hoping for some rebuke from the king. Many were jealous of him. But the king, who knew better, asked him for a reason.

Gopal told him what had happened to him on his initial visit and added, 'As I got better treatment when I came wearing my robe, I feel that the robe should have the sweets and not me!'

The patient laughs and says that he understands: inside the external status there is a human being and he has been ignoring that. He then says that he was actually asked to give out the awards.

A.B. points out that the club showed their appreciation of him in a different but nonetheless important way. This opens up an opportunity to talk about envy and jealousy in the here and now as well as in the past.

The patient says that on his way into the clinic, he has noticed that A.B. has a new car. He then admits that the events at the football club have made him sad and having seen the therapist's new car has made him feel extremely envious. He says how lucky he is to have gained so much in therapy as a way of reparation. This is discussed and he leaves with a new understanding.

In the heart of Freudian theory lies the triangular relationship between the child, the mother and the father. The jealousy of the child in discovering that he has to share the mother with the father sets up a series of emotional waves which comprise the Oedipal Complex. In adult life, this may mean that someone has taken or is threatening to take what by right belongs to the individual.

Essentially, jealousy involves three persons. Was Satan jealous because someone came between him and God?

An intense pathological condition described as morbid jealousy exists. It is also known as 'the Othello syndrome' because of Shakespeare's portrayal of Othello, epitomizing this emotion when Othello destroys the loved object and kills himself. In mythology, Medea kills her own children, symbols of her love for Jason.

Klein (1957: 182) draws attention to the difference in attitude between envy and jealousy and points out that 'the reason for this distinction is to be found in a universal feeling that the murder of a rival may imply love for the unfaithful person'. She goes on to say that Shakespeare left the definition between envy and jealousy unclear, and quotes from Othello:

Oh beware my Lord of jealousy;

It is the green-eyed monster which doth mock
The meat it feeds on.

Her interpretation is: 'One is reminded of the saying "to bite the hand which feeds one", which is almost synonymous with biting, destroying, and spoiling the breast.' That, to her, implies a more primitive and dyadic process, i.e. envy of the infant, without the involvement of the third person.

Early relationships determine the way one copes with 'the green-eyed monster'.

Case example

A couple who have married after a whirlwind romance come for therapy as the wife has become fed up with the husband's suspiciousness. Often he will turn up at her place of work or when she goes to play badminton with her female friends. She interprets this behaviour as lack of trust and feels oppressed. He says he does it to see if she is all right.

The therapist (A.B.) picks up the theme of trust and tells them the root story of the Arabian Nights. He relates how Shariayar, the sultan, is betrayed by his wife, and in disgust goes for solace to visit his brother, Shahjeman, a sultan in another land. There he finds out that his sister-in-law is also unfaithful. Both brothers leave in dismay, only to find a princess imprisoned by a genie but still having affairs with strangers as an act of revenge.

Shariyar returns home full of anger and distrust and begins the pattern of marrying a virgin every night and then beheading her the next day. Ultimately, he marries Scherazade, who enthrals him with her stories for a thousand and one nights, during which time the king falls in love with her and regains his trust in women.

The couple listen to the story and the man sighs. He then recalls his anger and sadness when his mother left him and his father for another man. This had been unknown to his wife, who only knew that her mother-in-law had died when her husband was little.

The husband explains the shame his father felt; this has been a family secret they have preserved. He apologizes to his wife for not having shared this fact with her. The wife now understands the origins of her husband's lack of trust.

In the story, the sultan split off parts of himself and projected all that was bad on to the woman; only by destroying her could he gain some control. Scherazade, through her love and her stories which depicted the good and the bad in all aspects of human nature, helped the king take back what he had rejected in himself, thereby restoring his sanity and wholeness.

To recognize jealousy in oneself helps one to come to terms with the jealousy in others. This acceptance can then lead to a review of past ways of functioning and subsequent change.

Case example

A man in his twenties hates his father who has always tried to diminish him in any competitive situation. As a result, the man has often withdrawn from ventures where he has to prove himself.

Once he went on a day trip and met a girl, distraught because her boyfriend had deserted her. Naturally and without any ulterior motive, he tried to comfort her. Unbeknown to him before the journey, his parents were going on the same trip. At a stop, his father came to meet him and then, having listened to the girl, made her sit near him and his wife. The patient was furious and presented this incident at the next session as an example of his father's behaviour towards him.

He does not want to see what motivated his father. All he can think of is his jealousy. A.B. tells him the story of Sohrab and Rostam from the Epic of the Kings. In this Persian story, the great warrior, Rostam, fights his son, Sohrab, without either of them knowing the other's identity. Sohrab gets the better of Rostam but spares his life, but Rostam kills his son. When he realizes what he has done, he is mortified. A.B. adds that if the father and son 'knew' each other this would not have happened.

The patient is obviously moved by the story but does not say much.

At the next session, he says he has rung his father who sponta-neously said that he and his wife deliberately took that girl away from him so that he could have some peace. Following this, the father said he had to build a garden shed but did not know how to go about it. Remembering the story, the patient, who has special skills in that sort of work, offered to give him a hand. This was a departure from their usual relationship. The father also promised to help him with decorating his house.

Where the roots of rivalry can be understood and accepted, a healthy co-operation may ensue. Rivalry can be replaced by competitiveness on the playing field and the destructiveness is channelled into something more positive.

A TUG OF WAR

Rivalry of the son has been talked about at length; not so much has been written about the father's jealousy of the son. Drona, the preceptor to the princes in the Indian epic the Mahabharata, says that he wishes for victory always, but for defeat when fighting his son or his disciple. In real life, this is often not so. Mythologies abound in stories illustrating this phenomenon. After all, Zeus, who emasculated his father, also happens to become jealous of his own progeny and tears open his wife's belly to swallow his own unborn child. In another Greek myth, attempts by Prometheus to bring fire to man result in his invoking the wrath of the jealous gods, and for this he is eternally punished.

Case example

A professional man, while playing football with his young boy, suddenly becomes aware of his intense jealousy towards the son. He wants to hurt him badly and is surprised and ashamed of his feelings. He considers himself to be an evil man.

In therapy, he is assured that it is not an unusual feeling and A.B. tells him the story of Zeus. He seems relieved and then starts talking of his own childhood. It emerges that he lost his own father at the same age as his son is now.

The connections are discussed and he realizes the origins of his jealousy: what he has missed out himself is available to his son. He takes immense pleasure that he can give his son what was denied to him.

Sibling rivalry has been a central theme in many stories. One of the most popular must be the story of Cinderella, so much so that it is again like a shorthand for all. The ugly step-sisters and their mother try their best to keep Cinderella down, but she triumphs in the end. There are many analytical expositions given to the inner meaning of the story, but the theme that truth will be out and wrongs will be righted seems to be the main message. There are many Cinderellas in real life who take heart from the story.

EACH MAN FOR HIMSELF

In this chapter, aspects of some early emotions have been described but by no means are they comprehensive. The main mental mechanisms that play important parts in these feelings, emotions, cognitions and fantasies are projection, projective identification and introjection. Only when these are understood can one take back what belongs to oneself and give back the rest where they should be. That way one becomes whole and split-off parts of the personality can be integrated. Thich Nhat Hanh (1987: 34–5) puts this beautifully in a story which was used in the following case.

Case example

A man coming to the end of therapy recalls how he used to be at the start of treatment. He describes how his whole existence was in terms of extremes, either bright as summer or bleak as winter, and how he would blame everyone else for all his ills without taking any responsibility himself.

A.B. tells him the story of a boatman who is sailing in the midst of a fog. He sees another boat approaching directly at him. He shouts abuse at the boatman of the other boat, fearing that they will collide. There is no response. He goes on shouting and steers skilfully to get out of the way of the other boat. When the other boat passes him, he notices that there is no one on the other boat, but that the tying rope has somehow broken and the boat has drifted. He then laughs loudly at his folly in shouting abuse at an imaginary boatman.

The patient laughs and says he understands exactly how the boatman feels, because that is what he has been doing all his life so far without ever looking at himself.

Similarly, as treatment helps one to take responsibility for oneself, so it enables one to reject what does not belong to one. In other words, the banished bits of self are accepted and the distortions in the self resulting from taking in projections and identifying with them are seen for what they are and are not incorporated.

Case example

A woman considers herself unloved and a failure. Her history shows a lack of early satisfactory relationships, and she has been blamed for everything that has gone wrong in the family. She has a poor image of herself and continues to feel responsible for mistakes others make. Any attempts to show this meet with resistance.

A.B. says it is as if everyone in the neighbourhood leaves his dustbin in her courtyard and the dustman blames her. She says how futile her protests would be in a situation like that.

A.B says that to protest she must be sure which bin belongs to her and which does not. He adds that otherwise she will be taking on everyone's rubbish as it is dumped in her yard.

He then tells a story from the Indian classic, the *Panchatantra*. There was a poor Brahmin, a pious man, who was given a baby goat by a benefactor. He was happily carrying the kid on his shoulders when three wicked men saw him and wanted to take the goat from him. The men placed themselves separately in the Brahmin's way.

When the Brahmin came near the first man, he exclaimed, 'Good morning, sir! Please tell me why you are carrying a dirty dog on your shoulders!'

The Brahmin responded angrily, 'Are you blind, man? Can't you see it is a goat?'

The man laughed and said, 'If you think it is a goat, you need your head examined.'

The Brahmin continued until he met the second man. The second man gave a sarcastic laugh and said, 'Shame on you! How can you, being a Brahmin, carry a carcass on your shoulders? I have never seen such abomination in my life.'

The Brahmin looked at the goat several times and feebly said, 'But it is a live goat that I carry . . . given to me by a kindly fellow. How can you say that I am carrying a filthy carcass? I am a pious man.'

The man said, 'You will know when your wife throws you out.'

By this time, the Brahmin had doubts in his mind. He had increased his pace to reach home quickly, when the third man accosted him.

Laughing aloud with derision, he said, 'What stupidity! A Brahmin carrying a dead donkey! This must be the age of fools and hypocrites. I must go and tell my friends not to acknowledge this impious Brahmin any more.'

At this, the Brahmin felt that there was certainly something wrong with his load. He dumped the goat there and then and hurriedly went home. The three crooks had a laugh at his expense, and collected the goat.

The patient laughs at the story, saying, 'You are right. I accept without question what others say about me.'

The Brahmin accepted the projections of the three men and his depleted ego became confused and coloured by what he had taken in from outside. True separation and individuation can occur when an individual can take back what he has projected and distinguish between what has been put in him from what actually belongs to him. Thus he can integrate the split-off parts of himself and become complete. That is maturity. It does not mean that the individual has to live in isolation. It means a new way of relatedness in co-operation with others who can be equally separate. Fairbairn (1952: 145) called it 'mature dependence . . . characterised by a capacity on the part of a differentiated individual for co-operative relationships with differentiated objects'. He goes on to say that this state cannot be fully realized, but is the ideal.

Storr (1960: 45) incorporates some ideas of Jung, expanding Fairbairn's intrapsychic concept to include the interpersonal relationships on the question of maturity: 'It is clear that the development of the individual and the development of his relationships proceed *pari passu*; and that the one cannot take place without the other.'

The dynamic therapies aim for this integration and depend on the relationship that develops between the therapist and the patient to give an indication of what has happened before and is happening now inside and outside in the life of the individual. Necessarily, this is unique and specific for the person. It is, therefore, difficult to use the measures common in other scientific studies to prove or disprove these theories. Is psychotherapy a science or an art?

CONCLUSION

The criterion of falsifiability may be applicable to some natural sciences dealing with generalities, but is it equally valid in assessing individual events? Bowlby (1988: 75–6) raises this issue and outlines 'two complementary disciplines' which need to be considered in the case of 'psychoanalysis'. He mentions a scientific criterion to understand general phenomena like personality development and psychopathology. He advocates a historical criterion to understand and help an individual as 'history . . . is always concerned with an appallingly complex sequence of highly specific interacting events which no amount of science can enable us to explain adequately, let alone predict'.

It is in the realm of the second category that clinical observations fall initially, but then a pattern begins to emerge from which theories can be and have been developed. The fact that these patterns repeat themselves so often cannot be ignored. How these patterns are interpreted may differ according to the interpreter's beliefs, but that does not nullify the patterns themselves.

If one has to make a meaning of the life story of another, that being an essential part of therapy, consideration has to be given to this historical perspective. A theoretical framework helps to create a structure. That is probably all, as each man has his own story to tell, individual, but always within the parameters of human experience. Myths, fairy tales and fables belong also to this historical perspective because that is what they represent, a sum total of human experience, retold in art form. That is why in therapy their use can be logical, legitimate and illuminating.

REFERENCES

Balint, M. (1968) *The Basic Fault*, London and New York: Tavistock Publications (reprinted 1979).

Bettelheim, B. (1976) *The Uses of Enchantment*, Harmondsworth: Penguin.

Bollas, C. (1987) *The Shadow of the Object*, London: Free Association Books, 52–4 .

Bowlby, J. (1988) *A Secure Base*, London: Routledge, 74–6.

Cade, B.W. (1982) 'The potency of impotence', *Australian Journal of Family Therapy* 4(1): 23–6.

Fairbairn, W.R.D. (1952) *Psychoanalytic Studies of the Personality*, London: Tavistock.

Gabbard, G.O. (1994) *Psychodynamic Psychiatry in Clinical Practice*, Washington DC and London: American Psychiatric Press.

Hanh, Thich Nhat (1987) *Being Peace*, Berkeley, California: Parallax Press (reprinted 1992, London: Rider).

Holmes, J., and Lindley R. (1991) *The Values of Psychotherapy*, Oxford: Oxford University Press, 18–21.

Kernberg, O.F. (1976) *Object Relations Theory and Clinical Psychoanalysis*, New York: Jason Aronson.

Klein, M. ([1957] 1993) 'Envy and gratitude' in *The Writings of Melanie Klein*, 176–235. London: Virago.

Kohut, H. (1971) *The Analysis of the Self*, New York: International University Press.

Mahler, M.S., Pine, F., and Bergman, A. (1975) *The Psychological Birth of the Human Infant*, New York: Basic Books.

Pines, M. (1984) 'Mirroring in group analysis' in T.E. Lear (ed.) *Spheres of Group Analysis*, Kildare, Eire: Leinster Leader.

Popper, K.R. (1963) *Conjectures and Refutations*, London: Routledge and Kegan Paul, 37–9.

Shah, I. (1968) *The Pleasantries of the Incredible Mulla Nasrudin*, London: Jonathan Cape (reprinted 1975, London: Pan).

Stern, D.N. (1985) *The Interpersonal World of the Infant*, New York: Basic Books, 248–50.

Storr, A. (1960) *The Integrity of the Personality*, Oxford: Oxford University Press.

Winnicott, D.W. (1960) *Ego Distortion in Terms of True and False Self*, reprinted in D.W. Winnicott (1965) *The Maturational Process and the Facilitating Environment*, London: Hogarth, 140–52.

Chapter 9

Separation, loss and bereavement

Sarah Hogan and Margaret Pennells

ATTACHMENT THEORY

The traditional psychological model postulated that there are two kinds of drives, primary and secondary, and it was thought that bonding between individuals developed because of these drives. Food and sex were considered as primary, and 'dependency' to have these met by others as secondary. However, in the work of John Bowlby (1950) on the ill effects on personality development from deprivation of maternal care, these beliefs began to be questioned as regards their adequacy in explaining attachment behaviour. Bowlby believed that the development of a human child's tie to its mother can be better understood in terms of a model derived from ethology and he outlined a theory of attachment.

> Attachment theory facilitates ways of conceptualizing the propensity of human beings to make strong affectional bonds to particular others and of explaining the many forms of emotional distress and personality disturbance including anxiety, anger, depression and emotional detachment to which unwilling separation and loss will give rise.
>
> (Bowlby 1969: 39)

Further work on attachment theory has been developed by Ainsworth (1978), Parkes and Stevenson-Hinde (1982) and Weiss (1982).

RESPONSE TO LOSS

Wishful thinking has probably contributed to the idea that children soon forget a lost person and so get over their pain and misery without any interaction. It was thought that grief in childhood was short lived. Now, however, this is shown to be not so. Bowlby noticed that, following deprivation of an attachment figure, a child becomes quieter and less explicit in their communications. Far from indicating that they have forgotten the attachment figure, they remain strongly orientated towards it. Bowlby's work with children's responses to maternal deprivation led to his controversial paralleling of the process to that of grief in adults and children's response to grief.

Parkes (1991) commented on Bowlby's work when discussing types of bereavement and pointed out that

> secure attachments in early childhood can be expected to give rise to a reasonable degree of trust in one's self with a reasonable degree of trust in others. Out of these two components of basic trust arises the confidence with which we attempt to cope with all the stresses of life. It is reasonable to suppose, therefore, that 'self trust' and 'other trust' will be important determiners of a person's reaction to bereavement. Lack of either trait is likely to give rise to special problems at a time of loss or change when a person's coping capacity is put to the test.
>
> (Parkes 1991: 271)

From the continued work of Parkes we realize the relevance of attachment theory and response to bereavement, loss and separation. He used attachment theory and research in developing programmes for the emotional care of the dying and bereaved. Weiss (1991) elaborated further on distinguishing characteristics of attachment theory, one of which he has termed 'inaccessibility to conscious control'. This supports the theory that attachment has a significant bearing on a child's response to loss and separation.

> Attachment feelings persist despite recognition that there can be no rejoining, as after the death of the attachment figure. Separation protest continues when an attachment figure has become inaccessible and adequate alternative figures are available.
>
> (Weiss 1991: 67)

Thus, children's initial attachment experiences can contribute to how they respond to loss and separation and that response is often exhibited through their behaviour. However, children differ greatly in their speed of development, and significant others in the child's life differ greatly in their willingness to communicate and in their skills in doing so. Children may face particular problems in grieving simply because they are children. As well as factors such as continuous development of cognition and language, other factors such as attitudes that do not encourage and acknowledge a child's role in the separation, loss and bereavement process can also add to the trauma of such events. When conditions are unfavourable for children to grieve they either express their emotions through their behaviour or they become guarded and internalize their real feelings. So how, then, is it best to support children and adolescents when faced with the trauma of bereavement, loss and separation? Traumatized children are vulnerable and bereavement, loss and separation bring with them implications that increase a child's vulnerability, increased stress levels, intensity of feelings and life-changing circumstances.

The emotional response to loss, separation and bereavement can seem overwhelming. The death or loss of someone close can further emphasize a child's helplessness, their dependency on attachment figures, their lack of control over life events, confusion over their role in the loss and also exposure of the threat of further loss and separation. However, children are resilient and can adapt to new situations, however painful the experience has been, but this is often a gradual process and only when it is complete might they relinquish absent attachments and form new ones. Elisabeth Kubler Ross (1970) recognized the importance of listening to and supporting children; without this they hold inside their own way of grieving, which she believed often became the roots for later emotional disturbance.

THE CONTEXT OF LOSS AND THE COURAGE TO CREATE

When children are trapped in the grieving process it activates the early responses of separation from the attachment figure, and they feel despair, isolation, anxiety and anger. For some children who have had benevolent and helpful relationships with significant others, they can develop a trusting and confident attitude towards supporting adults which fosters the necessary openness and receptivity for creativity and positive communication. However, if children have been denied this positive experience, or caring adults adopt an overprotective approach to the grieving child, or the significant adults are overwhelmed with grief themselves, then the grieving vulnerable child might remain locked in their inner world, distrustful of attempts to communicate with them directly or even fearing such attempts as something that threatens their fragile sense of self. Communication can then become not something that is creative or rewarding, allowing them to make contact with others, but something fearful and disturbing.

THERAPEUTIC USE OF STORY TELLING AND STORY-MAKING

Teaching tales, hypnotic fables, metaphors, parables and anecdotes have been used for centuries in stories that speak to the third ear of the unconscious and draw together the two 'languages' of the left and right hemispheres of our brain in order to create new possibilities, bypass rigid defences and strike a responsive chord in the listener. Creativity is 'the extent to which each individual can retrieve apparently irrational ideas, sift them and put them to some constructive use' (Francis Galton, cited in Hudson 1987: 172).

In a bereavement situation, story telling is a particularly useful way of dealing with the changes, pain and trauma it can bring (Gersie 1992). Stories form much of our childhood experience, especially in the telling of fairy stories. They often have deeper meanings or a moral. Stories may not only teach children, they can also heal (Davis 1990). Children lack the reasoning ability that adults have, and may employ different cognitive approaches depending upon their developmental stages; thus they may, for example, read reality differently. In a bereavement situation this can lead to them feeling they in some way caused the death, with the resultant feelings of guilt. Stories can work on the unconscious; they are not intended to deny the grief process but rather to help children through the process and hopefully towards some kind of resolution and healing.

We see story telling with bereaved children falling into three main categories:

1 use of stories – i.e. how we can use existing stories to aid the bereavement process for individuals or groups;
2 the making of stories – by individuals or groups;
3 stories for groups – these are for use therapeutically in a group situation.

Use of stories

Existing stories can be of therapeutic benefit when read to young children. These stories can capture the children's imaginations and invite the child to identify with the characters in the story. This process allows 'distancing' from the trauma as it may, for example, be an animal who is experiencing a bereavement similar to that of human beings. In *Badger's Parting Gifts*, Badger dies and his friends mourn their loss:

> Fox broke the sad news that Badger was dead . . . all the animals had loved Badger and everyone was very sad. Mole especially felt lost, alone and desperately unhappy . . . tears rolled down his velvety nose, soaking the blankets he clung to for comfort.
>
> Varley (1985)

Many children, on identifying with the situation, can work through their own grief simply by following the animals' process through grief: from sadness, anger, etc., to acceptance of the loss. From such stories children can see how animals solve their problems and it gives them confidence that they, too, can cope and manage their feelings. Workers with a child can use the stories by talking about the animals and their reactions, allowing the child to transfer this to their own situation. A child may say, 'I feel like Mole and cry in bed alone at night. I don't want my mummy to hear me because it might upset her.' Stories are often tools for opening up areas for discussion that may otherwise have been difficult by direct questioning.

A 'progression' in the therapeutic use of stories with bereaved children is next to use stories that still allow the distancing from personal experience but are more closely related to it: that is, the use of stories where an animal, as opposed to a human being, has died and people's reactions to this are described.

> One morning I woke up and discovered that Elfie [the dog] had died during the night. . . . We buried Elfie together. We all cried and hugged each other.
>
> (Wilhelm 1986)

> Our cat Fred has died . . . he got very ill . . . Fred won't be sleeping on my bed any more . . . we'll all miss him, won't we?
>
> (Simmonds 1989)

Children can quickly see that the feelings we have when a pet dies are the same, or similar, to those we have when a person dies, and thus it helps the children to come to terms with their personal bereavement.

Sometimes in working therapeutically with a child stories about a bereaved situation can be used directly. There are now many interesting and varied books written for children of all ages that can be enormously helpful. These include: Althea (1982), Selby (1975), Abrams (1992), Padoan (1987), Sims (1986), St Christopher's Hospice (1989) and Williams and Ross (1983).

Books, or sections from them, focus on different aspects of a bereavement and can help a child understand both the practical and emotional aspects. The stories help to normalize the situation for the child who can begin to see that bereavement happens not just to them alone.

In order to help bereaved children express their own feelings, there are work books which allow the children to write and draw their own bereavement story. Three such books are by Heegaard (1988), Van-Si and Powers (1994) and Barnardo's (1995).

The making of stories

Adults working individually with children can engage them in the task of making up a story, by using either an animal or a person. The adult can provide large sheets of paper and pens, or use a tape recorder. The adult begins the story, e.g. 'Once upon a time there was a girl (or rabbit) who was very sad . . . ' The story is then taken up by the child who says (or writes) as much as they want to, then the adult again adds a piece to the story and so forth, until the story comes to a natural conclusion. In this situation the child will often express worries and fears through the story telling as well as revealing what may have happened in the family, e.g. Child: 'Mummy Rabbit told little Flopsy that she must not cry any more and be brave, but inside Flopsy didn't feel brave at all but tried not to cry in front of her mother.'

The adult can use the story telling to guide the story in a certain direction with the aim of eliciting certain information and feelings from the child. It must be remembered, however, that the child may not be ready to face certain painful issues, even through the medium of a story, and this needs to be acknowledged and respected.

This same task can be adapted for use in a group, as each individual child can add something to the story as and when they wish. We have found that children enjoy the task when a micro-phone is passed around and the story taped. (Again, leave it for children to feel free to contribute or not.) Children will often relate what has happened in the story to their own experience.

Stories for groups

As well as the above exercise being useful for groups, the Bambi story has been found to be particularly relevant to bereaved children. We have used this exercise with children aged 10 upwards. It is taken from the book *Bambi* (Salten 1928), and describes the conversation between two leaves left hanging on a tree, wondering who will be the next to go and what it will be like. To begin the exercise the children are asked to close their eyes and get comfort-able; then the story is read to them. Afterwards everyone is given a piece of paper and a pen and asked to pretend to be the leaves in the story and write a letter to the tree. On completion of the letters the children are asked to fold them in half, and they are then collected, shuffled and given out again, making sure that no one gets their own letter back. Each child then reads the letter they received and writes an answer to the leaf as if it were from the tree. When they have finished writing their replies the children are asked to fold the letters back so that everyone can see their own handwriting; they then retrieve their own letter with its reply. Time is given for the children to read their replies and to discuss the task together. This exercise helps children to look at unresolved grief reactions and the difficulty of saying 'goodbye', and raises ques-tions about after life.

It is also possible to base a whole groupwork programme around the use of stories. This is very effective with young children. In our bereaved children's group for 6–8 year olds the story becomes the theme for the session, the impetus for ensuing work and the basis for discussion. The programme is as follows:

Session 1

Theme: change and loss
Read: *Lifetimes* (Mellonie and Ingpen 1983)
Draw something alive and something dead
What changes take place in things/people when they are dead?
How does it feel to lose something?

Choose a colour to represent a feeling and scribble it out on a piece of paper.

Session 2

Theme: positive memories
Read: *My Grandson Lew* (Zolotow 1976)
Discuss your favourite memory
Draw your happiest time with the person when they were alive.

Session 3

Theme: positive memories (continued)
Read: *Badger's Parting Gifts* (Varley 1985)
What have you learnt from the person who died?
Imagine meeting them again – what would you talk about?
Fill in pp. 15–17 in *A Keepsake Book of Special Memories* (Van-Si and Powers 1994) or p.19 in *When Someone Very Special Dies* (Heegaard 1988).

Session 4

Theme: the day it happened
Read: *Nana Upstairs and Nana Downstairs* (de Paola 1987)
Discuss how you were told about the death, what happened to you and how you felt
Draw on pp. 17 of *When Someone Very Special Dies*.

Session 5

Theme: negative feelings
Read: *Someone Special Has Died* (St Christopher's Hospice 1989) pp. 3–7
What feelings do you have?
Brainstorm feelings and then act them out
Fill in pp. 12 or pp. 20 of *A Keepsake Book of Special Memories* or pp. 11,12,13 or 14 of *When Someone Very Special Dies*.

Session 6

Theme: funerals

Read relevant sections in *When Uncle Bob Died* (Althea 1982) and *Remembering Grandad* (Padoan 1987)
Discuss whether your person was buried/cremated
Did you go to the funeral?
Read, when and where relevant: *Tell Me, Papa* (Johnson 1990)
A family book for children's questions about death and funerals
Act out a funeral.

Session 7

Theme: saying goodbye
Read relevant sections in: de Paola (1983), St Christopher's Hospice (1989), Sims (1986)
Write a letter to the deceased person (p. 24 *A Keepsake Book of Special Memories*) or design a headstone for the person who died; write a letter to them or a poem.

Session 8

Our own goodbyes
A goodbye ceremony, an outing or some way of saying goodbye to the group.

WORKING WITH ADOLESCENTS

Work with adolescents is often seen as more challenging and less fulfilling than work with adults and younger children. In part, such an attitude may be due to the cultural view of adolescence as a tumultuous time of rejection of adult values and formulation of self-identity. Often the view is taken that interactions will be conflictual and frustrating and thus approaches are adopted with such expectations. Parents, teachers and clinicians often fall into the trap of urging adolescents to adopt adult norms of behaviour. Adolescents are often bombarded from many directions with ideas on how to behave, think and construct values and priorities. Adolescents may be ambivalent about consulting with adults during times of distress, especially when it seems likely that adults will take a rigid stance on issues. Paradoxically, adolescents may both seek and resent intervention into their lives.

If adults are too rigid in advocating attitudes, the adolescent may become oppositional or simply stop listening, resulting in a conversational impasse. Anderson (1986) described such impasses as occurring in conversation where each of the participants believes that his or her description or explanation of a situation is correct and tries to convince the other. This causes the participants to become increasingly rigid in their own beliefs. Thus, the conversation becomes 'stuck' with little creativity or positive conversation.

Watzlawick (1978) links this with what he calls 'first order reality' and 'second order reality'. As cited in Guillaume (1996), this can be demonstrated by a scene in a movie *Rain Man* in which Dustin Hoffman plays Raymond, an idiot savant. Raymond is standing on a street corner, the 'Walk' sign illuminates, he steps off the kerb and proceeds across the street. However, before he gets to the other side the pedestrian sign switches to 'Don't Walk' and Raymond dutifully stops in his tracks. Moments later the traffic lights change and the drivers start honking their horns. The driver of the first vehicle gets out of his van and physically tries to remove Raymond from the street.

Watzlawick suggests that first order objective reality includes that portion of experience that is known through the senses. In this case Raymond's first order reality includes seeing the pedestrian sign change from 'Walk' to 'Don't Walk'. Second order reality is subjective to nature. This includes thoughts, feelings, interpretations and opinions that we hold about the first order reality. Therefore, Raymond's second order reality appeared to include an interpretation that he should follow the directions to the letter. It said 'Don't Walk' and so he stopped. It appears that, while both Raymond and the driver can agree on the first order reality, there is disagreement in their second order reality, namely their interpretation of the first order reality. Raymond is at odds with the drivers in the cars because they have different ideas about the appropriateness of standing in the middle of the street blocking the traffic. They might have interpreted the situation differently as there are at least three other responses available: turn back, run or continue to walk across the road.

Anderson (1986, cited in Biever *et al.* 1995: 492) suggests that the way to approach impasses in conversation is as a collaborative venture in which new stories or narratives are developed. This is based on the philosophy of social constructionism, suggesting that what we know as reality is the result of interactions with others. Therefore, meanings and understandings are fluid, determined by the social world of the individual and their first and second order of reality. Hence, as with Raymond, for any given situation there are many possible understandings.

THE NARRATIVE APPROACH

The narrative approach to therapy views meanings as developing out of stories people tell themselves and others (Hoffman 1990). It is not the role of the adult to edit the stories or to create more appropriate stories, rather to simply talk with the adolescent until new stories emerge. This strategy has been of particular use when working with adolescents who have encountered separation or loss within their lives.

Amanda was a 17-year-old who referred herself to a local voluntary youth counselling service. In her first session she told the story of how she and her mother had lived alone since her father had left when she was 4 years old. Amanda described her relationship with her mother as positive, her mother 'had always been there for her'. Recently Amanda had become pregnant and subsequently had a termination. Amanda was shocked by her mother's response, the person that she had seen as the 'tower of strength' had crumbled and consequently their relationship had been put into turmoil. For many weeks Amanda returned to re-tell her story. By adopting some of the conversation skills produced by Anderson and Goolishan (1991) the stories could develop. In order to achieve this we utilized the following guidelines:

1 Maintain the 'not knowing stance', adopting questions in order to elicit more about what had been said and what is not known.
2 Be open to and help to generate alternatives. Tom Andersen (1991) suggests two questions:
   • how else can this situation be explained?
   • how else can this situation be described?
3 Think in terms of both/and rather than either/or. Therefore the question becomes: how is it possible for the interests of all involved in the conflict to be served?
4 Assume the adolescent has strengths and resources. Emphasize the importance of asking about exceptions to the conflict and problem situation. Utilize the adolescent's own source of creativity.
5 Be aware of your own values and beliefs. It is not always the case that a clinician can remain neutral and unbiased, but it is important to be aware of how one's values are entering a conversation, and they can be introduced as just some of the many possibilities.
6 Work with the person, not a diagnosis or label. By utilizing the adolescent's own resources and creativity it is possible to reframe

experiences. For example, Amanda felt as if she was going 'crazy' with the loss of her attachment figure, but redefining her behaviour as normal for somebody who has experienced so many losses allowed her to develop more positive descriptions of herself.

7 Work towards understanding. When adolescents feel that they are being listened to by significant adults it helps them to build their confidence, and their abilities to work through the process of loss are boosted.

At the end of Amanda's sessions her story adapted a theme more appropriate to the separation of herself and her mother. She reformed her story of fear and anxiety to courage and challenge, adopting a more positive view that 'the sapling can no longer grow in the shade of the oak'.

This narrative approach can also be utilized in any adolescent situation, but we have found it most useful when dealing with the sensitive issues of loss, separation and bereavement. It allows us to enter the world of the adolescent and facilitate the generation of alternative meaning and understanding. We have found that it elicits co-operation and investment by the adolescent and circumvents the power struggles that can occur at this particular developmental stage. We know that adolescents will continue to generate new possibilities on their own when faced with other relationships and situations in life.

The usage of story telling and narrative approaches is a sensitive and creative tool designed to elicit children's thoughts, identify their distortions and help them to more accurately make sense of their world. We have found that there are many advantages of adopting this approach for children traumatized by loss and separation. The main benefits have included the familiarity of stories to children, their meaningfulness and flexibility and their ability to enhance relationships and enter into the inner world of the child or adolescent. We have found this allows creative and positive communication, allowing us to understand their experiences and therefore decreasing their need to express themselves inappropriately or, even worse, not to say anything at all.

REFERENCES

Abrams, R. (1992) *When Parents Die*, London: Lett.
Ainsworth, M.D.S. (1978) *Patterns of Attachment*, Hillsdale, NJ: Lawrence Erlbaum.

Althea (1982) *When Uncle Bob Died*, London: Dinosaur, Collins.

Andersen, T. (1991) *The Reflecting Team: Dialogues and Dialogues About Dialogues*, New York: Norton.

Anderson, H. (1986) 'Therapeutic impasses: a breakdown in conversations'. Unpublished manuscript cited in J. Biever, K. McKenzie, M. Wales North and R. Gonzalez (eds) (1995) 'Stories and solutions in psychotherapy and adolescence', *Adolescence* 30 (118): 491–9.

Anderson, H., and Goolishan, H. (1991) 'A collaborative language systems approach'. Paper presented at the Narrative and Psychotherapy Conference, Houston, Texas, May 1991.

——(1991) 'Human systems as linguistic systems: some preliminary and evolving ideas about the implication for clinical theory', *Family Process* 27: 371–93.

Barnardo's (1995) *The Memory Book*, Ilford, Essex: Barnardo's Publications.

Biever, J., McKenzie, K., Wales North, M., and Gonzalez, R. (1995) 'Stories and solutions in psychotherapy and adolescence', *Adolescence* 30(118): 491–9.

Bowlby, J. (1950) *Maternal Care and Mental Health*, Geneva: World Health Organisation.

——(1969) *Attachment and Loss. 1: Attachment*, London: Hogarth Press and Institute of Psycho-analysis.

——(1980) *Attachment and Loss. 3: Loss – Sadness and Depression*, Hogarth Press and Institute of Psycho-analysis.

Davis, N. (1990) *Once Upon a Time . . . Therapeutic Stories*, Oxon Hill: Psychological Association of Oxon Hill.

de Paola, T. (1987) *Nana Upstairs and Nana Downstairs*, London: Methuen Children's Books.

Gersie, A. (1992) *Storymaking in Bereavement*, London: Jessica Kingsley.

Guillaume, P. (1996) 'The change project: myth and metaphor and magic', published on internet journal, URL reference www.well.com/~bbear/myth_met.html.

Heegaard, M. (1988) *When Someone Very Special Dies*, USA: Woodland Press.

Hoffman, L. (1990) 'Constructing realities: an art of lenses', *Family Process* 29: 1–12.

Hudson, L. (1987) 'Creativity', in Richard Gregory (ed.) *The Oxford Companion to the Mind*, Oxford: Oxford University Press, 171–2.

Johnson, J., and Johnson, M. (1990) *Tell Me, Papa*, Omaha, NE: Centering Corporation.

Kubler Ross, E. (1970) *On Death and Dying*, London: Tavistock.

Mellonie, B., and Ingpen, R. (1983) *Lifetimes*, Surrey: Dragon's World.

Padoan, G. (1987) *Remembering Grandad*, Milan, Italy: Happy Books.

Parkes, C.M. (1991) 'Attachment, bonding and psychiatric problems after bereavement in adult life', in C.M. Parkes, J. Stevenson-Hinde and P. Marris (eds) *Attachments Across the Life Cycle*, London: Routledge, 268–92.

Parkes, C.M., and Stevenson-Hinde, J. (eds) (1982) *The Place of Attachment in Human Behaviours*, New York: Basic Books.

St Christopher's Hospice (1989) *Someone Special Has Died*, London: St Christopher's Hospice.

Salten, F. (1928) *Bambi*, London: Jonathan Cape.

Selby, J. (1975) *The Day Grandma Died*, London: Benjamin Books.

Simmonds, P. (1989) *Fred*, London: Puffin Books.

Sims, A. (1986) *Am I Still A Sister?*, Louisiana, USA: Big A and Co.

Van-Si, L., and Powers, L. (1994) *Helping Children Heal From Loss: A Keepsake Book of Special Memories*, Portland, Ore: Continuing Education Press.

Varley, S. (1985) *Badger's Parting Gifts*, London: Picture Lions.

Walzlavick, P. (1978) *The Language of Change: Elements of Therapeutic Communication*, New York: Basic Books.

Weiss, R.S. (1982) 'Attachment in adult life', in C.M. Parkes and J. Stevenson-Hinde (eds) *The Place of Attachment in Human Behaviours*, New York: Basic Books, 171–84.

——(1991) 'The attachment bond in childhood and adulthood', in C.M. Parkes, J. Stevenson-Hinde and P. Marris (eds) *Attachments Across the Life Cycle*, London: Routledge, 66–76.

Wilhelm, H. (1986) *I'll Always Love You*, London: Hodder and Stoughton.

Williams, G., and Ross, J. (1983) *When People Die*, Midlothian: MacDonald.

Zolotow, C. (1976) *My Grandson Lew*, Surrey: Windmill Press.

Chapter 10

Stories used therapeutically with children in educational settings

Sonia Compton

> Long before the invention of written language, fairy tales, legends and stories existed as a means to transfer knowledge from one generation to another. Transferring knowledge in this way was both entertaining and educational to children.
>
> (Davis 1990: 1)

Stories are used in educational settings to provide children with opportunities to view and hear language, and to develop an interest in reading. As has been stated:

> Reading is one of the most important life skills. The ability to read quickly and understand the myriad of written messages that surrounds us enables us to function in a literate society. Every day we read and act upon things as signs, directions and forms – an inability to do so could result in at worst, a traffic accident or at best, trouble with the Inland Revenue.
>
> (Bentley *et al.* 1995: 6)

There is the argument that stories should be told just to develop the skill of reading and for the enjoyment of hearing descriptive language. While acknowledging the importance of reading as stated in the above quote, it is also felt that different emotions, coping strategies and life experiences can be experienced alongside learning to read and hearing descriptive language.

Stories have been told for centuries. Originally stories were told orally by the older members of families or communities and the stories were passed down from generation to generation. As the stories travelled down the ages, each story teller would adapt and expand the story by adding elements from their unconscious. In today's society with television and less contact with extended families, stories are often told in the form of books. This unfortunately leaves little chance for the story teller to add their own individual elements to the story. However, Bruno Bettelheim (1976) believes that symbolic elements of stories connect with, in psychoanalytic terms, the conscious, the preconscious and the unconscious mind of the listener. The unconscious mind in human beings plays a large part in behaviour. Therefore, Bettelheim believes, original fairy and folk tales can provide the unconscious mind with different coping strategies, and stories can enable the unconscious thinking to come into the conscious mind and provide the person with insight about themselves or a solution to a particular difficulty. Also, stories have to contain both the good and the bad elements. Many of today's stories have been cleaned up and made nice, because, as Bettelheim (1976) noted, as a society we try to present the good side of life, hoping to shield children from the realities of life. However, by removing the gory and nasty parts (as society views them) from stories, we rob the listener of coping strategies to deal with the gory and nasty parts of life. As we all know, life is not a bed of roses. And as everyone who has read stories to children is aware, the parts they want to hear time and time again are the gory or nasty parts!

Stories can be used in many different ways: they can be told, read, dramatized, created and then enacted. On a variety of different occasions, stories may be used not just as educational lessons but also at points of crisis with children who are unable to orally express their distress safely.

Stories contain many symbols and messages and Bettelheim believed fairy tales contained symbolic messages which connected with the listener's unconscious. Bettelheim states,

> For a story truly to hold the child's attention, it must entertain him and arouse his curiosity. But to enrich his life, it must stimulate his imagination; help him to develop his intellect and to clarify his emotions; be attuned to his anxieties and aspirations; give full recognition to his difficulties, while at the same time suggesting solutions to the problems which perturb him.
>
> (Bettelheim 1976: 5)

The following story gives an example of a symbol within the story connecting with a child's unconscious and bringing the unconscious thinking into the conscious mind. I chose to tell this story to a group of eight children aged 10 and 11 years, as I felt the story contained ways of controlling and directing anger appropriately.

The children were from various backgrounds and differing levels of traumatic experiences. The majority of these children had been assessed to determine their special educational needs under the provisions provided by the Education Act (1993), and had been recognized as having emotional and behavioural difficulties. Many of the children within the group had either experienced inappropriate expressions of anger or expressed anger inappropriately to their peers, adults or property. One child within this group, Sam, had expressed his anger in verbal and/or physical aggression to peers and adults. He seemed to have limited conscious recognition of his behaviour and seemed to show no regret for any harm he caused others. He generated fear in others, but I wonder if this was a feeling he transferred from himself to others. During an English lesson I told this story; it had been told to me by Ted Wharem, who thought of it in conjunction with Mooli Lahad.

The story of Dracco

Once upon a time, a long long time ago but not that long ago, there lived a family of dragons. The dragons were green dragons. In this family there was a mum, a dad and three children: a boy, a girl and another boy. Now at the start of this story, Dracco was around the age of two and a half years. He had a bit of difficulty in controlling his fire. For example, he would try to build a tower of bricks, and when they fell over the odd brick would occasionally end up being burned or singed. His parents thought this would soon stop, especially once he started nursery school.

Things went well when Dracco started nursery school, but as time went by the teacher began to notice things being burned – the edges of the pages of a book, or the curtains in the home corner. However, the teacher did not know how these things were being burned. Until, that is, one day when there was a commotion going on in the home corner. The teacher went to investigate and found Dracco fighting with another member of the class. The teacher grabbed Dracco, but as she did so he turned round and a blast of fire shot from his mouth, and the fire burned the teacher's ear, hair and even melted her earring. As you can guess, the teacher was not very happy and she frog-marched Dracco by his ear down the street to his home. She told Dracco's mum exactly what had happened and Dracco was sent upstairs to his bedroom until the rest of the family came home. Dracco sat silently upstairs, waiting and thinking. He was feeling guilty about hurting his teacher. It seemed like a long time. Finally Dracco heard the front door open. He sat waiting and waiting until eventually his sister appeared at the door to say dinner was ready and that he was to come down. Dracco was feeling very frightened, because he did not know what was going to happen. He went slowly downstairs and sat quietly at the table. Everyone was silent.

Mum spoke up first and said, 'Your father and I have talked following today's uncontrolled outburst of fire, as it was a very serious incident. We have decided that fire will not be used ever again by any member of this family. We want your promises that you will never use your fire again.' Mum and Dad both promised and so did Dracco's brother and sister. Dracco also promised and said it would never happen again. Dad said he hoped that everyone would keep their promise and that the matter would not be discussed any further.

Dracco returned to nursery school and he really tried hard to control his fire. At first it was hard and occasionally the odd puff of smoke would leak out of his mouth when he felt upset, or a small whiff of smoke would sneak out when he was annoyed. However, he remembered his promise. As the weeks and months passed Dracco found it easier to control his fire.

Time passed, and fire was not used by any member of Dracco's family. Dracco's brother reached the age of 18. Now I don't know whether you know or not, but at the age of 18 dragons have to leave home and fly to another land to start a new life. So, at 18, Dracco's brother flew away and Dracco was sad to see him go. By the time Dracco's sister was 18, Dracco was doing his examinations. He was sad when his sister left. Time passed and Dracco passed his examinations; before he knew it, he was 18. Now it was time for him to leave home. He was feeling a bit frightened and sad about leaving his mum and dad, but he knew he had to leave. He kissed and hugged them goodbye. Then he flew off into the sky, high above the rooftops and trees until everything below looked like ants. He travelled over coloured fields, yellow corn ones, brown ploughed fields and green grassy meadows. He swooped down low over a bustling river where he could hear the swishing of the water. He travelled over seas, smelling the sea air, and could see dolphins playing and boats sailing. He travelled over blazing hot deserts with camels, and over the tops of snow-crested mountains, until he finally settled on a country in which to land.

He came down in a small town at the bottom of a hill. The town had a park in the middle, where Dracco landed. His first thought was to find a job and a home. So he walked over to a newspaper stand in the park and bought a local newspaper. He searched through the job vacancies, but could not find anything until he came to the last page. There, right in the bottom right-hand corner, was a small box that said:

DRAGON WANTED
TO
PROTECT
THE CROWN JEWELS

Please apply at
the Castle

Dracco thought, 'This is the job I want.' So he asked the newspaper seller where the castle was. 'At the top of the hill,' he was told. Dracco climbed the hill until he came to the large door of the castle. He knocked on the door. The door slowly creaked open and standing there was a very large old red dragon. Now this dragon was the keeper of the jewels and he was 178 years old. He had been looking after the jewels for 129 years, day and night. He wanted a rest. He explained to Dracco that nobody had ever tried stealing the jewels. He told Dracco about the job and then offered it to him. Dracco was very excited and signed the contract at once.

Over the next couple of weeks the old dragon taught Dracco the job, until one evening he decided Dracco was ready to look after the jewels during the night on his own. The old dragon took Dracco into the jewel room. It was full of beautiful jewels, gold goblets, silver swords, large shields encrusted with jewels and sparkling crowns. The room was so bright with the jewels. The old dragon reminded Dracco that he could not have the lights on at night in the jewel room. Dracco assured the old dragon that everything would be fine. The old dragon trundled off to his bed, where he briefly wondered if Dracco would be all right, but shortly he was fast asleep, snoring.

Now Dracco settled into the jewel room and he felt quite pleased with himself, but also a bit anxious. As the night went by, it became darker and the owls began to hoot. Dracco started to feel uneasy. There was the occasional glimpse of light from the moon as it came out from behind a cloud and shone through the window. Dracco began to feel more and more frightened. He started to hear sounds and see shadows. He kept telling himself he would be all right. At about twelve o'clock Dracco heard some whispering outside the door. He tried to crouch smaller and backed into the corner. He was very frightened, because he guessed the voices were jewel thieves. They opened the door. Dracco could feel his heart beat, thumping so loud he was sure the thieves would hear it. The sweat was dripping off him. Dracco tried to move further back but as he did he lost balance. He fell backwards, and as he did so – WHOOF! – a great blast of fire burst out of his mouth. The flames caught the jewel thieves and they turned and ran with their clothes on fire. Fortunately, because of the noise the thieves were making, the castle guards came running and caught them. Everyone woke up in the castle, and they all thought Dracco was a hero for saving the jewels. People were congratulating him on how brave he was. Dracco began to feel proud of himself. The king was so pleased with Dracco that he decided to hold a ceremony for him the next day.

The old dragon had woken up at the noise. He was pleased with Dracco, so he gave him the night off and sent him to bed. Dracco went proudly off to his bedroom. He was thinking about what had happened as he climbed into bed. Just as he was dropping off to sleep, he suddenly sat bolt upright and leapt out of bed, remembering his promise to his family. What was he going to do? He had broken his promise. He had used fire. He knew his parents would read about it in the morning newspaper. What was he going to do? He thought about it for a while and then he decided to write to his parents, so that they would hear from him first. He quickly got up and went to his desk and started writing. . . .

At this point in the story I stopped and asked the children to write a letter to Dracco's parents, pretending they were Dracco. The children were requested to respect other people's choice for privacy while preparing their letters. With this group the children were asked to write their letters; however, I have used this story with groups of children with learning difficulties, when instead of writing a letter the children have been given the option of drawing a symbol or a picture.

At the point in the story where Dracco's difficulty in controlling his anger at nursery school becomes apparent, the child previously mentioned (Sam) had interrupted the story and said, 'Like me'. He had then become completely engrossed in the story, and proceeded to write a letter apologizing to his parents for breaking the promise. Within the group the letters ranged from Dracco begging for forgiveness to explaining the situation and why he had used fire.

After the children had completed their letters from Dracco, they were asked to respond as if they were Dracco's parents. With this group the children were asked to respond to their own letters; however, if the group is safe enough, or perhaps if using this activity with adults, the letters to Dracco's parents may be placed in a hat for each group member to draw one and respond to. With this group it was felt that anxiety might be caused by the children feeling threatened if someone else responded to their letter. Also, within this group the self-esteem level was very low, and so the risk of having their work criticized by a peer was too high. Many of these children had failed in various aspects of their educational and social development.

When the letters were completed the children were given the choice of reading their letters to the group. Again the children were requested to respect other people's work and to listen to the letters. By listening to other group members' letters, they were able to observe different people's responses to the situation, with the aim of providing them with different ways of dealing with situations other than their previously learned behaviour. The responses to Dracco's letters varied from parents never wanting to see their son again, to parents not forgiving Dracco for breaking a promise, to parents accepting Dracco's explanation. In Sam's letter as a parent, he accepted Dracco's apology and said he was proud of Dracco for using his fire sensibly.

The story then continued after the children had listened to and discussed their letters.

Dracco sent his letter to his parents and then swiftly fell asleep. The next morning he got up and prepared himself for the ceremony. He polished his scales and cleaned his teeth. He was worried about his parents, but he felt excited about the ceremony. At eleven o'clock Dracco arrived at the banqueting hall, which was packed with guests who had come to congratulate him. Dracco walked slowly down the pathway to the king. He climbed up on the stage, and as he stood in front of the king he spotted his smiling parents sitting in the audience. The king congratulated Dracco on saving the crown jewels and tried to pin a medal on him. However, a dragon's skin is hard and scaly, so the king had to call for some Blu-Tack to stick the medal on Dracco. Everybody clapped and cheered.

Just as Dracco was leaving the stage, the old red dragon whispered in his ear, 'It is a good job you saved the jewels, because at the bottom of your contract, in the small print, it states that if the crown jewels were stolen, the keeper would have their head cut off.'

Like the writers cited earlier, Nancy Davis (1990) also states that stories can connect with a person's unconscious. I feel the above story may have connected with Sam's unconscious and brought his own behaviour into his consciousness. I have heard subsequently that with the support of the structured educational environment, he has found more socially acceptable ways to express his anger.

In times of crisis, I have used stories with children in an attempt to calm often aggressive and violent situations. Many times in situations like this the child is asked to verbalize the event and the feelings regarding the incident. However, the child may be too angry/too frightened/too out of control to communicate the event verbally.

> European educationists tell us that children cannot use words as tools to think with, until the age of about seven or eight; before that time, their use of language is similar to that of adults speaking a tongue which is only slightly known to them.
>
> (Lowenfeld 1948: 326)

It is during adolescence that the capacity for verbalization and inner thought becomes established (Ryan and Wilson 1996). Perhaps with this knowledge we need to find other ways to ask children to communicate, other than verbally, remembering that they may also not be ready to hear another's version of the event.

Sometimes stories may give the child time to gain control of their emotions and to distance themselves from the event. For example, I told a story to a child who had been removed from an incident where he had been physically attacking another child. He was extremely angry and was only just managing to remain seated. He looked like a coil about to spring. He had been questioned and spoken with about the event, but had remained silent. I used a Buddhist story about an anger demon (see chapter 5 in this volume). As I told the story, I observed Joseph become visibly calmer. His shoulders dropped and his fists became unclenched. By the end of the story, Joseph was able to verbalize his feelings and his version of the events leading to the physical attack. He was able to rejoin his group. On another occasion I used the same story with another child, who had been attempting to show his distress by destroying the classroom. I told the story to him once he was away from the classroom. He at first seemed not to be listening, but his body gradually uncurled and relaxed, leading to him being able to join the group safely. This story was remembered by the child, because following an incident with some of his peers I heard him re-telling the story and describing how he had originally heard it. The content of the story (that is, don't fight anger with anger) also helped me to handle the situation, calmly avoiding confrontation.

During a daily lesson that is aimed at encouraging recognition of feelings and the boosting of self-esteem, adapted from Circle time, (White 1991), I have used group stories with the children. Using Violet Oaklander's (1988) story technique, every week we had a group story. This involved the children sitting in a circle or round a table. One person started the story by drawing a picture and verbally beginning the story in whichever way they wanted. Then the picture was passed to the next person and they then continued the story. The story can either be written by an adult/child or it can be tape recorded. The group is asked to respect other people's work. Children are given the choice about whether they want to partici-pate. Some children find it very difficult to begin, because a blank piece of paper can be very daunting.

In our group, the story would sometimes come to a natural end with the last member of the group, but on occasions it would carry on to the next week. Initially the children found it difficult to make the story, but as time progressed the stories lengthened and became deeper in quality. This may have been due to the children feeling safer within the group situation and also to their self-esteem devel-oping. Due to the nature of the children's difficulties the stories at the beginning of the school year were disjointed and the stories did not flow. The children wanted to get what they wanted in the story and seemed unaware of where the story was before their turn. However, as the year moved on the children were able to work together to form a story. Also, because the children began to feel safe within the group they started to deal with their own issues, beginning to use the safety of symbolism to express them; for example, one child who had recently had a bereavement was able to express his family's distress about the bereavement by using the family in the story, where, in a previous child's turn, the dog had died. Another child brought the same theme, regarding a traumatic event, into his part of the story week after week, until he seemed to feel it was less important.

With the group story children are given opportunities to hear/view different ways to cope with their issues, because another child continues the story. As each child has their own individual ways of handling difficult situations, these are reflected in their part of the story. Also, in observing the group stories over a period of time, you see which role each child feels comfortable with; for example, one girl in the group would often take the rescue role and if this part of the story was taken by another child she would struggle to participate in the story.

The group stories also provide the children with an opportunity to express their feelings in a safe way and provide children with distance from their own real-life issues. For example, one child who had great difficulty controlling his anger safely was able to express this through the group story. His anger concerned an incident from the previous day, where a teacher had placed a boundary on him which he didn't like. This is his part of the group story.

Once upon a time there was a teacher called Mr James. He was strict and then one day he decided to take all the children on a trip to a land far, far away. While they were there, he threw three children in the sea, because they were being naughty. One of them drowned. Mr James was laughing at them when they were calling for help. He said he was not going to help them. The police put Mr James in prison. The child had not really drowned. He went under the sea and found he could breathe.

At this point in the story he passed the picture to another child, who then continued with the story. The boy was calmer for the rest of the day. He had been able to express his anger safely towards the teacher.

Stories can be used in many different mediums, such as tapes and dramatizing a story. Dramatization may reinforce the unconscious message of the story, as well as giving the child a chance to practise different roles. Taking on different roles may allow a child to view a situation from another's perspective, thus giving them an opportunity to see a different coping strategy. Also, dramatizing a story may enable something from the child's unconscious to be brought into their conscious thinking.

This was apparent in a story developed as part of a session called activity play. In this, a pair of children work together at their developmental level of play. Activity play is based on the theory that play is a developmental process and that play is children's natural medium to learn and discover. Therefore, with this in mind and also because many of the children's objectives on their annual special educational assessment review statements include 'through structured play children will learn to relate positively to other pupils and adults', we introduced activity play. There are three stages in the developmental process according to Sue Jennings (Jennings 1993). The stages are embodiment, projective and role play. In embodiment play, children usually within the first year of their life explore themselves and the world by using their senses. This generally leads to projective play, where the child begins to explore the world using toys and objects separate from themselves. These objects can also be used in embodiment play, dramatic play or in a narrative form. The third stage is role play. Children develop role play as a way of re-enacting real life events and stories, for example when children in a nursery play in the home corner and take on the roles of the adults in their lives. It is felt that some emotionally damaged children may need to re-experience the stages of play. The aim of activity play is to provide children with an opportunity to experience their developmental level of play. This follows an assessment of each child's individual level. This assessment is usually carried out from observations of each child playing and using the knowledge of the developmental stages of play. Following the assessment, play opportunities are provided to meet each child's level.

Using some of Sue Jennings' (1993) ideas along with help from the children, we created and enacted the following story, as it provides an opportunity to experience the embodiment stage where a child begins to explore themselves and the world using their senses. This story allows the children to use their senses and to develop trust within a relationship. It takes a lot of trust to allow another person to push you across the room, even though the floor provides safety.

The story of the tree

Once upon a time, there was a big strong old tree [one child stands as a tree]. It lived in a forest, near a river. The tree would sway in the wind, but it had big strong roots. The birds would nest in its branches. Foxes and rabbits would build their homes around the base of the trunk. Squirrels would hibernate in the tree. But one day a woodcutter [another child] decided to chop the tree down, to allow younger trees to grow. So she [he] chopped the tree down [the child becomes a log]. The woodcutter planted a new tree to replace the fallen tree. The woodcutter decided to have the log turned into a boat. So she [he] rolled the log to the river [log child lies on the floor and the woodcutter child rolls the log child]. The log floated down the river. [The woodcutter child now takes the role of the river and rolls the log.] Unfortunately the log got stuck in some mud and some reeds. The river tried to free the log. [The log child resists being moved.] The river pushed with all its might, but was unable to free the log. Luckily the woodcutter saw that the log was stuck and raced to the river. She [he] pushed the log and managed to free it. The log floated freely again down the river until it came to the boat-makers. There the boatmakers turned the log into a boat. The woodcutter was very pleased with the strong boat and climbed into it. [The children sit one behind the other and move forward together.] The woodcutter and the boat set sail on to the open seas and had many adventures together and lived happily ever after.

Prior to acting out this story, the children practised doing the actions and taking the different roles. One child, who presented as timid and found it difficult to stand up to other people, seemed to thoroughly enjoy the experience of resisting being rolled. At first she was unable to stop the other child pushing her over, but with encouragement she was able to resist being rolled over. Once she had achieved this she leapt off the floor and exclaimed excitedly, 'I did it.' Another child, who struggled with where his body began and ended, connected with his early development while enacting this story. He had many difficulties like bumping into things and being unaware of distances and his own strength, and was also reported to have had little opportunity to physically explore his environment in his early years. He stated while practising the physical actions of this story that he had never done anything like this in his early life and he then announced that he was going to ask his new family to practise this story with him. This story became important for all the children who contributed to it and led to them asking on many occasions to repeat the story and to show other children and adults. Six months after enacting the story, one child began making a book and writing the story out, remembering it accurately. The children were able to add to the story, either with verbal elements or by developing their role in the enactment of the story.

Many children who hear a story that connects with their unconscious may request to hear the story time and time again. So many of us adults have become bored with telling the same story repeatedly, but still the child requests it again and again. It is thought that if the child is given the opportunity to hear the story as often as requested, finally the child may find solutions to their particular difficulties/conflicts. Berne (1964) believes the story is connecting with the child's unconscious mind, because it may mirror the child's life script at that time. As the child's life script changes, so may the story.

The following example shows how a story may have been a symbolic mirror to the child's life script and how she received some resolution from hearing and enacting the story. The child had a six-month-old sibling. She seemed to cope with having a baby sibling who demanded so much attention from her mum, as babies do. But at times, especially around feeding time, she would sometimes display behaviour that required attention, either in the form of 'I have a tummy ache' or by doing something she had been asked not to do. However, she rarely showed any feeling other than happiness and love towards her baby sibling, except that on the odd occasion she would clamp her teeth together and clench her fists when looking at the baby. She asked for a story and was read *The Tunnel* (Browne 1989), and then over a period of weeks she requested the story constantly. She even took the book with her wherever she went. She enacted the story by using a gap between two chairs as the tunnel and a male figure doll as the brother and herself as the sister. When satisfied with this, she then requested the adults around to play roles from the story. Eventually the story became less important, leading to the belief that she had resolved her conflict. However, as she did not verbalize her conflict, I can only surmise that it was to do with her sibling.

CONCLUSION

In this chapter I have attempted to show how stories are beneficial for the child as a whole and not only as a learning tool for reading in educational settings. Stories have the ability to by-pass the conscious thinking of the listener and connect with the unconscious mind, therefore giving the opportunity for unconscious thinking and behaviour to come into the conscious mind. Also, stories can provide resolutions to conflicts and different coping strategies. In an educational setting, too, the stories can be used in many different ways, from telling a story to making a new story. I have only shown a few ideas of how stories can be used, but I have found that my best source of ideas is from the children themselves. Invariably the children give suggestions about how to adapt and enhance an activity. Children know what they need if given the environment to explore their ideas.

REFERENCES

Names and other identifying details of children referred to in the chapter have been changed to ensure their confidentiality.

Bentley, D., Birchall, C., Flew, A., Karavis, S., Lowry, J., and Reid, D. (1995) *Scholastic Teachers' Resource Book for Fiction* (Purple set, boxed resource, Literacy Centre), Leamington Spa: Scholastic Ltd.

Berne, E. (1964) *Games People Play*, New York: Grove Press.

Bettelheim, B. (1976) *The Uses of Enchantment*, New York: Grove Press.

Browne, A. (1989) *The Tunnel*, London: Walker Books.

Davis, N. (1990) *Once Upon a Time*, Oxon Hill: Psychological Associates of Oxon Hill.

Department for Education (1993) Education Act, London: HMSO.

Jennings, S. (1993) *Playtherapy with Children, a Practitioner's Guide*, Oxford: Blackwell Scientific Publications.

Lowenfeld, M. (1948) 'The nature of the primary system', in C. Urwin and J. Hood-Williams (eds) (1988) *Child Psychotherapy – War and the Normal Child: Selected Papers of Margaret Lowenfeld*, London: Free Association Books, 325–45.

Oaklander, V. (1988) *Windows to our Children*, New York: The Gestalt Journal Press.

Ryan, V., and Wilson, K. (1996) *Case Studies in Non-directive Play Therapy*, London: Bailliere Tindall.

White, M. (1991) *Self Esteem (A)*, Cambridge: Daniels Publications.

Chapter 11

Stories in the context of family therapy

Barry Bowen

They come to you, as you are an expert in story telling.

(Cecchin 1988: 9)

Lena was all but invisible underneath the three large beanbags in the playroom. She was 15 years old and in her short life she had experienced early childhood sexual abuse, neglect, fostering, adoption and latterly, adoption breakdown. The world had proved both unsafe and unpredictable. Somehow the world had to become safe again and she had to change her status from victim to survivor. This meant challenging the dominant story she had of herself (see, for example, White and Epston 1989; Epston and White 1992). To do this in a direct way would have been an experience too frightening and too overwhelming to contemplate. Instead, Lena could experiment with a metaphorical challenge, in the form of a story.

'I'm in my house. You've got to try to blow it down,' said the muffled voice from underneath the beanbags. 'Go away, go away.'

'You want me to go away?' I asked.

'No,' said the exasperated voice, 'Not by the hairs of my chinny-chin-chin.'

Slowly the story came back to me from the depths of my childhood, and from hers.

'Not by the hairs of my chinny-chin-chin,' I said in my best stage-villain voice. 'I'll huff and I'll puff and I'll blow your house down.'

As the story progressed I blew down houses of straw and sticks, before Lena escaped to her safe brick house, which could not be blown down. The story ended with me, the big bad wolf, being burned to death in the chimney.

With the story ended, Lena went on to talk, still underneath the beanbags, of her birth father and some of her early childhood memories. The story had been the door through which the memories could be introduced into therapy. It had also allowed her to challenge her victim status, for in the story Lena had triumphed. She had survived.

At the beginning of teaching workshops on the use of therapeutic stories I sometimes divide participants up into pairs and ask them to tell each other their earliest remembered story. Mine was told repeatedly, in exactly the same way, by my father, to my sister and me when we were quite young children. It always began the same way:

> Not last night, but the night before,
> Two big tom-cats came knocking at our door.
> They said, 'Are Barry and Jacqueline coming out to play?'
> I said, 'No, it's too late, they're both in bed.'

So the two tom-cats climbed up the drainpipe and tapped on the window. Barry and Jacqueline woke up and the two tom-cats led them down the drainpipe and into the garden.

There in the garden was a magic ring of toadstools and Barry and Jacqueline and the two tom-cats all sat on toadstools and waited. Before very long they were joined by fairies and elves, who brought with them all sorts of wonderful foods and drinks. An elf played magic elf-music and some of the fairies danced in the magic circle. They all had a wonderful time.

When it was nearly morning the two tom-cats led Barry and Jacqueline up the drainpipe and back into their bedroom. The next day their mum and dad couldn't understand why Barry and Jacqueline were so tired. But Barry and Jacqueline knew!

My father may have made up this tale, or it might have been a remembered story from his childhood. As he and my mother are now dead I shall probably never know. It remains, though, an important ritual from my childhood and carries with it a feeling of safety and warmth. It also features within it some of the important elements of story telling: repetition (e.g. two tom-cats), identification (e.g. Barry and Jacqueline), a ritual opening (e.g. 'Not last night. . . . '), fantasy (e.g. the fairies and the fairy ring) and, the added bonus in this case, children outwitting the adults ('their mum and dad couldn't understand'). It was my first experience of the importance of stories in family life and family communication.

As I began my career as a therapist I became aware of influential writers in the field whose work featured the use of metaphor and story telling. My first major influence was Jay Haley's account of the techniques of Dr Milton Erickson (Haley 1973). Erickson used his knowledge of hypnotherapy to help his patients use his stories at the metaphorical level, opening up new options and offering up solutions to previously perceived insoluble problems. Erickson often incorporated his patients' interests and preoccupations into the subject matter of his stories. For example, he used a metaphorical story about a tomato plant to help a dying florist reduce his perceived pain (Haley 1973: 300–6). As my interest grew I sought out other examples of story-centred writings.

Callow and Benson (1984) continued the theme of hypnotic story telling; Davies (1988) and Creedy *et al.* (1993) were excited by the use of fairy tale (as in 'The three little pigs' above); Wood (1988), as in the work of White and Epston (1989), combined the use of stories with letters to children; Speed (1990) wrote of a day in her own life and Spellman and Scott (1993) looked at therapy itself as a story. Elsewhere, Milton and Crowley (1986) were using stories formed of therapeutic metaphors framed in the child's own language. Influences abounded.

As a family therapist, my interest lay in the incorporation of metaphor and story into therapeutic work with families.

Some of my earlier work, with my co-therapist Gini Nimmo, was published in a 1986 paper dealing with the active use of metaphor and analogy in family therapy (Bowen and Nimmo 1986). This involved families acting out a metaphorical description of their family situation. The example used was that of an adolescent boy in the voluntary care of the local authority, or 'accommodated', as it would now be called. His mother described how he was so removed from the family as to be 'over the bridge'. This was a reference to the Runcorn bridge, which connects Runcorn with Widnes. The two towns had been united into the district of Halton in the local government changes, but as the two communities remained firmly separate the only reason most people travelled over the bridge was to collect their benefit from the Widnes office. Thus 'over the bridge' was to be no longer part of the local community, or in this case, of the family. The metaphor of the bridge was utilized in the session by the building of a bridge made from chairs. The boy had to cross blindfolded, guided only by instructions from the family, while at the same time ignoring the shouts and calls made by his peers from outside the room, which was part of the children's home.

Part of this work, although not included within the paper, was the beginning of my use of story telling within family therapy.

Over the years I have collected a library of therapeutic stories which can be adapted for use with various family situations and at various points during the therapeutic journey. During our work with the 'bridge' family I used the following story, called 'The little red engine', based upon the stories of the Revd W. Awdry (e.g. Awdry 1946). To maintain the family connection, I first met Awdry's stories through the medium of radio and the programme *Listen with Mother*, when I was only three or four years old.

The little red engine

Once, in the time of steam trains, there was a little red engine. He lived in the engine sheds with all the other engines, but he was so small and looked so weak that no one ever used him, neither to carry goods nor to carry people. All the other engines went out every day, laden with goods wagons or passenger coaches, but the little red engine stayed in the sheds, feeling lonely and sad and helpless and useless. After a few months [or years, depending upon the history of the family's problems] the little red engine did not only feel useless, he believed he was useless.

Then, one day, when the little red engine was all alone in the sheds yet again, there came a message from the big factory in the big town. They needed seven goods carriages of iron rods and they needed them straight away. But who was to carry them? All the other engines were out for the day. There was only the little red engine. Well, thought the railwaymen, he will just have to do it.

So they linked up the seven heavy goods carriages, filled with heavy iron rods, to the little red engine. And off he went, out of the sheds and on to the track that led to the big town.

The first thing the little red engine saw was a mighty gradient. His first task would be to climb this hill, pulling his heavy load behind him.

The little red engine believed he was helpless and useless, so it was with a downcast heart and a fear of failure that he began the ascent. As he went he repeated, over and over again: 'I-can't-do-it, I-can't-do-it, I-can't-do-it . . . ' [the sound of an engine struggling].

With each turn of his wheels his voice became slower and weaker:

'I-can't-do-it, I-can't-do-it. . . . '

Finally, he stopped, applying his brakes to avoid slipping back all the way to the sheds. Not that his brakes would hold, he thought. As a final disaster he would be dragged helplessly back to the sheds, to remain there until he rusted away. The sound of his brakes sounded like a long drawn-out sigh . . . sssssshhhhhhhh.

Just then, over the hill came the biggest brightest strongest engine in the whole sheds. He came confidently along the line, pulling behind him the best and newest passenger carriages, a reward for good service. He drew to a dignified halt beside the little red engine, he on the down line, the little red engine on the oh-so-steep up line.

'What seems to be the trouble, little red engine?' said the strong measured tones of the pride of the sheds.

'Oh, I have to carry this heavy load to the big factory in the big town, but I am so weak and helpless and useless that I am going to be dragged back to the sheds. This was my chance to prove myself, but I am just a failure.'

'And what was that I heard you telling yourself just before you sighed to a stop, my friend?'

The little red engine should have been cheered by the mention of 'friend', for he truly believed he had no friends, certainly not this big glistening and powerful engine. He was small and inadequate; everyone looked down on him.

Still, he answered the question.

'I was saying: I-can't-do-it, I-can't-do-it.'

'Then that is what is wrong,' said the glistening engine. 'You must say instead: I-can-do-it.'

'Must I?' said the little red engine.

'But of course. Not only that, but you must say it clearly and with a strong confident voice. Now try it.'

So the little red engine tried it: 'I-can-do-it, I-can-do-it . . . ' [the sound of an engine moving].

Slowly, he began to move up the hill. Soon he was picking up speed and his voice began to shout, more and more loudly and more and more quickly, the exhilarating words: 'I-can-do-it, I-can-do-it . . . ' [the sound of an engine picking up speed].

Then, surprisingly soon, he reached the crest of the hill and he could see the big town laid out below him, with the big factory right there at the bottom of the hill as he plunged down the other side, shouting out by now: 'I-did-it, I-did-it, I-did-it, I-did-it . . . ' [the sound of an engine rushing downhill].

Versions of this tale have been told to families experiencing many varying problems. What they had in common, though, was a belief that they were helpless and that all their endeavours would inevitably lead to failure. Not uncommonly there would be a family member, often a child, who believed themselves to be useless and friendless, just like the little red engine. Just as I did as a small-for-age child so many years ago.

I was often faced with families containing a small child or toddler described by the parents as 'out of control', or as 'a monster'. These problems were usually best tackled by the use of behavioural techniques such as effective praising and mild social disapproval (see Eimers and Aitchison 1978). By the time I saw the family, however, it was often the case that the parents were in a fairly high state of stress. My message was always for them to work at relieving their stress levels before attempting any behavioural change. To reinforce this message it was necessary to offer a simple explanation of the physical and psychological mechanisms of a stress reaction. I found that by using a story I held their attention (and often that of their child) while offering a mnemonic to trigger the memory during the earlier stages of a stress-provoking situation.

The cave-man

Once long ago, in the age of cave-men, there lived a cave-man, a cave-woman and three little cave-children. Also, a cave-dog, a cave-cat and a cave-budgie. They lived in a first-floor cave in a good neighbourhood [or whatever was most like the family's own residence] and were particularly proud of their wall-painting, which stood in the corner of the room and at which they stared, mesmerized, for most of the evening.

One morning the cave-man got up, opened the fridge, and was shocked to discover that they had run out of food. So he picked up his club, which had nails stuck in the end, and marched off down to the deep dark forest in search of a small dinosaur. The family were particularly fond of fried dinosaur steak for breakfast.

Now as you walk deeper into the deep dark forest two things happen: it gets deeper and it gets darker. When the cave-man got to the deepest and darkest part of the forest, guess what happened! You can't guess? No? Well, I'll tell you.

What happened was that a giant sabre-toothed tiger jumped out from behind a tree. Now, there are only about three things that someone can do when faced with a giant sabre-toothed tiger. What are these?

[At this point I would welcome suggestions. These were often: 'You could run really fast'; 'You could kill it with the club'; or 'You could play dead'.]

All these ideas are quite possible, although each person might tend to choose one of these ways instead of one of the others. To explain I need to tell you something about myself. [I would now take out a paper and pencil and start to draw.]

Anywhere over the line (b) is 'awake' and anywhere below it is 'asleep'. Now I wake up fairly quickly in the morning and become more and more awake until just after lunch, when I feel a bit less awake, before becoming a lot more awake in the late afternoon and early evening. From there on it is all downhill until I fall asleep in the late evening. [I would then ask each family member to tell me about their levels of 'awakeness'.]

Let's say that the cave-man had a very similar awake pattern to me. He goes in search of dinosaur meat in the early morning and meets the giant sabre-toothed tiger at about 11.00 a.m. At this point he can hit, run or do nothing. To make the right decision he has to be very very awake. More awake, in fact, than at any other time of the day. Once he is really really awake (which takes much less than a

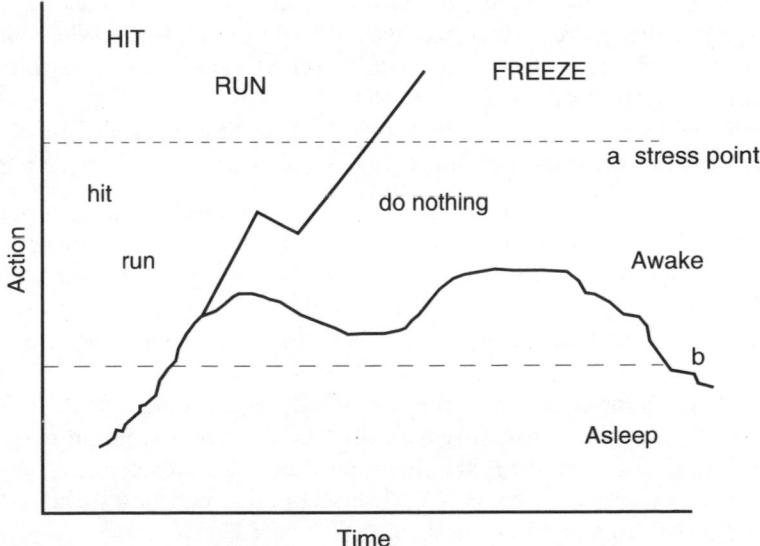

Figure 11.1 Stress diagram

second) he can make his decision and avoid becoming cat-food. [I would sometimes add here something about adrenaline, etc.]

Now, why is it a bad idea for the cave-man to go back to his normal awake level straight afterwards? [The usual answers were: 'Because if he hit the tiger it might wake up'; 'Because if he ran away it might chase him'; 'Because the tiger's mate might be behind the next tree', etc.] So the cave-man returned to his normal awake level slowly, by which time he was sure he was safe.

If something happened before he was back to his normal level, though, his level of awakeness would shoot up, but this time it would shoot up faster and higher. The problems started either if the cave-man was in a situation which went on for a long time, or if he met lots of worrying situations. [I would here place emphasis upon whichever fitted best with the family's history.] In these cases he might find himself crossing the stress point (b). Once over the stress point he might still hit, run or do nothing (or 'freeze'), but as he would be thinking with his emotions, and not with his brain, he would lose control over the decision. Some people tend to hit more, some to run more and some to freeze. Once someone was over the stress point, how might they hit? [Answers included: 'Punch someone', 'Slam doors', etc.] How might they run? ['Leave the house', 'Take an overdose', etc.] People who froze might not make a decision. By not making a decision they were in fact making a decision not to act. When all this happens it isn't too long before the whole family is hitting, running and freezing – at each other.

Now, let's see if we can find ways to help this particular family move below the stress point. . . .

Once a family was ready to seek solutions they would need to begin to think in different ways. Families beset by problems have usually become blinkered to solutions, focusing largely upon problems; or they would be attempting the same failed solution over and over again. To help families to reframe their thinking I would encourage the use of lateral thinking.

What follows are two examples of lateral-thinking stories. The first, 'The pebbles', was first published in a paper I wrote on using the externalization of problems (e.g. White 1988) to overcome problems of anxiety (Bowen 1996b). The second, 'A puzzling suicide', I first heard from my friend and colleague, Alec Clark.

The pebbles

Once, many years ago, in ancient China, there lived a beautiful and gentle girl named Su Lia. She and her elderly father lived together in a small hut in the coastal province of Chii. This province was under the rule of the wicked despot Hui La.

One day, the soldiers of Hui La came to the hut and carried off the honoured father of Su Lia and threw him into the darkest dungeon. The next day, the beautiful Su Lia met with Hui La on the pebbly beach which bordered the province to the east.

'I have an offer I would wish to make,' said the oily pimply and disgusting Hui La. 'You will see that I have in my hand a leather pouch. In this pouch are two pebbles. One is white, the other black. You may place your hand – and such a beautiful hand,' he dribbled, 'into the pouch and draw out one of the pebbles. Should it be the black pebble you draw out I will release your honoured father and give you a fortune in gold and silver. However,' he leered, 'should you be so unfortunate as to draw out the white pebble,' and here he paused to scratch his dirty robe with an even dirtier fingernail, 'I will behead your most honourable father and you will become my concubine.' He paused. 'A good deal, don't you think?'

The alert Su Lia had noticed, however, that the evil and wicked Hui La had placed two white pebbles in the bag. It was then she remembered the two laws of honourable behaviour. First, it was forbidden to accuse another person of lying or deceit (the penalty being 150 years in the deep dark dungeon) and, second, elderly relatives must be protected, no matter what the cost (the penalty being 200 years in the even deeper and darker dungeon). What was the beautiful and gentle Su Lia to do?

Slowly, she placed her hand in the leather pouch [at this point the family are invited to guess what Su Lia must do] and dropped a pebble on to the pebbly beach beneath her.

'Oh dear,' she said, in that sweet plaintive way of hers. 'Never mind. If you look into the pouch, dear honourable Hui La, you will find a pebble. If the pebble is black, then I picked the white, but if the pebble is white, then I picked the black.'

Inside the pouch, of course, was a nice rounded white pebble. Hui La thought of the laws of honourable behaviour . . . and set the father of Su Lia free, with a fortune in gold and silver [adapted from Bowen 1996b].

A puzzling suicide

There was a man who had been blind from birth. He lived in Manchester and he heard that there was an operation, available only in a prestigious London hospital, which would allow him to see. So one sunny morning in June he took the train and travelled down to London. Within three weeks he was discharged from hospital with perfect eyesight. He looked in wonder at the sights around him (the Houses of Parliament, Buckingham Palace and all the other places he had heard of, but never before seen) and then boarded his train for the return journey to Manchester. He was so happy. About halfway home, he killed himself. Why?

I now invite the family to come up with the answer (just as I would with the pebble story). As the family struggle to find the solution, at least three things are happening. The mood of the session changes, becoming lighter and more positive; the family practise looking for solutions outside their usual frame of options; the therapist can also observe the family interactions around problem-solving, while noticing which member or members of the family possess potentially good lateral-thinking skills, for they may hold the key to the opening up of new options for change. This second story, moreover, has an ending which makes it particularly useful at the end of the last family session.

The man killed himself because he went through a tunnel. He, of course, thought he had gone blind again. He had never gone through a tunnel while sighted and to him there was no such thing as a temporary loss of vision. (He had even started to dream in pictures.) Now, I'm fairly certain that this family will go through tunnels at times. I don't know whether they will be short tunnels or long tunnels. I also don't know how fast you will be travelling, or even if all members of the family will be travelling at the same speed. What I do know, though, is that you will come out through the other side, back into the light.

This story helps to prevent molehills becoming mountains, or re-referrals.

The Israel Association for Family Therapy held a conference in 1994 which concentrated on therapists' own families (Amias 1994). Ten per cent of delegates even took members of their own families to the event! Family therapists do well to remember that they too come from families: those that may be current, those that may reside in the past and also families of origin. Stories from this mass of family experience can sometimes be used, with care, to enliven therapy, normalize family difficulties, offer hope and sometimes open up options for change. (There is, I know, some considerable debate about self-revelation within therapy. Like most things, though, I think it is a matter of degree. Most of all, I think we need to ask ourselves, 'For whom am I telling this story?') These are a selection of my favourite family stories.

My father was an immensely practical man. He could cobble shoes, decorate, mend anything electrical; if a job needed doing he could do it. Like many another practical man, however, he had no patience with anyone less skilled than he. I can remember his voice, as if today, saying, 'Oh, give it to me, I can do that while you're looking at it.' You know, I was 25 before I could change a plug.

I went to a single-sex school in a run-down part of a northern city. It was an old Victorian building, with thick walls and a head-master who went around school in his academic gown. The masters used only our second names and seemed to expect trouble from us at all times. Corporal punishment was a daily occurrence and some teachers ruled by fear. I hated it. Even now when I hear someone say, 'I was hit as a child and it never did me any harm!' I think of the harm it did to me, destroying my confidence and turning me off school to such a degree that it was not until my twenties that I felt like learning again. My most vivid memory is of my second year at the school. I can remember sitting on one of the two buses which took me on my one-hour journey to school. I remember saying to myself, 'This year I am going to try really hard.' Then, at the end of that academic year, we received the examination results. These were read out in front of the whole class (a public humiliation for boys like me who usually came thirty-first out of a class of thirty-two). This year, though, I came fifth. In science I came first! I sat proudly in the science class as Sir read out the results. I can remember his exact words: 'Bowen has come first. [Pause] Must have been a fluke.' With those words he condemned me to three more years at thirty-first place.

I had only just met Ann, the woman who was to become my wife. She has two children, Robert and Frances. At that time Frances was 8. She had gone to see a pantomime with the Brownies and I agreed to pick her up after the show. She left the theatre with nothing more than a 'Where's Mummy?' to warn me of what was to come. Two minutes later she was running around a large car park in the centre of Northampton shouting out, 'I'm not getting in that car, you're not my dad!' I had a vision of the headlines in the next day's local paper: FAMILY THERAPIST ARRESTED FOR FORCING BROWNIE INTO CAR. Luckily for me, Brown Owl came round the corner and saved the day. Frances still screamed all the way back to her mother's house.

For two years I had been visiting Ann and the children. At least once a week we sat down together for a snack of boiled eggs. Each time, I cut the top off my egg with a knife while Robert and Frances broke theirs with the back of a spoon. The first sign I had of being accepted by the children was when Frances asked me to cut off the top of her egg. Then Robert wanted his egg decapitated too. I was beginning to be a member of the family. (Adults make relationships with each other quite quickly, children make relationships with children very quickly, but children make relationships with prospective step-parents very slowly – and who can blame them?) All things have their down-sides, though. I cut the tops off the children's boiled eggs every week for another two years!

Stories told in the context of family therapy can be many and varied. I have mentioned fairy stories ('The three little pigs'), childhood ritual stories ('The two tom-cats'), metaphorical stories ('The tomato plant'), acted out stories ('The bridge'), stories adapted from children's literature ('The little red engine'), stories offering hope ('The cave-man'), lateral thinking stories ('The pebbles' and 'A puzzling suicide'), and personal stories ('The practical father', 'The fluke', 'The Brownie in the car park' and 'The right way to eat a boiled egg'). I would add to those stories taken from the media and personalized stories.

I have written elsewhere (Bowen 1996a) of my use of the television and comic character the Incredible Hulk to help a boy who had problems with aggression. Like others (e.g. Jones 1995) I have also written a number of stories specifically for certain children and families. Sometimes, children or families have co-written stories with me. The whole field of stories in therapy is filled with inventiveness and creativity, the very antithesis of the problem-centred helplessness sometimes encountered in presenting families. However, I close with a warning to would-be inventive therapists. I call this (true) story 'The revenge of Big Ted'.

Alec Clark (from whom I heard 'A puzzling suicide') wrote a paper in the early 1980s (Clark 1981) in which he told of some innovative work with a family who had a child with an eating problem. This concerned a child named Tony, who was being long-term fostered along with his brother. Tony was refusing to ask to get down at the end of family meals (a strong family rule) and even if given permission he would continue to sit and say nothing. Clark and his co-therapist joined the family for a meal, together with a large teddy bear belonging to the family's birth child, Paul. At the end of the meal it was noticed that Ted said nothing and did not leave the table, even when asked. This then led on to a family conversation about why someone (Ted or Tony) should act in this way. There emerged a lot of different stories to explain why Ted (and Tony) remained silently at the table.

Several years later I was working with a 5-year-old girl with an eating problem. Her father (a local general practitioner) and her mother (a senior nurse) were very worried about her extremely limited intake of food. In a flash of inspiration I remembered Alec Clark and Ted. I arranged a family meal, to which I invited myself and Big Ted (a 14-year-old giant teddy bear which once belonged to my step-son). We all sat around the table watching Big Ted not eating. After a few minutes of this inactivity, I ventured the question: 'Why do you think Big Ted isn't eating?' There was, as the novelists say, a pregnant pause. Then up piped a little female 5-year-old voice: 'Because it's stuffed!'

I now use this story with families who believe they have found the only possible solution to their problems.

REFERENCES

Amias, D. (1994) 'Therapists and their own families', *Context* 19: 43–4.

Awdry, W. (1946) *Thomas the Tank-Engine* (new edition 1985), London: Octopus.

Bowen, B. (1996a) 'Externalising anger', *Context* 26: 30–3.

——(1996b) 'Zapping anxiety', *Context* 28: 8–11.

Bowen, B., and Nimmo, G. (1986) 'Going over the bridge – A practical use of metaphor and analogy', *Journal of Family Therapy* 8(4): 327–37.

Callow, G., and Benson, G. (1984) 'Hypnotherapy with delinquents and acting out adolescents', *British Journal of Experimental and Clinical Hypnosis* 1: 19–27.

Cecchin, G. (1988) ' "Old wine in new bottles" – Hypothesising, neutrality and circularity revisited', *The Association for Family Therapy Newsletter* 8(4): 9.

Clark, A. (1981) 'Therapy – that's a different story', *Journal of Family Therapy* 3(3): 211–25.

Creedy, K., Bunch, J., Lawrence, B., and Nemeth, B. (1993) 'Missing granny – wood-cutter suspected', *Context* 14: 44.

Davies, E. (1988) 'Reframing, metaphors, myths and fairy-tales', *Journal of Family Therapy* 10(1): 83–92.

Eimers, R., and Aitchison, R. (1978) *Effective Parents – Responsible Children*, London: McGraw-Hill.

Epston, D., and White, M. (1992) *Experience, Contradiction, Narrative and Imagination: Selected papers of David Epston and Michael White 1989–1991*, South Australia: Dulwich Centre Publications.

Haley, J. (1973) *Uncommon Therapy: The psychiatric techniques of Milton H. Erickson MD*, New York: W.W. Norton.

Jones, M. (1995) 'The story without an end: multiple magical use of metaphor in hypnosis and family therapy', *Context* 23: 30–4.

Milton, J.C., and Crowley, R.J. (1986) *Therapeutic Metaphors for Children*, New York: Bruner Mazel.

Speed, B. (1990) 'Mum's the word – a family therapist's diary', *Context* 5: 20–2.

Spellman, D., and Scott, C. (1993) 'An everyday story of systems practice', *Journal of Family Therapy* 15(1): 23–34.

White, M. (1988) 'The externalisation of the problem and the re-authoring of lives and relationships', *Dulwich Centre Newsletter*, Summer; reprinted in M. White (1989) *Selected Papers*, Adelaide: Dulwich Centre Publications, 5–28.

White, M., and Epston, D. (1989) *Literate Means to Therapeutic Ends*, Adelaide: Dulwich Centre Publications.

Wood, A. (1988) 'King Tiger and the roaring tummies: a novel way of helping young children and their families to change', *Journal of Family Therapy* 10(1): 49–63.

Chapter 12

The use of stories to help children who have been abused

Suzanne Lawton and Susan Edwards

All children who have been abused are harmed. Generally, the damage to a child's emotional well-being caused by abuse can be long lasting and traumatic. Finkelhor (1984) has analysed the damage caused by sexual abuse and identified several effects:

- the child has had his or her trust betrayed;
- the child feels stigmatized and suffers a negative view of self;
- the child asks: 'Why me?' 'What did I do wrong?' and feels guilt for not stopping the abuse;
- the child suffers a sense of powerlessness through the betrayal of trust and through losing control over his or her body;
- poor relationships and confusion around appropriate affection may be features later in life;
- some children feel 'unclean' and show inappropriate sexualized behaviour.

Most of these effects can also be seen in a child who has been subject to emotional abuse, neglect and physical abuse.

HELPING CHILDREN WHO HAVE BEEN ABUSED

The aim of therapy is to address the effects of abuse. Finkelhor (1984) suggests that the child's trust in people needs to be restored. 'Blame' and guilt need to be addressed through ensuring children grasp that they are not to blame for the abuse. If the child has disclosed abuse, blame should be removed and an affirmation of the importance of telling needs to be given. Family systems theory is useful in helping to remove blame. Therapy must also address the powerlessness the child experiences by aiming to increase a level of control through the promotion of a positive self-concept. Above all, the therapy must help the child recover from feelings of fear, sadness, anger and shame. This may in turn help restore a healthy development of the caring sharing relationships the child encounters.

Children may present a variety of behaviours as a result of abuse. Some may show a lack of concentration, particularly at school, moving from one activity to another, and appear 'day dreamy'. Children may cling to identified people, even the perpetrator, withdrawing from social situations. Sleep may be affected and there may be eating difficulties, physical health problems, enuresis/encopresis, inappropriate sexual behaviours, psychosomatic symptoms, running away, lying and stealing, and aggression.

The worker needs to develop a comfortable relationship with the child which is conducive to therapy. Underpinning therapy with children should be a fundamental belief system based on the principle that children have rights. So, the worker should:

- support the right of the child to be heard and respected;
- present opportunities for the child to share feelings;
- respect the child's opinions and views;
- accept children for 'who' they are; and
- recognize that the worker is privileged to have the opportunity of entering the child's world, that this privilege should always be negotiated and checked out with the child and that the situation should not be exploited.

The worker also needs to accept that children need rights and power in order to realize a sense of 'self-determination'. The worker needs to be aware of the imbalance in the working relationship: that is, to recognize that the worker has power which is greater than the child's, since that power determines the choice of setting and the choice and nature of intervention. Therefore, the worker needs to recognize power and use it in a positive way which gives power back to the child. Only then can the intervention be based on empowerment. The worker should respect the child's level of ability, offer positive feedback and encouragement at all times and project a feeling of warmth and empathy towards the child.

The venue for therapeutic work should be comfortable and safe for the child. A room which is neither too big nor too small is desirable, with comfortable chairs and sufficient comfortable floor space. The room should be designed for children and not adults. Natural air and light is important. The walls should be colourful and be both stimulating and relaxing. The worker needs to ensure that there will be no interruption during the session and that privacy is ensured. Suitable play materials should be provided to stimulate the child's imagination and aid self-expression. A number of suitable toys should be provided in the playroom or carried to the venue in a toy bag (Bray 1991). Gentle vulnerable objects should be provided as well as frightening or aggressive ones. Many and various items should be included, of interest to children of both sexes over a wide age range and to children of different cultures. Frightening objects may be kept separately and under the child's control.

The importance of planning should not be underestimated or overlooked. Planning needs to incorporate an evaluation of the previous session as well as planning for future sessions. The worker should develop good working relationships with other professionals involved. During liaison with agencies and professionals the worker needs to maintain a sense of loyalty to the child, promoting the child's well-being and challenging attempts to undermine the rights of the child and respect for the child.

Liaison with those with parental responsibility is crucial in successful therapeutic intervention with the child. Partnership with parents or guardians is important and needs to be worked at for the well-being of the child. The worker needs a consultant for support in the work. A key to the planning of the sessions with the child is consistency. A regular time needs to be maintained and the length of time should remain constant, as should the venue and the materials available.

Assessment is fundamental to the planning of the intervention, the methods employed and evaluation of the work. The purpose in undertaking assessment is to guide the intervention (Reder *et al.* 1993). In guiding intervention, the worker goes on a journey of collating information, making sense of information and sharing the information with others in order to make decisions about the nature of intervention. The child should not be excluded from the assessment process and, depending on age and development, should be given the opportunity to speak freely and in confidence to the worker, in the absence of those who may choose to speak on behalf of the child. The parents or substitute parents also need to be involved in the assessment, as do other family members and those who play significant roles in the child's life. The use of genograms (a family tree) as an assessment tool provides the worker with a framework which steers the worker into an awareness of a historical as well as present context. Genograms of the child's lost or abusive family need to be made with sensitivity, as this will be stressful for the child.

The timing of therapeutic intervention with children who have been abused is important. The worker needs to gauge the 'right time' to begin the work on past trauma. To do this the assessment needs to be thorough, concise and accurate. If the worker assesses that the child is not secure, perhaps because of forthcoming court cases, the intervention should be deferred until decisions have been made (Cattanach 1992). However, if the child is safe and secure from abuse, therapy may begin. Cattanach (1992) suggests that intervention should not be ruled out as a way of helping the child cope with court proceedings and could form part of the therapy.

The nature of the work needs to be explained to the child and checked out to ensure that the child has grasped what will happen. Confidentiality issues need to be explained in an effort to begin the delicate process of intervention. It needs to be made clear to the child that, should abuse or the identity of an abuser be disclosed, the worker must inform the relevant professionals with responsibility to protect the child (Cattanach 1992).

A contract may be made with the child so that both the worker and the child understand their roles and the child feels safe (Cattanach 1992). As part of the contract, 'ground rules' are defined and explained to clarify the nature of the intervention. Rules include no hitting, fighting or touching each other. It is particularly important when working with sexually abused children that there is a rule of not touching the private parts of the body (Cattanach 1992). The purpose of meeting should be established at the beginning of each session.

Virginia Axline is a pioneer of the non-directive approach to play. Essentially, this approach is based on the belief that children hold the key to the solution of their problems and have the ability to solve them (McMahon 1992). Within this approach, the child is provided with a wealth of play materials and is free to choose where to begin. The role of the worker is to adopt reflective listening, to recognize the child's feelings and to reflect these back to the child, in order that the child develops an understanding of his or her behaviour (McMahon 1992). The therapy is geared to move at the child's pace and not the worker's. McMahon (1992) suggests that the pace of intervention can be very slow and that this is – or may be – a drawback of the process, as many workers do not have the time to offer it.

Children like to create what they see as their own world by using paper, drawing different shapes, colours, lines, etc. (Oaklander 1988). Children can be asked what their world looks like (Oaklander 1988). It is important that the worker does not try to interpret for the child the meaning of drawings. This would result in the worker imposing his or her own value base on the play. Braithwaite (1986: 16–17) suggests a non-directive role for the worker while the child draws: 'The art is to be non-directive but to "actively listen", confident that the process in itself is sufficiently therapeutic to redress imbalances and provide the impetus for progress.'

USE OF STORIES

Oaklander (1988) suggests that the worker can use stories in different ways. This can involve enabling the child to create a story or perhaps to write his or her own life story, or it can involve the worker telling a story to a child, writing stories or using pictures to stimulate stories. McMahon (1992) suggests that story telling can be useful to help children work through their feelings; older children may prefer fairy stories such as 'Snow White' or 'The Ugly Duckling' while younger children may prefer stories nearer to home, such as *Can't You Sleep, Little Bear?* (Waddell 1988).

If a child is creating a story, it is important that the worker writes down the story as the child is telling it. This will ensure that the story remains as the child told it, without a second interpretation by the adult.

Another way in which stories can be used is as a metaphor reflecting and explaining the child's own life and experiences (Bray 1991). The worker writes an original story which parallels the child's life story. This enables the child to address and understand stressful experiences in an indirect way. This approach is shown in the case of Anita (names and some details have been changed in the interest of confidentiality).

Anita

Anika was the name on the file of the tall thin 8-year-old with big blue eyes, but she was known as Anita. She was a clever girl with an attractive personality, but she was anxious and clingy. Her concentration was poor and she could be demanding and atten-tion-seeking. Her self-esteem was low and she had sexual interests beyond her years. She had been placed for adoption and had been with her proposed adoptive parents for nearly two years when therapeutic work began with her. However, her paternal grandparents were contesting this adoption. They had taken an interest in Anita since her birth and had fostered her themselves in the past on more than one occasion. They had not opposed her adoption until they met the proposed adoptive parents (of whom they did not approve) and saw that there was no role planned for them as grandparents.

Anita's natural father had left when she was a baby. As a toddler she was found to be neglected and bruised and her younger sibling had a burn. A Place of Safety Order was taken in respect of both children, and led to Care Orders. Anita was placed with several foster parents, including her paternal grandparents, before being placed for adoption in her present home at the age of 6. Anita's foster family were anxious about the contact with her grandparents ordered by the court and she was also affected by their stress. It was felt that she should have the opportunity to express her feelings and to have her voice heard in her own way in a child-centred setting.

The genogram had revealed that Anita was very confused about her life story and the structure of her family. For example, she had close paternal relatives who she had thought were maternal and she had siblings of whom she had no knowledge. She had met her father many times without knowing her relationship to him. It was felt that life story book work would need to be done and indeed she was learning new things about her past every day. This was, however, left for later, when her future was settled. It was intended that it would be made in her own home, with her new parents closely involved. The current priority was to allow Anita the time and space to express her present concerns so that she could lead the conversation with the therapist and others, which in turn could assist the court in reaching the right decision.

These sessions, therefore, took place in a non-directive way in a small playroom at the clinic which had an abundance of small toys, a low table and chairs and plenty of drawing materials. Her social worker brought her to and from the sessions and also maintained a close liaison with her foster parents, school and the therapist. At the beginning of each session the social worker and therapist sat with Anita at the little table, having a drink and exchanging news. Anita would often draw and they would share with her their wish to understand what she felt about her life and what she wanted to happen. Anita would then begin to play while one or the other closely attended to her and also reflected back what she was doing and saying. This was in order to show Anita that they were interested in what she was doing and also in trying to understand.

She used dolls' houses and farm and zoo animals to create worlds on the carpet and made it clear that she wanted to remain in her present world with her proposed adoptive parents. She made this clear also in her drawings on a large white board and on paper. Anita used symbols in her communication, a cat to represent herself, an elephant for her natural family and animals or dolls to represent herself and her foster parents lovingly together. Witches were often in her mind. She was obsessed with Roald Dahl's (1983) book called *The Witches* and played the story tape of this over and over. She played it on the car journeys to and from the sessions and during sessions read extracts from the book to the therapist and her social worker. She liked to read them a passage describing the transformation of seemingly kind women into horrible witches. They made comments about the difficulty of trusting people and mentioned that she had been let down many times. These comments were acknowledged with looks and nods by her.

It was in this context that Anita then told an elaborate story using toys from a bag containing toy dinosaurs and snakes, figures of wrestlers, spacemen and witches, and also a plastic toilet which had contained a play material called Slime. There was a Boglin family in the bag with a baby Boglin in its plastic egg and some miscellaneous objects including a plastic dish, a straw and a mirror. Anita arranged these on the floor and moved them about as she made up her story and recounted it out loud. She was pleased to have the therapist write down the story as she told it. An extract is reproduced here. It expresses her feelings about the court battle going on for possession of her.

> Once upon a time in the sewerage drains there lived a daddy and a mummy Boglin. They were expecting an egg to hatch. The monster caught Mummy but she escaped and she ran back and told Daddy. Daddy killed the monster. When he got back the baby had hatched from the egg.
>
> The wicked witch asked the magic mirror how to find their enemies. 'I would like to see what they are doing in their drain. Are they having a baby?' She made a plan with two of the monsters, a snake and a wrestler. She threatened to eat them up if

they did not get the baby's power for her. She taught them how to get the power with a tube and a bowl.

The snake went to the Boglins' home but failed to get the baby's power because the Boglin mummy was minding it and keeping it safe. The mummy stroked the baby Boglin. The witch asked the wrestler to get the baby and offered a lot of money. The wrestler went to the Boglins' home and stole the baby's power. The witch was pleased and gave him ten million trillion rubies. The snake escaped and went to the Boglins' home and gave the baby back its power.

The witch was angry and killed both monsters and got the rubies back.

The daddy Boglin and his friend went to the witch's house and put her in jail. They fixed the mirror wires to make it into a goodies' mirror and they all lived happily ever after.

Anita was pleased to have the story typed from the therapist's jottings and wanted to share it with her proposed adoptive parents. Thus the therapeutic atmosphere enabled Anita to express her feelings and wishes very clearly through the medium of a story which was extremely helpful in making a decision about her adoption. It confirmed her expressed wishes about her adoption which could otherwise have been seen as only reflecting what had been said to her by others. The story she had created was a metaphor expressing her feelings concerning the contest regarding her adoption. It enabled the court to understand her perception. She was therefore adopted and she also shared her delight with her therapist and the social worker.

Now it was time to discontinue the playroom work, and after a break, to begin to facilitate the next phase of the work in her own home with her parents in order to help her create a life story book.

Her two names (Anika and Anita) symbolized her dual heritage which it was important to acknowledge and sustain. Her parents had initially thought that she would have a new identity on adoption and that her past could be forgotten. During the two years she was with them they came to understand the issues and to favour an open adoption. They had a good relationship with Anita's mother, and after the adoption bridges were built with her paternal grandparents, who were able to continue in the role of grandparents. It was likely that later she might meet her natural father, sister and brother. For these reasons it was considered necessary for her to know and come to terms with all aspects of her own life history and of the history of both her natural and adoptive families in developing an integrated identity as she grew up.

The therapist made up a story for Anita which was a metaphor of the beginning of her life story. It is very difficult to explain to a child how he or she came to be in local authority care. The therapist thought that the story might give Anita some understanding of the therapist's perception of this, in the same way that her story had given the therapist some understanding of her own perception of the court battle.

The first part of the story was received so well by Anita that the therapist wrote further episodes to give to her each time the therapist and the social worker visited her. The work on her life story book was being undertaken by her parents and her social worker and was not limited to the therapist's visits to the home. Photographs were collected into an album, scrapbooks were made beginning with her present situation and experience. Visits were also made to relatives of natural, adoptive and various foster families. The story made up by the therapist for Anita was as follows:

The pedlar man and his wife found a baby under a gooseberry bush in a lane. 'You will be our Gypsy Princess,' they said. The Gypsy Princess travelled the world. When the Gypsy Princess grew up she met a handsome prince and fell in love. Goblins already plotted to spoil their happiness. They had poisoned sweets to sell. The Gypsy Princess married Prince Charming and they had a baby girl. They called her Beauty. The King and Queen came to see Beauty and brought presents for her.

Prince Charming lived with baby Beauty in a cottage. They were very happy and the Gypsy Princess sang to baby Beauty all day long.

Mr Big is the rich goblin who organizes the business of selling poisoned sweets. Once the sweets are tasted people want more and more of them, however much they cost to buy and however badly they make them behave. This makes Mr Big very rich. The Gypsy Princess and Prince Charming ate the poisoned sweets. They tasted wonderful but they made them quarrel. Prince Charming went away with some wandering musicians. The Gypsy Princess was very lonely and sad. She became very poor.

Prince Charming married another young woman. They had a baby called Merriment. He ate more poisoned sweets, quarrelled again and left them too.

The Gypsy Princess left Beauty with other people while she went out to beg for money for more poisoned sweets. All the Gypsy Princess's friends ate poisoned sweets. She married another man and they had another baby girl. They called her Treasure.

Beauty and Treasure lived in a house where people behaved very badly. Both children were hurt and Treasure was burnt by a hot sausage.

The Fairy Godmother rescued the little girls and took them to a place of safety. Beauty and Treasure lived with a woman who lived in a shoe for a little while. Then Beauty and Treasure went to live in a far-off kingdom with the King and Queen, who were Prince Charming's mother and father. Prince Charming returned to the far-off kingdom and helped to look after the little girls for a while before he went away again to seek poisoned sweets.

The Fairy Godmother arranged for the fairies to take Treasure to a new mummy and daddy. Beauty wanted to live with her mummy, the Gypsy Princess. So the Fairy Godmother arranged for her to live again with the woman who lived in a shoe while she waited for her mummy to stop eating the poisoned sweets and to get better.

Beauty went to live with her mummy but she began to eat poisoned sweets again. She neglected Beauty and Beauty was hurt. The Fairy Godmother took Beauty to live in the house that was a shoe again, but the Gypsy Princess wanted her. She took Beauty and ran away with her. The Fairy Godmother was worried. When Beauty was found she took her to live again in the far-off kingdom with her Granny and Grandpa, the King and Queen.

Beauty missed her mummy. Sometimes she felt left out when her young aunt and uncle, Princess Graceful and Prince Brave, were playing together. Sometimes she was cross.

The Queen was too busy ruling her vast kingdom to look after her properly. The Fairy Godmother arranged for Beauty to leave the palace and she began to look for a new mummy and daddy for her. Beauty waited again in houses that were shoes.

Beauty met Mr and Mrs Good who were to be her new mummy and daddy. 'You will live with us for ever and ever,' said Mr and Mrs Good. Beauty went to live with Mr and Mrs Good. She chose a new name – 'Prittie Ann Good'.

She saw her mummy, the Gypsy Princess, sometimes. She visited the King and Queen in the far-off kingdom sometimes.

Prittie was happy in her new home. She had lots of friends and relations and she was happy at school. She missed little Treasure and she did not even know that she had a sister called Merriment. She also had a new little brother because Prince Charming had married again.

The Queen said that she was no longer so busy ruling her kingdom and she would like to have Beauty back at the palace and bring her up as a princess. 'It is too late,' said the Fairy Godmother. 'Prittie wants to live happily ever after with Mr and Mrs Good.'

This made the King and Queen very upset. 'She is a princess and our grandchild and she must be brought up in the palace.' So they all decided to go to ask the Wizard what was the best for the little girl.

The Wizard had wise old women to help him to find out all about it. The King and Queen and Mr and Mrs Good had elves and fairies to help them to tell the Wizard what they thought was best.

Prittie talked to the wise old women who were helping the Wizard. 'Tell him I want to stay with my new mummy and daddy. Tell my Gypsy Princess mummy that I love her and will never forget her.' So they all went to the top of the mountain to see the Wizard. The Wizard decided. Prittie was adopted by Mr and Mrs Good.

Prittie was very happy. She sang and she danced. The Fairy Godmother danced. Prittie said, 'Thank you' to everyone who had helped her. Mr and Mrs Good planned a party. Prittie was sitting by the fire cuddling her cat one day and she said to her mummy, Mrs Good, 'For a happy ending I should have become a princess.' But then she added thoughtfully, 'There are more important things than being rich and living in a palace.'

'You are a princess to us,' said Mrs Good. 'You are our beautiful princess. We are your mummy and daddy and we love you very much.'

Anita was delighted with the story written for her. It was illustrated profusely with pictures taken from a nursery rhyme book. She kept the story by her and read it over and over again to her parents and to her social worker and asked them to read it to her. Roald Dahl's book *The Witches* was no longer read. The new story may have helped to change Anita's perception of her natural grandmother, who was transformed from a witch to a queen. As the story unfolded Anita made comments and asked questions to indicate that she understood that the story paralleled her own life: for example, 'I thought he took one look at me and left' – a reference to her father leaving when she was a baby; 'So it was all the Goblins' fault'; 'That's like me visiting Granny and Grandpa.' She identified strongly with Beauty, missing her mother and feeling left out and cross when she was at the palace the second time. She asked questions about her own life which were stimulated by the story.

When the story was finished it was clear that the therapist's task was done. The therapeutic work undertaken by her parents would continue over the years to come as Anita gained in knowledge and understanding. Her social worker would be available for some time to provide information and support in the making of a book of her life story. Anita's behaviour had improved during the period of the play sessions directed by her, in spite of the stress and insecurity leading up to the adoption hearing. This may have been because she had an appropriate way to express her feelings and to be heard. There was a dramatic improvement in her demeanour after she was adopted. She was more relaxed, better behaved and she gained in weight.

CONCLUSION

Stories made up by a child while drawing, painting, playing imaginative games or playing with small toys and objects can be therapeutic to the child and allow them to communicate their feelings, perceptions and wishes. A worker can use imaginative metaphorical stories, both old and new and sometimes original, to communicate difficult information 'one step removed'. They can be used to change a child's perception and understanding of past events as well as to prepare the child for events to come, such as a court hearing or a move to another care giver.

The preceding examples in the case of Anika/Anita demonstrate that stories greatly increase our power to help children who have been abused.

REFERENCES

We are very grateful to Anita and her family for their kind permission to use their case in this chapter.

Braithwaite, C. (1986) 'Art always reveals truth . . . ', *Community Care* 622 (31 July): 15–17.

Bray, M. (1991) *Poppies on the Rubbish Heap – Sexual Abuse: The Child's Voice*, Edinburgh: Canongate Press.

Cattanach, A. (1992) *Play Therapy with Abused Children*, London: Jessica Kingsley.

——(1994) *Play Therapy Where the Sky Meets the Underworld*, London: Jessica Kingsley.

Dahl, R. (1983) *The Witches*, London: Jonathan Cape.

Dwivedi, K.N. (ed.) (1993) *Groupwork with Children and Adolescents. A Handbook*, London: Jessica Kingsley.

Finkelhor, D. (1984) *Child Sexual Abuse – New Theory and Research*, New York: Free Press.

McMahon L. (1992) *The Handbook of Play Therapy*, London: Routledge.

Oaklander, V. (1988) *Windows to our Children*, New York: Gestalt Press.

Reder, P., Duncan, S., and Gray, M. (1993) *Beyond Blame – Child Abuse Tragedies Revisited*, London: Routledge.

Waddell, M. (1988) *Can't You Sleep, Little Bear?*, London: Walker Books.

Chapter 13

Stories for children with disabilities

Ruchira Leisten

INTRODUCTION

This chapter is for ordinary people who care for children with disabilities. It is intended to encourage people to develop a strategy for story telling for their particular child. It is not prescriptive because it is not possible to be specific about approaches that are suited to all people. Everybody is different, and the existence of disability in society increases that diversity. However, it does seek to help the carer prepare a thoughtful and informed strategy of story telling that is beneficial to the particular child. Story telling is an art, an act of creativity, which relies on the talent of the story teller. To make this chapter applicable to children with all types of disabilities, we rely on the ability of the reader to be imaginative and develop appropriate story-telling practices and to elicit story making practices from the general methods we identify. The important point for the reader to grasp is the therapeutic nature of stories. If this chapter serves to help focus the wit and charm of the story teller to enhance and develop the life of the child with a disability, then it has served its purpose admirably.

The birth of a child with a disability presents to parents and carers many challenges of adaptation, acceptance, management, accommodation and fulfilment. The emotional needs of all concerned can be most fully satisfied if these challenges can be met positively and the life of the child with the disability be made as rich as is possible. There are many aspects of story telling which can enhance these prospects, and to understand these we must first look at the emotional and physical needs of the disabled child.

PSYCHOLOGY OF DISABILITY

As the baby with a disability develops conscious thinking, it begins to experience frustration at not being able to achieve certain goals. The essential difference between the 'normal' developing child and the development of a child with a disability concerns the comparative extent and duration of these feelings of frustration and anger. The 'normal' developing child will, in time, experience the thrills of accomplishment. However, in respect of activities which are impaired by the disability, the child with a disability will often experience lingering and heightened feelings of frustration and rage. This frustration often manifests itself in tantrums or forms of attention-seeking behaviour which are common in all children who lack the ability to express themselves or do the things that they can imagine. It is important for the carers of such children to be sensitive to this quite understandable emotional problem and to try and compensate for it.

An adult person experiencing the sudden onset of disability has the task of understanding and accepting their disability before a stable level of life fulfilment can be attained. However, the developing child with a disability needs to come to terms with the disability with only partial understanding of life itself and their role in the world. The understanding and support that the child needs to meet these challenges without frustration can be given by parents or carers using the medium of story telling. Various strategies for using story telling as a method of communication that is considered interesting and understood by the child have been developed. These strategies will be examined in the context of the therapeutic purpose that they serve.

IMPORTANCE OF STORIES

As the child with a disability develops into a social human being with an interest in friendship and group play there is a possibility that feelings of loneliness or isolation will occur. Worse, the child may actually experience social rejection and may require a compensatory relationship with carers which is more intense than normal. Story telling can fulfil this need by providing a warm and loving form of contact with a child in which communication occurs through both the content of the story and the rapport between the story teller and the child. It creates a much needed sense of belonging and self-worth for the child and is also an opportunity to secure empathy between the story teller and the child. This is the first, the most basic and probably most important benefit of story telling.

Story telling as a therapy addressing many of the developing child's needs is a comparatively recent extension of play therapy which has been used for decades. In fact, according to Millar (1968), psychoanalytic explanations of the use of play as a technique to be used 'with disturbed children' was an element in Sigmund Freud's development of psychoanalysis. In the 1920s Sigmund Freud made fleeting references to play but it was not until later that play was recognized as a therapeutic tool. Influential workers included A. Freud (1946), Klein (1955) and Isaacs (1946). Their presumption was based on the observation that the amount of play is generally seen to decrease as the child becomes more competent at coping with the world.

In her book *The Psychology of Play* Millar (1968: 25) describes the therapeutic action of play: 'The child distinguishes play from reality, but uses objects and situations from the real world to create a world of his own in which he can repeat . . . order and alter . . . events. In play this is possible.'

As psychoanalysis grew as a subject, so did the application of psychoanalytic thinking to child psychology, particularly in the quest for ideas on how to help more demanding or less able children. This thinking led to the development of play and story telling as educational therapeutic tools. If the opportunity to play is impaired by disability then the developmental function of play has to be provided by other means, such as story telling.

Psychologists studying play in the early years tended to classify play descriptively (Buhler 1935). An important step was made by Jean Piaget (1951) when he began to examine play in terms of child development (particularly intellectual). Piaget postulated that development was passed in the twin processes of assimilation (processing information and building up a knowledge base) and accommodation (adjusting to external influences in order to make sense of the assimilated information). These twin processes were considered by Piaget to lead to intellectual development through a continued and active interplay between assimilation and accommodation. Obviously play and story telling are sources of learning and experience which promote this development process. In children with disabilities, story telling or story making can compensate for the reduced ability to play, despite its seemingly non-active status.

Buhler (1935) has classified the listening to or telling of stories as 'passive play'. It is an extension of pretend play which is crucial in social and cognitive development. These forms of play act directly to increase concentration span and ability to communicate while also enhancing the development of the child's reasoning, ordering and social awareness. In fact it may be sensible to respectfully disagree with Buhler's characterization. Stories are far from 'passive' but are active without the physical exertion. They are at least as psychologically stimulating as pretend play. Story telling as a therapy is seen to serve an educational/developmental purpose which is utilised by the story teller proactively.

STORY TELLING AS THERAPY IN ACTION

The important thing that concerns us in this chapter is the nature and purpose of story telling, particularly in the context of children with a disability. These are areas of psychology which do not enjoy the conventionally held level of scientific proof. The reader is therefore invited to evaluate the argument more on its 'applied relevance' than authority. There is a lot of experience, in fact, and much of it is very well founded and wise.

There is nothing new about story telling as a means of communicating about the world to young people in a manner that they find interesting. Bornstein (1988) has pointed out that what the tribal elders were trying to do with their story telling was essentially developmental in that:

> The history of the tribe, descriptions of the world and how things work, and stories about tribal heroes and their adventures were included in story-telling sessions around the camp fire. When young people asked questions about life and its meaning, the tribal elders often answered with a story.
>
> (Bornstein 1988: 102–3)

The child was learning wisdom, cultural conventions, a sense of right and wrong and a sense of belonging or tribal identity. For example, in the story *Grandma's Bill* (Waddell 1990), Bill and Grandma look at photographs of the past and the present, and discover the reassuring sense of continuity and security they bring. Perhaps after this story the carer and the child can go through their family pictures. It is important to recognize that modern society has developed story telling away from these profound and valuable

objectives to those that are often of a more immediate and essentially entertainment-oriented character. Children with disabilities
require some compensatory development assistance, with respect to
unimpaired children, and therefore it is sensible to recommend that
the human wisdom stories have greater benefit than those which are
excessively 'technological', such as Sonic the Hedgehog.

Children entering the world with disabilities will generally need
to develop coping strategies to deal with the 'injustice' of their
disabilities. Stories with a moral tone or fables can help to install a
compensatory sense of fairness in the child's thinking. Such stories
are often fairy stories and have a structural simplicity that is
portrayed to the stark relationship between good and evil. The
wicked witch or the evil step-mother contrasts absolutely with the
innocent child. The 'good' character is anticipated by the child to
win the struggle in a most pleasing way, so that the bad character
holds no fear or respect in the eyes of the child. The triumph of
good over evil and the selfless moral behaviour of the heroes and
heroines are messages which build a faith in justice.

In the fairy story of Beauty and the Beast (Southgate 1968), the
beast has to suffer the indignity of looking repulsive before he wins
the perfect princess's love. Similarly in the tale of the Sleeping
Beauty (Southgate 1965), Beauty has to stay asleep until she is
kissed by a handsome suitor. The child identifies in both these
stories with the fair outcomes and also with the sufferings of the
'good' main characters. Perhaps the sympathy the child feels for the
good selfless main character is heightened by the disability, and
consequently the pleasure associated with the 'happy ever after'
ending is magnified. In the case of the child with a disability there
may also be subliminal connections between the disability and the
'bad' main character. If this latter association exists then the
triumphant message of good fairy stories may signify the release of
hope in the child. In the story of the Ugly Duckling (Bradbury
1979), it is possible that the child may identify with the isolation
experienced by the Ugly Duckling prior to becoming a swan.

Bornstein (1988) has many interesting things to say about fairy
tales. She points out that fairy tales connect with the unconscious
mind, a theme that is important to psychotherapists, and describes
the action of fairy tales:

> The language and imagery of fairy tales create a dream-like
> atmosphere, where ordinary concerns of rationality and logic do

not apply, and important messages are conveyed through symbolism. When people listen to these stories they willingly suspend disbelief, as they would in nocturnal dreaming or day-dream activities; strange coincidences, morphologic transformations, and other magical phenomena are accepted as normal events. Symbolism is the language of the unconscious mind, imagery is more emotionally evocative than language-based thought. Thus people are drawn into the stories and become emotionally and mentally engaged very rapidly.

(Bornstein 1988: 107–8)

Bornstein adds that:

Fairy tales make use of the same day-dreaming process that most children and adults use to cope with psychological pressures, and because the stories are entertaining, the messages embedded in characters and plot are accepted by the listener without resistance.

(ibid.: 112)

This insight into the action of fairy tales or simply fantastic stories is helpful when we consider how children with disabilities may be feeling.

To progress a relationship with a child with a disability using the medium of shared story experiences it is necessary to start with stories that vividly capture attention. It may be sensible to use a character that is already known to the child, but in a plot that is more interesting than the context of the character that is known to the child. An example of this is Trivizas and Oxenbury's (1993) delightfully funny book *Three Little Wolves and the Big Bad Pig*, which is a reversal of the traditional tale, with a different ending. Alternatively, it might be effective to challenge the child's knowledge of the story that conventionally uses the character in question with a modified story. For example, it might be more captivating to tell a version of the Little Red Riding Hood story (Southgate 1988) in which the wood-cutter and the grandmother are just finishing eating the wolf when Red Riding Hood comes with even more food! The laugh, giggle or even reluctant smile will signify approval – we have built a fairy-tale pathway to the unconscious mind. Of course, if the child does not notice the change to this well-known story, then it is necessary for the story teller to search for stories which are more familiar and accessible to the child.

Before using the more sophisticated medium of stories with a degree of realism, it is wise to build up a solid experience of sharing stories. These are not demanding of the child's conscious mind and are aiming to build a relationship in stories which can develop through trust and curiosity to other media. This process permits a slow development of themes which are therapeutic to the child's particular needs. At all stages a sensitive consideration of the child's needs and the nature and severity of disability should ensure that appropriate progress is made.

Story telling and the child's telling of stories do not have to be based on story books alone. Video recorders, tapes and children's television programmes provide excellent sources of therapeutic story telling, with the advantage that these media can animate familiar characters to develop a uniquely vivid character identity in the mind of the child. In developmental significance the visual media can probably only be surpassed by the skilful use of story telling between carer and child as a means of communication. For example, in the Thomas the Tank Engine videos (Allcroft 1991) all the trains have strengths, weaknesses and often playful personalities. While watching this type of video a carer can emphasize that despite the child's disability or weakness the child still has areas of strength. The story teller has the opportunity to modify the story/video to enhance or heighten aspects of the story which are meaningful to the child.

THE ROLE OF CARERS

Of course, a well-founded strategy for story telling for children with a disability has to be absolutely child-centred. There is no point in telling stories which do not interest the child or which they cannot grasp. It is a good practice to involve the child in story invention and to invite frequent feedback and comment from the child. This can be a demanding task. Young children usually have short attention spans and the trick is to capture the child's imagination and to hold it until the story is told and the point of the story is grasped.

There are some matters of importance with regard to the special relationship that exists between the story-telling carer and the child with a disability. It is a primary purpose of the carer to fulfil the emotional needs of the child, because when that is done all the secondary benefits of learning, rapport and contentment ensue. A child with greater emotional needs is more likely to desire the form of intense attention of the story-telling experience. The corollary of this is that such a child is also more motivated to hold concentration for (in infant terms) sophisticated stories. This second point really distinguishes children who almost always yearn for attention from those whom, we might say, as a result of their disability have a special need for it. Of course, each child is different and the story teller should experiment with the extent to which the individual child can be invited to contribute, by comments or drawing pictures or simply pointing to pictures. Always involve the child to the maximum extent that is possible.

Let's go back to the beginning again. A young child is trying to make sense of the world that it finds itself in and with which it is gaining familiarity. Because the child's knowledge of its environment is incomplete, it cannot vividly imagine how to react to circumstances. In this context story telling can be viewed as a problem-solving tool.

This is a particularly important theme in the case of children with disabilities, because the ability of a human being to solve problems reflects their capability in society. Stories which impart solutions, told to young children, help engender a problem-solving mind that is more able to cope with disability and more likely to achieve success and fulfilment. The book *Seal Surfer* (Foreman 1996) is an imaginative story about the friendship that is created between a disabled boy and a baby seal.

The longer-term benefit that story telling can give the child with a disability should influence the story teller not only in terms of choice of story but also the strategy for story telling. In addition to the purposes of developing a special rapport and a helpful sense of identity the story teller should attempt to weave in themes of emancipation and of elegant solutions. The more vividly a child can derive from the stories the answers to the many questions, the more quickly the child can develop a problem-solving confidence. The importance of this cannot be overemphasized because the foundations of experience installed at childhood determine the character of a person in later life in certain ways. The level to which things are held in awe and avoided or feared by adult people is associated with their confidence at problem-solving. People with disabilities generally have impairments which adversely affect certain capabilities and it is this disadvantage that the story teller can equip the child to overcome.

Of course, stories project the issues of 'who am I?' and 'what can

I do?' into the form of characters (animals, humans, inanimate objects like cars) that represent the child and significant issues in the child's life. Excessive reality tends to confuse the child because it raises too many questions that the child finds frightening or difficult to understand. In a sense a degree of abstraction or unreality is reassuring to the child, because it does not raise conflicts of experience and anxiety in the mind of the child. This enables the story to be formulated in a way which holds the child's interest and conveys simple messages that are valuable to the child in fantasy and in reality.

Before addressing the sensitive issues concerning childhood disability and its influence or incorporation into stories, it is helpful to attempt a short summary of the argument that has been presented so far. All people have a certain fear of the unknown and for a child, with limited knowledge, there is much confusion and awe in their experience of the world. Stories for children use characters or plots sufficiently removed from reality to project messages which help to order the thinking of the child and impart information that clears confusion and solves problems in the child's experience. These stories enhance development and the self-identity of the child and help to create a confidence in imaginative thinking. All of these benefits are general and available to all children, including those without disabilities, and it is the role of the carer to use stories to benefit the child.

STORY TELLING AND STRATEGIES OF PRESENTING DISABILITIES

We must now face the difficult question of whether the medium of story telling should be used as a tool to hasten the development in the mind of the child of the nature and ramifications of its disability. There is the obvious risk that the knowledge of such adversity will knock the child back in its development. Yet if we keep faith with the generally true statement that knowledge can help overcome fear, we see that the child can benefit from such disclosures. The difficulty of this question cannot be overlooked or trivialized because it is no less stark than the decision of Balloo the Bear (in Kipling's *Jungle Book*) to tell Mowgli that he cannot, after all, consider himself to be a bear and must actually go to the man-village. There is a risk of rejection of the rapport that the story teller enjoys and recognizes if the content of the story develops emotional pain in the child. However, young children are more resilient than adults and a caring sensitive approach to disclosures can help the child adapt to the knowledge of its disability and surpass the learning by developing some indifference to it.

A sensible way to approach the question of disclosure is to invert the process of the story telling in the fashion of Richard A. Gardner (1971) or Brooks (1993). Gardner has published much on a technique that he calls mutual story telling, which he has established as a psychotherapeutic tool. A similar method which seems to require a less brilliant level of intellectual ability from the child is advocated by Brooks. Gardner prompts the child to tell a story which he analyses and then re-tells in a more sophisticated and psychologically reassuring way. Brooks requires a lower level of involvement in his approach, in which he invents a therapeutic story based on a character that is named by the child but whose nature is intended to address the psychological need of the child. To a degree that is possible within the inventive skill range of the child, these methods invite the child to use story telling, or simple character naming, as a way of communicating their feelings, worries or understanding to the therapist or carer. One of the case studies used to illustrate the 'creative characters' technique is that of a 7-year-old girl who has an attention-span problem. Over many sessions of therapy 'Hyper' the dog was invented to take the little girl's place. Hyper had the same problems as the girl and was helped by Dr Bark (the therapist) to learn to concentrate. The impact of creating the story not only improved the girl's attention span but also increased her sense of pride and self-esteem.

It should be admitted that Gardner and Brooks are skilled therapists who utilize clever techniques very effectively. However, their methods are worth considering in the context of children with disabilities because they focus the mind of the carer on what the child is thinking.

Just as the story teller uses allegory to make a story seem unthreatening to the child, so the child, (who may have difficulty rationalizing feelings of pain or anguish) may also communicate these worries in story form if encouraged to employ metaphor. The stories may be confused or unstructured, but more than likely the psychological meaning will be blunt and direct. The carer and child can discuss the story to clarify the psychological meaning of the story if necessary, but great care should be exercised to ensure that the abstraction is retained. The wisdom that the carer may be able to impart to the child can then be communicated in the form of a more sophisticated version of the child's story, with a wise message woven into it. This is the method of mutual story telling that is proposed by Gardner. The important things here are that it is the child who is able to pull the experience of the story and its message back into its conscious life at its leisure. Also, the worries that occur to the child are being addressed, not the worries of the caring adult, which ought not to add to the child's burden of anxiety.

Back again to the matter of disclosure – we are now equipped with a better answer to these questions. Our approach should not be intrusive. These stories should only address the issues that occur to the child with the disability. Children are very direct in their appraisal of problems because, relative to adults, they lack ability to perform deductive reasoning and will therefore often relate exactly what is troubling them. For example, a paraplegic child's story may reflect an inner fear of steps and specifically a step between the back garden and patio of the child's home. For the optimum therapeutic benefit, the story teller should address only the solution of problems that are occurring to the child.

Telling stories containing a specific message to children is a task requiring a great deal of creativity. It is worth while striving for a unity in this creative pursuit between the story teller and child. Both partners are engaged in an intellectual exercise, both tuned consciously to the communication of constructive fantasy. This has to be an act of play and not condescension on the part of the story-telling carer. Jump, laugh and cry – whatever it takes to make fun. The more appealingly the story is presented, the more memorable it will be and the greater its impact.

Stories can help to give children with disabilities certain coping skills which will be of great benefit to them throughout life. Escapist stories with warm and fantastic themes, in which the story creates an empathy between the child and the adventuring main character, are especially good in this regard. A good example of this sort of story is *Penguin Small* by Mick Inkpen (1992). Penguin Small feels ostracized by his society on account of his small size and fear of water. However, Penguin Small is involved in a series of adventures which get more and more fantastic until he learns to fly and returns to the colony making a spectacular flying display. This is a well-told and beautifully illustrated story of fantastic liberation from insecurity. The child who has enjoyed the story has encountered hope, happiness and perhaps temporary relief from insecurity that may be heightened by the disability.

CONCLUSION

In all children a balance has to be struck between the reassuring themes of the favourite books and stories and the stimulating experience of new stories. The child with a disability may benefit from a little more diversity. Stories may well be acting rather more as a 'prop' for a child with a disability than they may for an able-bodied child. Alternatively, the child may well be diverting energy that it cannot perhaps direct towards physical pursuits towards intellectual and fantasizing activities. Whether the child possesses a physical or a learning disability, it is likely to have a more thoughtful interest in stories than children of similar intellectual ability without disability. A wide variety of stories of good quality can provide a strong development stimulus to give strengths in imagination and thinking of which the child can ultimately be proud. The effort needed to mount this story-telling campaign can be rewarding to the carer because it creates a unique bond with the child. This can help to present a positive aspect to the disability which makes it easier to bear for both child and carer alike. The effort gives the child a confidence in its vivid imagination and the carer a fulfilling relationship without the negative feelings of failure, which can arise in both the child and the carer who are striving to 'achieve' normal things.

The most magical thing about stories is that they serve to remind us that the human spirit rises above adversity in ways equal to the most fantastic of them. People can adapt to all manner of circumstances and overcome all forms of obstacles through the power of their minds. Build the mind and the character of the child with the disability and the child will gain abilities and fulfilment. Let the stories lay the foundations for a life that is wonderful, miraculous and inspirational. Above all, have fun.

REFERENCES

Allcroft, B. (1991) *Thomas the Tank Engine and Friends* based on the Railway Series by the Revd W. Awdry, Watford: Britt Allcroft (Thomas) Ltd.

Bornstein, E.M. (1988) 'Therapeutic storytelling', in Rothlyn P. Zatiourek (ed.) *Relaxation and Imaginary Tools for Therapeutic Communication and Intervention*, London: W.B. Saunders, 101–18.

Bradbury, L. (1979) *The Ugly Duckling* from the Well-Loved Tales series, Loughborough: Ladybird Books.

Brooks, R. (1993) 'Creative characters', in Charles E. Schaefer and Donna M. Cangelosi (eds) *Play Therapy Techniques*, Northvale, NJ: Jason Aronson, 211–23.

Buhler, C. (1935) *From Birth to Maturity: An Outline of the Psychological Development of the Child*, London: Kegan Paul.

Foreman, M. (1996) *Seal Surfer*, London: Anderson Press.

Freud, A. (1946) *The Psychoanalytical Treatment of Children*, London: Hogarth.

Gardner, R.A. (1971) *Therapeutic Communication with Children: The Mutual Storytelling Technique*, Northvale, NJ: Jason Aronson.

Inkpen, M. (1992) *Penguin Small*, London: Hodder and Stoughton.

Isaacs, S. (1946) *Social Development in Young Children: A Study of Beginnings*, London: Routledge.

Klein, M. (1955) 'The psychoanalytic play-technique', *American Journal of Orthopsychiatry* 25: 223–37.

Millar, S. (1968) *The Psychology of Play*, Harmondsworth: Penguin.

Piaget, J. (1951) *Play, Dreams and Imitation in Childhood*, London: Heinemann.

Southgate, V. (1965) *Sleeping Beauty* from the Well-Loved Tales series, Loughborough: Ladybird Books.

——(1968) *Beauty and the Beast* from the Well-Loved Tales series, Loughborough: Ladybird Books.

——(1988) *Little Red Riding Hood* from the Well-Loved Tales series, Loughborough: Ladybird Books.

Trivizas, E., and Oxenbury, H. (1993) *Three Little Wolves and the Big Bad Pig*, London: Heinemann Young.

Waddell, M. (1990) *Grandma's Bill*, London: McDonald Young.

Chapter 14

New perspectives
Stories and life stories in therapy with older adults

Damian Gardner

OPENING COMMENTS

This chapter is concerned with the value attached to the lives of older people. Running throughout is a concern to legitimize the spending of time on listening to their life stories, and of listening to them being told as far as possible in the words and style of the teller. The 'therapeutic format' (i.e. the who, where, when, what and how long of therapy) can be variable – from one conversation at a hospital bedside through to twenty or more sessions over weeks and months or longer. The approach described is 'metatheoretical' and can therefore be integrated with a range of therapeutic orientations. It is anticipated that many readers may be familiar with the *substance* of life story work but perhaps not have conceptualized their practice in metatheoretical terms. Pseudonyms are used throughout for clients' names. The terms 'older people/adults' and 'people in late life' are used interchangeably and can be interpreted flexibly as applying to people in their sixties or seventies and older. Furthermore, there is no reason why the approach may not be used at other stages of the lifespan – particularly at points of development and transition. Readers interested in applying the ideas in this chapter to older adults with significant cognitive impairment are referred to Cheston's (1997) work on story and metaphor with people with dementia and to selected references from the bibliographies produced by Richardson (1995) on psychotherapy with people with dementia and Bender (1995) on reminiscence.

Why life stories and older adults?

Many psychotherapeutic approaches are formulated, more or less explicitly, around a narrative model: that is to say, our lives can be seen as lived stories and the processes of psychological therapy as involving the telling, retelling, editing and exchanging of those stories.

It is no accident that therapists of differing models or orientation working with older adults have highlighted the significance of life stories (e.g. Viney 1993, Garland 1994, Hildebrand 1995). There are a variety of reasons for doing this. Most central is the truism that if life is 'lived narrative' (MacIntyre 1985) then people in late life are nearing the final chapters of their story. And while much can happen in the closing chapters, the simple knowledge of an approaching ending carries an urgency, finality and weight of its own. The pressure to find coherence and completion to a life story, while there is still time to do so, urges a recognition of narrative processes in therapeutic encounters with older people.

Associated with this pressure is the escalation in the number of adverse life events that comes with late life (Murphy 1982) and possible changes in the family constellation (Herr and Weakland 1979). Bereavement, physical illness, loss of the freedom to drive, etc., often lead people to take stock of their situation and integrate their current life circumstances with their sense of self. These experiences may occur against a background of economic deprivation and social isolation.

The losses of old age bring with them opportunities for change, growth and the achievement of an integrity of identity (Erikson 1951; Hildebrand 1995). Nevertheless, life events for older adults often initially have an adverse impact. The individual may feel overwhelmed – unable to weave a coherent account of what has happened and thus unable to make sense of their life and move forward. Alternatively, the event may be experienced as confirming culturally held negative stories of ageing (Viney 1993: chs 5–7) and leave the person anxious or depressed. For yet others, life events activate powerful constellations of thoughts, sensations and emotions which may constitute quite severe disorder in individuals who have led well-adjusted lives for many decades but experienced significant abuse or neglect early in their life. For these people the 'why' questions of therapy (why me? why now?) can be pressing and may involve revisiting and making new sense of the opening chapters of their story.

There will often be successful adaptations to loss without dislocations or loss of coherence to a life story. Therapists most frequently hear the negative stories, the stories that close down possibility or the stories that are heading for tragic endings (Berne 1972; Steiner 1974). It is important, therefore, to retain a perspective that sees loss and development as two sides of the same coin – the 'negative' experiences of old age as also being opportunities for integration and growth.

Where there are changes in family constellation late in life there may be systemic problems in the family which lie behind the referral for psychological treatment. Invariably, working with such families necessitates a telling of the story of what has happened from the differing perspectives of the family members. This can then lead into an exploration of family-held stories which may be affecting the current problem. These may be linked with ageing, mental illness or death or be more concerned with other family members or relationships generally. Families and individuals may also spontaneously outline a history of the family – or of its name – tracing their origin back several generations. Such narratives often carry both geographical and historical elements of a 'plot' (Brooks 1984) linked via the relationships and movements of family members down the generations. The telling of conflicting stories or of stories which have 'lost the plot' can form the first steps in a search for a 'better story' (Pocock 1995).

The *process* of story telling provides further justification for a narrative approach to psychotherapy with people in late life. The role of story teller confers a valued status to older people in many cultures. The association is with wisdom and being the bearer of cultural history. The modern Western world has downgraded these attributes of society's elders and conversely values the attributes of youth (Jacobs 1993). In the context of psychotherapeutic encounters and mental health services these societal prejudices can be exacerbated by imbalances of power and the use of alien languages (Masson 1990; Amundson *et al.* 1993). Listening to a person's story and stories is in itself affirming of their experience and status.

HEARING THE STORY

The stories heard by therapists will be understood in terms of the therapist's own stories. The degree to which these stories are accommodating of others' experience will influence the subtle and not so subtle ways that the therapist prompts, edits and validates the client's story. Thus therapists need to be sensitive to their own stories and the ways these may affect their clients' freedom to find their own voice.

Therapists' stories operate at various levels. There are their own stories which may contain similar or differing experiences to their clients' and, at the very least, are likely to be grounded in a more recent historical context. The importance of being aware of personal stories and the ways these may work for or against the client's interests is well understood in psychotherapy. It may, however, help therapists to look again at their life stories and the way the telling of these is affected by one's current life context. Paradoxically, the starting point for autobiography is the present and the frame of reference it supplies (Freeman 1993). By beginning with a problem, dilemma, diagnosis or pathology there is an inherent danger of forcing a retrospective evaluation of a life constructed in terms of vulnerability, weakness and failure. If therapists are sensitive to the way their retrospective evaluation may be influenced by their current life situation they will be more likely to help clients 'free up' their own perspectives on their pasts.

In addition to their personal story, therapists' own stories about therapy, healing and mental dis-order and dis-ease may impose readings or meanings on a client – leading either to breakdowns in communication or to uneasy hybrid accounts of autobiography and 'psychologese'. Of course, therapists can help clients reconstruct their narratives by drawing on established therapeutic orientations. such as cognitive therapy (Gonccalves 1994). Caution is needed over whether these meanings are being truly co-authored or – as is easily done – the search for a satisfying and theoretically coherent account for the therapist is pursued at the expense of truly listening to the story being told.

A third set of stories for the therapist to consider concerns stories of ageing. In her book *Life Stories: Personal Construct Therapy with the Elderly* Viney (1993) identifies three common 'self limiting' stories of ageing: life being worthless, anxiety about the future and fear of being a burden. These are contrasted with positive stories of enhanced freedom and deepening relationships. In an ageist society it is not always easy to hold on to realistic but hopeful stories of ageing, especially if the therapist's contact with older people is confined to clients referred for help with their problems (Genevay and Katz 1990).

Finally, and most challenging to the therapist, there is the exploration of the 'invisible' stories collectively held in cultures. Despite the popularity of post-modern and social constructionist accounts of society it remains difficult to function as a therapist and simultaneously be aware of the assumptions of both one's profession and one's culture, and how these directly impact on one's clinical work. There are, however, emerging signs of the need and possible benefits of doing so (Hacking 1995). If this is to be anything other than a purely intellectual exercise then it is likely to involve some discomfort. Therapists may wish to explore the way age and older people are defined, devalued and marginalized by ubiquitous social constructs (for example, the very grouping and labelling of people by their age as a distinct population entity).

WORKING WITH LIFE STORIES

It has been suggested already that therapy with older adults inevitably involves elements of life story work. Nevertheless, there are approaches that make the process more explicit, particularly personal construct therapy (Viney 1993) and life review therapy (Garland 1994). In practice these two approaches have much in common. Essential to them both is the notion that by telling/hearing and re-telling their stories clients gain new perspectives which open up choices and options in the present. Thus, while the content may be largely historical it is crucial to draw links between the events of the past, how these were understood, interpreted and managed, and the dilemmas facing the client in the present.

In terms of narrative identity the process of life review can be seen as moving between the particular and the general. Memories are explored in detail and depth, told as stories, episodes or chapters in themselves and then the perspective shifted to allow reintegration of the overall narrative or plot of a life (or family).

In fostering these processes the therapist inevitably becomes engaged in a dialogue, questioning, acknowledging and highlighting elements of the clients' stories. At times the response evoked in the therapist will be that of silence; at others, the therapist may interrupt and bring the client back or take them forward to a new point in their story.

In a paper entitled 'Doing Life Review' Garland and Kemp (1996) discuss a range of practical guidelines for engaging clients in a life review process. The authors recommend the use of structured interviews (e.g. Haight 1992); taping sessions (for both client and therapist to review); use of different media such as drawing or music; and the incorporation of objects or personal belongings into the therapeutic process. Leaving tapes, notes or other products of the session with the client allows them to retain ownership of the process of storying their life. The authors also recommend a balance between focused and open questioning and being prepared to be directive if the situation calls for it.

Clients may spontaneously introduce objects and mementoes into sessions without prompting. Mrs Stevens was a 77-year-old lady referred for anxiety related to several health complaints that had troubled her in recent months. A retired businesswoman, she had been happily married but had lived alone for fifteen years following her husband's death from a heart attack. At our third session (which happened to fall on Valentine's Day) she told how her husband had proposed to her in a letter after he had stayed with her family one weekend. Mrs Stevens was very much in love with him but irritated and concerned that he had proposed by post. She wrote back and said she had adopted a child called 'Tommy' and could not consent unless he was willing to accept this. He in turn arranged a visit the following weekend. When she saw that he was still keen she took him to meet Tommy – a baby tortoise in a box of straw. At this point in her story Mrs Stevens stood and walked over to the mantelpiece. She said that her husband never referred to the incident again, but a few months before his death had given her a china tortoise which she now picked up and showed me. As she did so her face and demeanour transformed from a pallid, restrained and isolated expression to one full of life, light and vitality. She laughed and said, 'I still have Tommy.'

MISSING NARRATIVES

Therapists and clients may 'miss each other' and clients may choose to miss out parts of their story. While the therapist may encourage a story to be told, there is also a time when the 'eloquence of silence' (Barker 1991: 238) must be respected. Mr Goodwin was referred for post-traumatic stress symptoms, especially nightmares, following a head-on car crash. At our assessment he mentioned that he had seen active service in the Second World War in the Marines but did not wish to talk about it. He had, he said, put that behind him. The following eighteen months necessitated regular contact as he adjusted in turn to his wife's death, having a heart attack, an enforced house move and being burgled. Towards the end of this period the D-day celebrations appeared to trigger a series of deeply disturbing nightmares. In our session he declined to discuss his nightmares but one day said, 'I was trained to walk a foot behind the enemy, treading in their footsteps, but so as they wouldn't hear', and, after a pause, 'some of those Germans were just kids'. After a long silence he said he did not want to talk further. In the following weeks he established contact with an ex-servicemen's organization and met up with two men he had served with and not seen for four and a half decades. Over this period his nightmares gradually abated.

IMAGES AND METAPHORS

The images and metaphors that permeate the narratives of clients can be a potent means of exploring the particular in order to throw light on the general. In the case study described at the end of this chapter the client was asked to close his eyes and visualize his life as a picture or image. He described a felled tall oak tree.

Another example comes from Mrs Peters, a woman suffering from emphysema and a heart condition who was referred for panic and acute anxiety. She knew she had only months and possibly weeks to live when, in our third meeting, she anxiously described her perspective on life as being confined to seeing between the pages of a book which were rapidly folding in front of her. As we explored this image she talked to her husband for the first time of how she hated to think that her final days were passing her by. In doing so she calmed down visibly and again connected with the open pages of her story.

CAUTIONS IN LIFE STORY WORK

Life story work is under-evaluated as a clinical approach and is not a panacea (Garland 1994; Garland and Kemp 1996). Some cautions are necessary.

First, not all people want, need or are able to review their life (Coleman 1986). People with pasts that they do not wish to review may be particularly unsuited to this approach, while those with cognitive impairment may not see its relevance. The best guide is likely to be that of asking the client if they are interested in or actu-ally already reviewing their life. If the answer is yes then clinical experience suggests they are likely to be good candidates for the approach.

A second caution is that of negative memory bias. It is well established that depressed individuals are more likely to access more negative memories (Teasdale 1983) This places an onerous task on a therapist using memory and life review to help a person who is in a state of low mood or demoralization. It helps if the therapist is comfortable with interrupting and restructuring global negative evaluations while remaining sensitive to the client's narrative 'autonomy'. For this to be successful it is important to have the strong sense of shared endeavour implied by the earlier caution concerning willing engagement.

A third concern is that of seeing life story telling as automatically of benefit. The work of Viney, Garland and others draws on long experience of trained and supervised clinical practice. Listening and recalling stories with older people with serious mental disorders is likely to require a thorough grounding in psychological assessment and intervention to be safe and effective. With such clients the approach may again be used alongside other therapeutic interventions – including medication – in either a concurrent or sequential fashion.

A final point concerns 'narration and difference'. Clients and therapists differ in many ways including their gender, culture and class. These and other more subtle differences are further influenced by likely differences in age. To take gender, for example, there is evidence that older men are more inclined to give chronological and women thematic accounts of their life (Hockey 1989). Therapists can learn to be careful of imposing a gendered structure unsuited to their client. More generally there are well-known, but often ignored, issues of gender matching and the concern that women may not wish to discuss some experiences with a male therapist or that, if they do so, then these may not be truly 'heard'. Similar sensitivities are required when working with older adults from different races, cultures and class backgrounds. When such differences are openly acknowledged and the potential barriers overcome, one may feel tremendously privileged to be invited into previously unknown worlds – these often being most powerfully described through the telling of vivid autobiographical or family accounts.

LIFE STORY WORK: MR HAMLYN

Mr Hamlyn was referred by his GP with a diagnosis of clinical depression. Aged 66, he had in recent years suffered a series of losses, including being made redundant from his post as head graphic designer for a food packaging company, moving house and developing arthritis. Throughout this period he felt the financial pressure of paying for his mother's care in a local residential home following the onset of Alzheimer's disease. He complained, too, of finding life dull and unsatisfying in recent years and had for many months felt unable to carry out his life-long hobby of painting in watercolours. His frustration had led to irritable outbursts with his wife which left him feeling sad and concerned.

A life story narrative

There are narrative conventions to describing 'psychiatric cases' – for example the separation of background facts and observations from conceptualization, and an organized chronological treatment account. These conventions carry implications of how people's stories are renarrated by experts (Susko 1994). It feels uncomfortable to rework the life story told by Mr Hamlyn into this format. Instead, there follows a summary prepared for our penultimate (eighth) session. The impressionistic account reflects the process of the work – namely a sensual indeterminate patchwork of memories, images, thoughts and feelings.

A few preliminary comments may be helpful. Mr Hamlyn, as already mentioned above, visualized his life as a fallen tree. After forming this initial image he visually stripped and cut the tree into segments which he sketched on paper. The separate segments were broadly allocated as phases in his life for review, and annotated as we went along. During the sessions he sometimes sketched scenes from the memories explored. At other times he drew between sessions. The account given here summarizes the life story and is a version incorporating his editions to my initial draft.

Mr Hamlyn's story

Introduction

How to condense a life into eight one-hour sessions? How to condense this life which has been unusually full into that time? And how to summarize that summary on a page?

A solution would apparently lie in producing a sketch, i.e. suggesting the whole with a few key details.

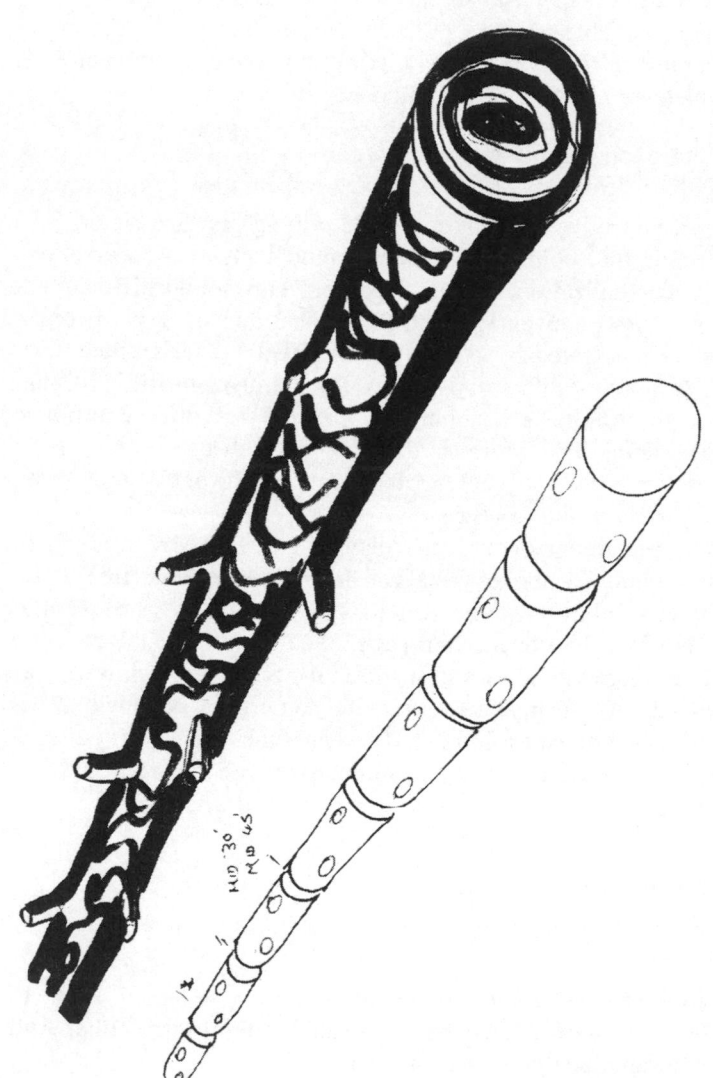

Figure 14.1 The tree of life

But we begin with a picture of a life as a tree (figure 14.1). The image implies growth and evolving stability – layers of learning and experience building on previous layers. And it recognizes too the importance of roots and the varied multiplying offshoots of branches. But this tree has been chopped down.

Early years

The first image, a kitchen. Warm, colourful, nurturing. Papers and print in the hands. Laundry overhead, cheese on a wooden board. And others emerge: the Coronation parade (the imposed maternal demands of dress unstoppable). A teddy bear's ear is torn in an argument; an aunt is 'not quite right' and disappears for periods without explanation.

Grandparent presences are felt as much as parental ones. Expectations are there, influences are around.

The early messages combine nurturing with duty, encouragement with warnings of the world's brutality: 'Be straight in life', and, unsaid, the rider 'because you're Jewish and cannot afford not to be' (Father). 'Have another portion' (Grandmother). 'Keep on practising' (Grandfather). 'Keep your fingers out from the bricks' (Mother, taken from advice on how to castrate animals).

After this home world, junior school comes as a shock. Fear and sadness (and later on bullying) are encountered. But good teachers are found and talents discovered, developed: the talent to draw and the talent to talk.

The themes continue into grammar school but become overshadowed by the war. On the Isle of Wight a strange combination of anticipation, excitement and deadly seriousness heralds the outbreak of war.

Young adulthood

Art college is a world of paint and smells and innocent discovery. Freedom, delight and companionship, within the safety of a disciplined, structured system.

And then the RAF. The exotic sights, sounds, smells of India. A new fear on sentry duty. And the rites of death, fire, water and vulture-picked bones.

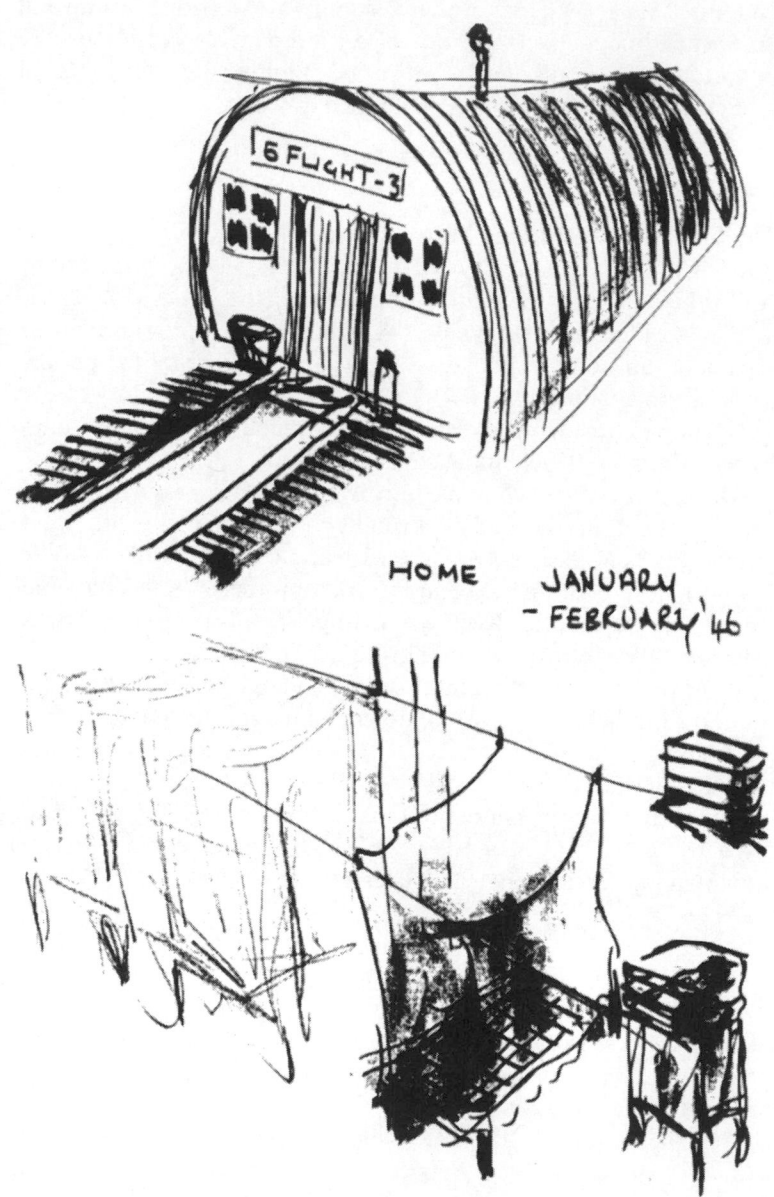

Figure 14.2 Life in the barracks

Full adulthood

Art college again and then work – work for more than thirty years, drawing, designing, planning, inventing, talking, visualizing. Bad experiences with supportive bosses and the satisfaction of seeing projects completed.

And over these years a life outside work, family growing up, swimming, life-saving, Rotary, archery, old beautiful cars. A broad full and vivid immersion in life.

And then a series of blows (chops of the axe?): the discovery, abroad, that the job was being advertised, moving house and the old house not being treated with dignity while the new one disappointed; the exhaustion of caring for Mother, whose stroke seemed to strengthen those traits of her character which were always hard to carry; the diagnosis of arthritis.

Finances took up time and energy and the position of head of the family threw up more and more demands.

And with the changes came time and a frustration that the world is turning wrong, that problems could not be fixed so quickly, that the just world where, if you do things right you will be rewarded, did not after all exist.

And through this a strong desire to do the right thing and to learn and adapt.

Now

The various blows of recent years took a toll. Pleasures (painting, creating, stimulating conversation, exercise) got squeezed out. Time as a couple also suffered – outings to the country, with vivid memories of scenery and villages – had become less frequent. The irritations of a world with different standards seemed to overpower the vitality to continue a life once so full.

The future

Reviewing this life has been an exhausting process. Not just because it is full but because the emotion of past events has been rekindled in the telling.

There is a future to make. Perhaps the next steps are to make small plans to fill out and enrich the days. Or to plan a holiday, a move, a sequence of paintings? Or to offer your rare combinations of skills to people who will value and use them properly?

By the time of this review Mr Hamlyn's mood had begun to lift, and while he still became irritable this was less frequent and intense and no longer felt to be a problem. Both his wife and children had now become keen to find out more about the family history and a visit was being planned to see the home of his childhood and the local area.

A further session was agreed, focusing on action planning to maintain the changes that had occurred (plans made included going on a painting holiday, setting up a room for drawing, weekly trips out with his wife, regular swimming, etc.).

CONCLUSION

It is hoped that reading this chapter will alert the reader to the richness of the narratives that permeate work with older people. Awareness of the centrality of stories in this work can help both client and therapist to find new ways of describing and understanding their lives. The conclusion of Mr Hamlyn's life story narrative gave a beautiful and pertinent illustration of this process. At a follow-up meeting six months later, Mr Hamlyn was continuing to do well and painting regularly (though he still had 'off days'). He proudly informed me that his art had developed in a new direction: he was now revisiting favourite landscape subjects and painting them several times over, but always from a new location, achieving differing perspectives.

REFERENCES

Amundson, J., Stewart, K., and Valentine, L. (1993) 'Temptations of power and certainty', *Journal of Marital and Family Therapy* 19: 111–23.
Barker, P. (1991) *Regeneration*, London: Viking.
Bender, M. (1995) *Bibliography No. 1: Reminiscence* (PSIGE bibliographies), Leicester: British Psychological Society.
Berne, E. (1972) *What Do You Say After You Say Hello?*, New York: Grove Press.
Brooks, P. (1984) *Reading for the Plot: Design and Intention in Narrative*, Cambridge, Mass: Harvard University Press.
Cheston, R. (1997). 'Stories and metaphors: talking about the past in a psychotherapy group for people with dementia', *Ageing and Society* 16 (forthcoming).

Coleman, P.G. (1986) *Ageing and Reminiscence Processes: Social and Clinical Implications*, Chichester: Wiley.

Erikson, E.H. (1951) *Childhood and Society*, Granada: Triad.

Freeman, M. (1993) *Rewriting the Self: History, Memory, Narrative*, London: Routledge.

Garland, J. (1994) 'O what splendour, it all coheres: life review therapy with older people', in J. Burnet (ed.) *Reminiscence Reviewed: Achievements, Evaluations, Perspectives*, Milton Keynes: Open University Press.

Garland, J., and Kemp, L. (1996) 'Doing life review', *Psychologists' Special Interest Group in the Elderly Newsletter* 56: 9–11.

Genevay, B., and Katz, R.S. (eds) (1990) *Countertransference and Older Adults*, London: Sage.

Gonccalves, O.F. (1994). 'Cognitive narrative psychotherapy: the hermeneutic construction of alternative meanings', *Journal of Cognitive Psychotherapy* 8: 105–25.

Hacking, I. (1995) *Rewriting the Soul: Multiple Personality and the Sciences of Memory*, Princeton: Princeton University Press.

Haight, B. (1992) 'The structured life-review process: a community approach to the ageing client', in G.M.M. Jones and B.M.L. Miesen (eds) *Care-Giving in Dementia Research and Application*, London: Routledge, 272–92.

Herr, J., and Weakland, J.H. (1979) *Counselling Elders and Their Families*, New York: Springer.

Hildebrand, P. (1995) *Beyond Mid-Life Crisis: A Psychodynamic Approach to Ageing*, London: Sheldon.

Hockey, J. (1989) 'Residential care and the maintenance of social identity: negotiating the transition to institutional life', in M. Jeffries (ed.) *Growing Old in the Twentieth Century*, London: Routledge.

Jacobs, R.H. (1993) *Be An Outrageous Older Woman – A RASP*, Connecticut: K.I.T.

MacIntyre, A. (1985) *After Virtue* (second edition), Guildford: Duckworth.

Masson, J. (1990) *Against Therapy*, London: Fontana.

Murphy, E. (1982) 'Social origins of depression in old age', *British Journal of Psychiatry* 141: 135–42.

Pocock, D. (1995) 'Searching for a better story: harnessing modern and postmodern positions in family therapy', *Journal of Family Therapy* 17: 149–73.

Richardson, C. (1995) *Bibliography No. 5: Psychodynamic Psychotherapy with People with Dementia* (PSIGE bibliographies), Leicester: British Psychological Society.

Russell, R.L. (1991) 'Narrative in views of humanity, science, and action: lessons for cognitive therapy', *Journal of Cognitive Psychotherapy* 5: 241–56.

Steiner, C. (1974) *Scripts People Live: Transactional Analysis of Life Scripts*, New York: Grove Press.

Susko, M.A. (1994) 'Caseness and narrative: contrasting approaches to people who are psychiatrically labelled', *Journal of Mind and Behaviour* 15: 87–112.

Teasdale, J.D. (1983) 'Negative thinking in depression: cause, effect or reciprocal relationship?' *Advances in Behaviour Research and Therapy* 5: 3–25.

Viney, L.L. (1993) *Life Stories: Personal Construct Therapy with the Elderly*, Chichester: Wiley.

Index